MONASTIC LIFE
IN THE MEDIEVAL
BRITISH ISLES

MONASTIC LIFE IN THE MEDIEVAL BRITISH ISLES

Essays in Honour of Janet Burton

EDITED BY
KAREN STÖBER, JULIE KERR
AND EMILIA JAMROZIAK

UNIVERSITY OF WALES PRESS
2018

www.uwp.co.uk

British Library Cataloguing-in-Publication Data
A catalogue record for this book is available from the British Library.

ISBN: 978-1-78683-322-8 (hardback)
            978-1-78683-318-1 (paperback)
e-ISBN: 978-1-78683-319-8

The right of The Contributors to be identified as authors of this work has been asserted
by them in accordance with sections 77 and 79 of the Copyright, Designs and Patents
Act 1988.

Typeset by Marie Doherty
Printed by CPI Antony Rowe, Melksham

CONTENTS

Part III: Women in the medieval monastic world

ACKNOWLEDGEMENTS

The editors are indebted to the help and encouragement of many people in the making of this book. We would like to thank the University of Wales Press and especially Llion Wigley and Siân Chapman for their support and patience throughout this project. We are grateful to our contributors for producing their chapters cheerfully despite the tight deadlines and strict word limit, and to all those who have participated in the *Tabula Gratulatoria*.

Our thanks to Dani Leiva for his evocative drawing of Byland Abbey which is on the front cover and which Dani drew specifically for this Festschrift. Byland Abbey holds a special place in Janet's heart and in her research, making this a fitting tribute. We are indebted to William Marx, Our Man in Lampeter, for without his conspiratorial help and support this project would not have been possible. Throughout, William has provided us with the necessary names, facts and figures, and he moreover compiled the list of Janet's publications – no mean feat. We thank Paul Watkins for the photograph of Janet in the Founders' Library. Paul managed to dupe Janet into posing for this picture: we commend his guile.

Finally, we would like to thank everybody who has helped to keep this project a secret from Janet, allowing us to surprise her with the presentation of this book.

ILLUSTRATIONS

ABBREVIATIONS

BL	London, British Library
Bodl.	Oxford, Bodleian Library
Burton, *Monastic Order*	Janet Burton, *The Monastic Order in Yorkshire, 1069–1215* (Cambridge, 1999)
Cal. Close Rolls	H. C. Maxwell Lyte et al. (eds), *Calendar of Close Rolls preserved in the Public Record Office, AD 1227–1509*, 61 vols (London, 1902–63)
Cal. Papal Registers	W. H. Bliss, C. Johnson, J. A. Twemlow and M. J. Haren (eds), *Calendar of Entries in the Papal Registers Relating to Great Britain and Ireland*: papal letters (London, 1893–in progress)
Chron. Melsa	E. Bond (ed.), *Chronica Monasterii de Melsa a fundatione usque ad annum 1396, auctore Thoma de Burton, Abbate*, RS, 43, 3 vols (London, 1866–8)
Giraldus Cambrensis Opera	J. S. Brewer, J. F. Dimock and G. F. Warner (eds), *Giraldi Cambrensis Opera*, 8 vols, RS (London, 1861–91)
JMMS	*The Journal of Medieval Monastic Studies*
Mon. Ang.	William Dugdale, *Monasticon Anglicanum*, J. Caley, H. Ellis and B. Bandinel (eds), 6 vols in 8 (London, 1817–30)
ODNB	Colin Matthews and Brian Harrison, Lawrence Goldman and David Cannadine (eds), *Oxford Dictionary of National Biography*, 60 vols (Oxford, 2004); online version 2005 with updates, *www.oxforddnb.com/*
OMT	Oxford Medieval Texts

PL	J. P. Migne et alia (eds), *Patrologia cursus completes, series Latina*, 221 vols (Paris, 1844–64)
RCAHMW	Royal Commission on the Ancient and Historic Monuments of Wales
RS	Rolls Series
TNA	The National Archives
VCH	The Victoria History of the Counties of England and Wales

CONTRIBUTORS

David Austin is professor emeritus at the University of Wales Trinity Saint David and director of the Strata Florida Research Project.

Edel Breathnach is CEO of The Discovery Programme.

Michael Carter is senior properties historian at English Heritage.

James Clark is professor of history at the University of Exeter and associate dean for research and knowledge transfer.

Claire Cross is professor emeritus at the University of York.

Kimm Curran is an affiliate researcher in the Medical Humanities Research Centre at the University of Glasgow. She is publicity officer and on the steering committee for the History of Women Religious in Britain and Ireland.

Marsha L. Dutton is emeritus professor of English at Ohio University and executive editor of Cistercian Publications.

Brian Golding was formerly reader at the University of Southampton.

Martin Heale is reader in medieval history at the University of Liverpool and director of Liverpool Centre for Medieval and Renaissance Studies.

Philippa Hoskin is professor of medieval studies at the University of Lincoln.

Colmán Ó Clabaigh O.S.B. is a Benedictine monk of Glenstal Abbey, Co. Limerick.

Veronica O'Mara is professor of medieval English literature at the University of Hull.

Andrew Prescott is professor of digital humanities (English language and linguistics) at the University of Glasgow.

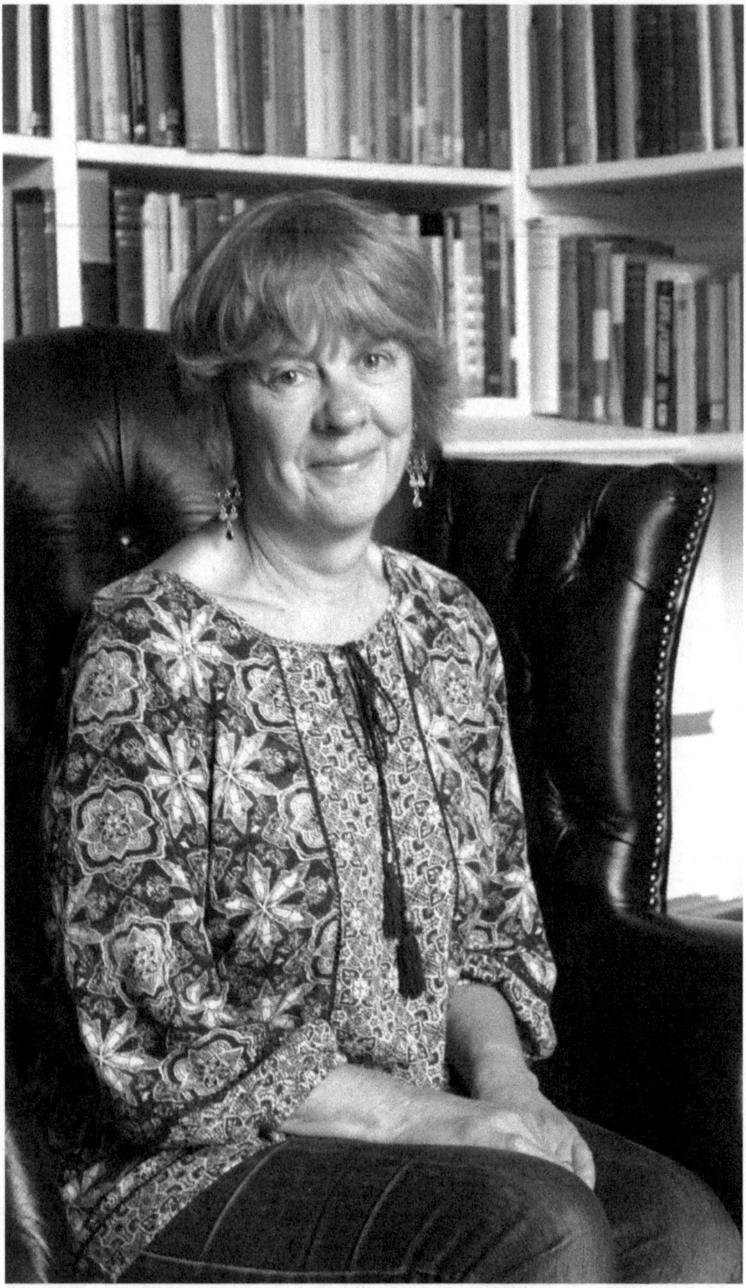

Janet Burton

INTRODUCTION

Karen Stöber and Emilia Jamroziak

The present book has come into being to pay tribute to a very special person, scholar and teacher, Professor Janet Burton. Janet graduated from Westfield College, University of London in 1973 where she was taught by two distinguished medieval historians, Christopher Brooke and Rosalind Hill. After London, she completed her DPhil in the Department of History and Centre for Medieval Studies at the University of York. Her thesis on the development of monasticism in Yorkshire in the century and a half after the Norman invasion of England was supervised by Professor Barrie Dobson. Janet subsequently worked for several years as an archivist, first at what was then known as The Borthwick Institute of Historical Research at York and thereafter at the Ceredigion Record Office in Aberystwyth, an experience that helped to shape her subsequent research. In 1994 Janet was appointed lecturer at University of Wales, Lampeter (now University of Wales Trinity Saint David), then senior lecturer, reader and, from 2006, professor of medieval history. Throughout her long teaching career Janet has been dedicated to her students. Her charisma and encouragement have brought the medieval period alive to undergraduates and postgraduates who are indebted to her for kindling a keen interest in the subject.

Janet's contribution to British medieval monastic studies is as far-reaching as it is profound and over the past forty years she has contributed substantially to our knowledge of a wide range of aspects relating to the study of monastic history in medieval Britain, especially in Yorkshire and Wales. This is reflected in her long list of publications, which is appended to this volume. Janet is a fellow of the Society of Antiquaries, a fellow of the Learned Society of Wales and a fellow of the Royal Historical Society of which she is a former member of council and vice-president. As well as writing and publishing her own research, Janet has been instrumental in fostering the work of others through the publication of a series of edited volumes. She has been especially encouraging to junior academics, involving them in conferences and helping them to get a foothold on the academic ladder. The *Journal of Medieval Monastic Studies* which she founded with Karen Stöber in 2010 and which has been published by Brepols since 2012, and the accompanying book series Medieval

Monastic Studies (Brepols), both aim to be an international platform for the dissemination of current research. Moreover, since 2008 Janet has been the co-director of the *Monastic Wales Project* (*www.monasticwales.org*), together with Karen Stöber. This project combines scholarly rigour with accessibility and reflects Janet's commitment to stimulate new and interdisciplinary research and to make this available to the public and relevant to the wider academic world. It has been an inspirational model for similar endeavours on regional approaches to monastic culture.

Janet's scholarly activity has not been limited to academic publications and she has had more than her five minutes of TV fame, notably when she accompanied Dan Snow on his *Norman Walks* in Yorkshire and explained to Huw Edwards the importance of Strata Florida Abbey in the BBC documentary *The Story of Wales*.

Despite her busy professional schedule and such a prolific scholarly output, Janet has never neglected her active personal life and has always made time for family, friends and travel. She is a regular swimmer, an intrepid ice-skater and has often graced the dance floor at the annual International Medieval Congress at Leeds; and she has been known to explore Catalan cities on the back of a motorbike. Not least she and her husband William Marx have been generous and warm hosts to many colleagues and acquaintances over the years and many of us who have contributed to this volume have been recipients of their kind hospitality.

The impact of Janet's scholarship has made itself felt in the study of medieval monastic history in general, but has perhaps been strongest in those fields that she has predominantly focused on over the decades, namely monasticism in Yorkshire, the Cistercian Order, the regular canons and the religious houses of Wales.

THE CISTERCIANS AND YORKSHIRE

The DPhil thesis Janet completed in 1977 at the University of York on 'The origins and development of the religious orders in Yorkshire *c*.1069 to *c*.1200' was a major turning point in the historiography of the medieval religious history of northern England, but it also opened a new perspective on the development of monasticism in the British Isles from the eleventh to the late thirteenth century. This work has set a new agenda for the study of Cistercian history and this subject area has remained an important strand of Janet's work for decades. The thesis was revised and published as a monograph study in 1999 but in the interim Janet published extensively on monasticism and Yorkshire; this early work reflects her expertise in the source material related to the Yorkshire religious houses. In most cases Janet's work provides the first new interpretations of this material since the era of antiquarian studies, such as her studies on the charters from Byland Abbey and Lenton Priory, the confraternity list of St Mary's Abbey, the cartulary of the York Minster treasurer, as well as her pioneering work on Yorkshire nunneries in the twelfth and thirteenth centuries, published in 1979.[1] These early publications bear the hallmarks of Janet's impressive scholarship, namely, in approaching monastic material within a wider social and cultural context, as well as offering detailed examinations and an often innovative approach to neglected sources. Beginning with her DPhil thesis and continuing with her publications in the late 1970s and early 1980s, Janet steered the approach to Cistercian history in the north as well as the religious history of Yorkshire away from both antiquarian approaches and the separation of monastic history from its wider socio-political context. The transformative impact of Janet's work on Cistercian monasticism was recognised by the inclusion of her chapter on the foundations of the British Cistercian houses in the 1986 volume on *Cistercian Art and Architecture in the British Isles*, edited by Christopher Norton and David Park, an important work and the first systematic study of this subject, which has remained current for several decades.[2] Janet's chapter in this volume encapsulates her novel approach to the foundation processes and complex interrelationship between monastic communities and their founders, bishops, benefactors and other authorities, which can no longer be seen as a simple linear development. The theme of foundation and its mechanisms, as well as the formation of monastic estates, is the subject of her 1998 article on 'The estates and economy of Rievaulx Abbey in Yorkshire', which became a definitive study of the chronology of the early years of Rievaulx and the complexities of its 'foundation charter'. Janet returned to these issues in the article she contributed to the Festschrift for Peter Fergusson, an eminent scholar of Cistercian architecture, with whom she collaborated in the early 1990s. In this article she explains the importance and complexity of social networks for the development of Rievaulx Abbey in its social context.[3] During the first twenty years of her career, Janet continued to explore the wider monastic history of the north from the Norman Conquest to the end of the thirteenth century. Her articles on Benedictine, Cistercian and Augustinian communities are deeply engaged with the regional context of these institutions as well as more distant connections and influences, for example with Scotland.[4] In this work she continues and develops an approach to monastic patronage first explored by Christopher Brooke, among others, and embedded monastic history within the social context of twelfth-century English society as examined by, for example, Judith Green.[5] Janet's work also resonates with other early studies on the motivations of secular patrons and benefactors by Brian Golding, Emma Mason, Benjamin Thompson and David Postles.[6] This approach, which Janet Burton has pioneered in relation to the Yorkshire material, later became the hallmark of her work on Wales (see below). Moreover it was the material relating to the north of England that Janet first used to argue for a new understating of the relationship between the Cistercian Order and female communities. She has shown that the 'Cistercian status' of the nunneries in Yorkshire was not something permanent but was subject to change over time: while twelve communities claimed at various times to be Cistercian, others started doing so only in the late Middle Ages. Some of these communities followed Cistercian customs without being formally part of the Order. Janet has shown convincingly that the reasons cited by historians for the nuns' claim of Cistercian status – financial considerations and in particular freedom from the payment of tithes – were not much in evidence in the Yorkshire cases. Rather, it was the interest of patrons and the personal connections with neighbouring male and female houses that influenced the nuns' desire to follow the Cistercian way of life.[7]

In 1994 Janet Burton published *Monastic and Religious Orders in Britain 1000–1300* in the Cambridge Medieval Textbooks series.[8] This was the first of several synthesis works which she produced in the course of her career, and one that has not been superseded by other publications. It not only explains the pre-Conquest Benedictine communities, but also the role of twelfth-century reform, the emergence of the communities of canons and the arrival of the White Monks. Whilst this volume examines the monastic economy, intellectual life, ideas of reform and the role of tradition, it is a particularly significant contribution to the debates about the role of monastic patronage in the development of monastic networks across the British Isles. The relationship between religious communities and their patrons and benefactors was also central to Janet Burton's next monograph, *The Monastic Order in Yorkshire 1069–1215*.[9] It built on her doctoral work, combined with two decades of further research. It is not only an excellent study of a specific region and its monastic culture in the process of change, but it is also a very important contribution to the discussion about the place of monasticism in medieval society. Why did lay people found monasteries? What were the expectations of benefactors from the monks, and vice versa? This approach was taken up and developed further by Emilia Jamroziak in her monographs on Rievaulx Abbey and on Cistercian communities on different types of medieval frontiers.[10] Janet's most recent synthesis on Cistercian history and culture was published together with Julie Kerr in 2011.[11] It builds on Janet's extensive knowledge of Cistercian sources, archaeological evidence and regional dynamics of the Cistercian network, combined with Kerr's in-depth understanding of Cistercian daily life, and brings material from the British Isles into dialogue with evidence from other parts of Christendom.

Source editions have always been a very important strand of Janet's work as a medieval historian. Very unusually, she combines an impressive portfolio of editions of different types of medieval sources with publications of monographs and edited volumes. In this way the editions and monographs inform each other and give Janet's work unusual methodological strength: drawing on a detailed and sophisticated understanding of the sources, she pushes the boundaries of interpretation and contextualises even the most minute evidence. Janet's knowledge of administrative documents, charters and cartularies, as well as narrative texts is exceptional. Amongst her most important editions of primary sources are the volume of documents of the archbishops of York from 1070 to the mid-twelfth century for the English Episcopal Acta; the cartulary of the treasurer of York Minster, for Borthwick Texts and Studies; the cartulary of Byland Abbey for the Surtees Society; *The Foundation History of the Abbeys of Byland and Jervaulx* for Borthwick Texts and Studies; and the *Historia Selebiensis Monasterii* – an historical narrative from Selby Abbey, for Oxford Medieval Texts.[12] Her edition of the Byland Abbey cartulary set new standards for editing cartularies that have not survived in their original form, whilst the introduction to the edition of the narrative foundations from Byland and Jervaulx remains the crucial reference point for any discussion on institutional memory, founding myths and the transmission of Cistercian narrative models.

The impact of Janet Burton's work on both the study of the Cistercian Order in the British Isles and on monasticism in Yorkshire has been transformative for both. Her regional focus, her sophisticated and rigorous approach to the primary sources, as well as her attention to the multifaceted social context have set the standards for all those working in the same area, many of whom have been directly influenced by Janet's work.

WALES

The study of the history of monastic Wales has been a very uneven affair, and Janet has played an instrumental role in rectifying this. For a long time scholarly interest in Welsh monastic matters tended to focus on certain aspects of monasticism in Wales while disregarding others to a greater or smaller extent. This was frequently due to the uneven distribution of the sources; thus we find some religious orders much more fully represented in the historical writings than others, just as we find a tendency among historians to concentrate on particular facets, notably the economy, or the 'Welshness' of a religious group.

In 1976, when Glanmor Williams published the English-language version of his magisterial *The Welsh Church from Conquest to Reformation*, a book that was to become one of the key works on the medieval church in Wales, he stated that 'there were in all some forty-seven religious houses left in Wales by the beginning of the Tudor period'.[13] By this count he failed to include no fewer than eight Benedictine priories (Bassaleg, Cardiff, Carmarthen, Goldcliff, Llanbadarn Fawr, Llandovery, Llangenydd and Llangua), a Cluniac house (St Clears) and two houses of Augustinian canons (St Tudwal's and Puffin Island). He moreover included the Premonstratensian abbey of Talley with the houses of Augustinian canons. Fortunately, the state of our knowledge of the Welsh monasteries has been steadily improving over the past decades and is continuing to do so. Janet has played a leading role in this development.

Several general works about the Welsh monasteries have emerged over the past decades. David Knowles and R. Neville Hadcock's reference work on the religious houses of England and Wales, first published in 1953, has very short summaries of the histories of the Welsh monasteries and nunneries, including most of the Benedictine houses omitted by Glanmor Williams (all except Llangenydd and Llangua, which can be found in their list of alien priories), though these are in need of updating; and 1992 saw the appearance of R. Cooper's guide to the abbeys and priories of Wales, being one of very few books dedicated specifically to Wales's religious houses, aimed at a broader audience.[14] To this we can now add Janet's guide to the medieval Welsh monastic communities, written together with Karen Stöber.[15]

The Cistercians in Wales

The imbalance in the scholarly interest in medieval Welsh monasticism is very visible in that particular attention has long been paid, for example, to the Cistercian Order, while other religious groups have lingered on the margins in terms of academic publications or archaeological excavations. This is not altogether surprising, given that the White Monks were one of the numerically strongest of the religious groups in medieval Wales, and considering the standing remains of their monasteries, which include some of the most impressive and beautiful in the country, such as Tintern Abbey or Valle Crucis. The Cistercians in Wales have always received a great amount of attention from scholars, poets and artists alike. They have fuelled the imagination and inspired study like no other religious group in medieval Wales. Arguably the most prolific among the scholars of the Welsh Cistercians is David Williams.[16]

Williams's extensive work on the Cistercian Order in Wales has had its critics and needs updating in many respects, yet, and despite its uneven thematic coverage, it remains an important reference work. Alongside David Williams mention must be made of David Robinson, who, as well as publishing, in 2006, his masterful and richly illustrated work on Welsh Cistercian archaeology and architecture, is the author of a large number of outstanding guidebooks to individual Welsh Cistercian monasteries, including the abbeys of Tintern, Basingwerk, Cymer and Neath.[17]

One key aspect at the heart of many studies of the Cistercians in Wales has been the issue of patronage and political loyalties among the White Monks; another, that of filiation and the Cistercian family tree. Janet herself has a long-standing interest in the White Monks in Wales, reflected in both her teaching and her research. In 2007, she published an important article on 'The Cistercians in England and Wales' in *Archaeologia Cambrensis*, in which she traces the foundations of the Welsh Cistercian abbeys.[18] Filiation is also the focus of Emilia Jamroziak's recent study of Clairvaux in the British Isles, which discusses the Welsh monasteries alongside those in England and Scotland.[19]

Individual Welsh Cistercian monasteries have also received considerable attention among historians and archaeologists. Perhaps in many ways the most iconic Cistercian house in Wales is the abbey of Strata Florida. Associated since the Middle Ages with cultural production and political involvement, this monastery has long occupied a special place among the houses of White Monks in Wales in the imagination of the populace. At this point it is opportune to mention the ongoing Strata Florida Project, directed by David Austin, which not only seeks to 'preserve for the benefit of the people of Ceredigion and of the Nation, the historical, architectural and constructional heritage that may exist in and around the Great Abbey Farm of Strata Florida', but within the framework of which significant excavations have taken place at the site of the former Cistercian abbey of Strata Florida in Ceredigion.[20] In this context note especially the work of Jemma Bezant, one of the leaders of the Strata Florida excavations.[21]

Neath Abbey in Glamorgan has also been the focus of a recent research project, led by Daniel Power at Swansea University.[22] The abbey has moreover attracted ongoing attention on account of its surviving medieval floor tiles.[23] The study of monastic estates – identifying them and mapping them – has been a key aspect of the study of monastic houses in medieval Wales for many decades.[24] And the monastic buildings, too, where they survive, have been the source of much scholarly debate, as the work of CADW and architectural historians and archaeologists like David Robinson and Stuart Harrison has shown.[25]

The Welsh friars

Other monastic orders have attracted rather less scholarly attention. Thus the Welsh houses of friars, for instance, have provoked considerably less historical debate. Admittedly, the limited surviving documentation and the fact that their buildings have in most cases all but disappeared make their study a somewhat greater challenge than is the case with the Cistercians, Augustinian canons or Benedictines. Nonetheless, there were ten houses of friars in medieval Wales: five Dominican friaries, three houses of Franciscans, and one house each of Carmelites and Austin friars. In 1914, Ruth Easterling wrote her important article on 'The Friars in Wales', a work which for a long time stood more or less on its own.[26] Only occasional publications made reference to the friars in Wales over the following decades.[27] More recently, the friars in Wales have received renewed attention, thanks to the work of Frances Andrews on the Austin friars, that of David Williams on the Carmelites, and that of Jens Röhrkasten on 'Monasteries and Urban Space in Medieval Welsh Towns', though the friars remain on the margins of monastic studies in the context of medieval Wales.[28]

Nunneries in medieval Wales

Similarly on the margins of monastic studies in Wales are the female religious houses. This is in part understandable as there were so very few of them: no more than three nunneries, two Cistercian and one Benedictine, ever flourished in medieval Wales, and these were mostly very small foundations. The foremost scholar of female religiosity in Wales, Jane Cartwright, has studied these communities, the Cistercian houses of Llanlugan and Llanllŷr, and the Benedictine priory of Usk, in both English and Welsh.[29] Cartwright's work aside, publications on women's monasticism in medieval Wales have been patchy indeed, though the problem lies with quantity rather than quality. In some cases the Welsh nunneries appear alongside female houses in England or on the Continent. Thus Roberta Gilchrist, in her work on *Gender and Material Culture*, mentions all three female houses, albeit briefly.[30] The year 2007 saw the publication of Madeleine Gray and John Guy's study of the Welsh Cistercian nunneries;[31] an article by Richard Morgan, published in 1983, discusses the early documentation of Llanllugan;[32] and David Williams mentions both Llanllugan and Llanllŷr in his *Welsh Cistercians*, and he also published an article dedicated to the 'Cistercian Nunneries in Medieval Wales' in *Cîteaux: Commentarii Cistercienses* in 1975.[33] Usk Priory has been the subject of a number of studies as well as excavations;[34] while all three of the Welsh nunneries have also been included in online resources such as the *Monastic Matrix* website, and on *Coflein*, the online catalogue of the Royal Commission on the Ancient and Historical Monuments of Wales.[35]

Medieval Welsh poetry has long been appreciated as a rich source for the study of Welsh monastic history, and this is true also for the female houses. In 1991 Helen Fulton discussed Welsh poetry that mentions nuns, and more recently Jane Cartwright has investigated similar source material.[36] Janet treats the Welsh nunneries in several of her works, including her *Monastic and Religious Orders in Britain*, her chapters on '*Moniales* and *Ordo Cisterciensis* in medieval England and Wales', and on the Benedictines in Wales; and (with Karen Stöber) in the introduction to *Abbeys and Priories of Medieval Wales*, but more work remains to be done on nuns in the principality.[37]

The military orders in Wales

Another religious group that has been less thoroughly treated by scholars in the Welsh context than elsewhere are the military orders, whose presence west of Offa's Dyke was limited indeed. Helen Nicholson has published very widely on the military orders, including in Wales, noting that of the two groups that were present in medieval Wales, the Knights Hospitallers and the Templars, only the former 'held substantial property there'.[38] Apart from the Welsh lands held by the military orders, only one commandery was ever established in the principality, namely the Hospitaller commandery of Slebech in Pembrokeshire. At the turn of the nineteenth century, J. Rogers Rees published his research on the Knights of St John in Wales in a book and an article, emphasising the importance of Slebech Commandery.[39] Knowles and Hadcock say about Slebech that it was 'the largest preceptory of the west'; and F. G. Cowley includes the commandery in his list of appropriated churches in the dioceses of Llandaf and St Davids.[40] More recently Kathryn Hurlock dedicated a chapter to the military orders in Wales and the March in her study of Wales and the Crusades; but the above aside, publications on the topic have to date been limited.[41]

The Benedictines in Wales

Neither have the Benedictines, despite being one of the numerically strongest religious orders in medieval Wales in terms of their monasteries, attracted as much attention from scholars as one might expect. Glanmor Williams talks about most of them in his *Welsh Church*, but fails to include some of the dependent priories, as has been noted above.[42] Martin Heale, on the other hand, has treated those Welsh dependent priories that were subject to English mother houses, including those that do not appear in Williams's list, like Bassaleg (a cell of Glastonbury Abbey), Cardiff (a cell of Tewkesbury Abbey) and Goldcliff (a cell first of Bec Abbey and later of Tewkesbury).[43] And since the Benedictine monasteries of medieval Wales (with the exception of

Llanbadarn Fawr), were all situated in the south, they feature in F. G. Cowley's study of the monastic order in south Wales, which is arranged thematically.[44] Some work has moreover been done on individual Welsh Benedictine houses, including Brecon, Chepstow, Ewenny and Goldcliff.[45]

Against this rather uneven background, Janet's contribution to the study of the Benedictine Order in Wales is noteworthy. Considering the Benedictine houses both as religious communities and as part of a wider political strategy by the new Norman elite, Janet has explored the foundation of Benedictine cells, dependent on French or English mother houses, alongside their new castles as another 'symbol of conquest'.[46]

WALES AND THE REGULAR CANONS

Similarly, Janet's research on the regular canons in medieval Wales has contributed to our understanding of this complex religious group, notably her article on the Augustinian priory of Haverfordwest.[47] She co-edited a substantial volume dedicated to *The Regular Canons in the Medieval British Isles*, about which more below; this includes a chapter on the regular canons in Wales by Karen Stöber.[48] Our knowledge of the regular canons in Wales owes much to David Robinson's decisive work on the geography of their settlement, published in 1980.[49] As in the case of other religious orders, interest in the regular canons has tended to favour some monasteries over others. Thus Llanthony Priory in Monmouthshire, so admired by Gerald of Wales, has received the lion's share of scholarly attention, followed by the priories of Penmon and Beddgelert.[50] The northern Augustinian houses have moreover been discussed by David Austin and Karen Stöber, but overall the regular canons in Wales, including the only Welsh Premonstratensian monastery, Talley Abbey in Carmarthenshire, remain an understudied group.[51]

While the religious orders in medieval Wales have in the past often been studied as groups (of Cistercians, friars, nuns and so forth) or by regions, as we have seen, much recent work has tended to take a more thematic approach, considering the role of monastic communities or individuals in subjects such as cultural production, hospitality or burial. This concept opens up a whole spectrum of interdisciplinary considerations, approaching the Welsh monasteries through literature, art or architecture, for instance. The scholars working at the Canolfan Uwchefrydiau Cymreig a Cheltaidd in Aberystwyth, for example, have appreciated medieval Welsh poetry as a unique and important source for Welsh monastic history for a long time, as is evident in the work of Dafydd Johnston and Eurig Salisbury.[52] The important role of the Welsh monastic *scriptoria* has long been appreciated by scholars, including Daniel Huws, who saw the compilation of the Welsh *Chronicle of the Princes* (*Brut y Tywysogyon*) at Strata Florida as 'evidence of national consciousness at the abbey' at the time.[53] In 2013 Ceridwen Lloyd-Morgan, formerly of the National Library of Wales, published a study on manuscript production in the *scriptoria* of Welsh religious houses.[54]

Monastic patronage and hospitality, also seen through the eyes of the medieval Welsh bards, and monastic burial culture, have all recently been explored in a Welsh context. In 2007 *Archaeologia Cambrensis* published a very fine article by Huw Pryce on 'Patrons and patronage among the Cistercians in Wales', a topic also treated, among others, by David Stephenson (with special focus on Gwynedd and Powys), by Jemma Bezant (concentrating on grants to Strata Florida), by Julie Kerr, whose significant work on monastic hospitality considers Wales as well as England, by Karen Stöber, who has studied patronal networks in England and Wales, and by Andrew Abram in his study of monastic burial in Wales.[55]

The monastic history of medieval Wales thus has a long history of scholarly publications, but what was lacking for a long time was a way of bringing all the existing, but dispersed, information together. Aware of this problem, Karen Stöber and Janet created the *Monastic Wales Project* in 2008. The *Monastic Wales Project* was developed with the aim of providing a platform for medieval Welsh monastic history, both as a research tool and as a reference site, bringing together the histories of the religious houses of Wales and a regularly updated bibliography of relevant literature and sources on its website.[56] The website itself was developed by Nigel Callaghan of Technoleg Taliesin and was designed by Martin Crampin, while Julie Kerr was responsible for the immense task of collecting, processing and inputting the data on each of the sixty monastic sites currently on the website. As well as maintaining and expanding its website, the *Monastic Wales Project* also leant its name to a number of workshops on *Monastic Wales* (Aberystwyth, 2009) and on *Monastic Wales and Ireland* (Lampeter, 2011). The former resulted in the publication of a volume entitled *Monastic Wales: New Approaches*, edited by Janet together with Karen Stöber and published by the University of Wales Press in 2013, while the latter gave birth to the *Monastic Ireland Project*, which was launched in Dublin in 2014.[57] Together with the publication of *Monastic Wales: New Approaches*, the University of Wales Press commissioned the editors to write a guide to the monasteries of medieval Wales for a wider audience, which was published in 2015 under the title *Abbeys and Priories of Medieval Wales*.[58]

Janet has taken a much more holistic approach to the writing of Welsh monastic history than her predecessors. She has made a marked contribution through her own publications but also encouraging and facilitating the research of others, notably her students, and promoting the publication of their work.

THE REGULAR CANONS IN THE BRITISH ISLES

Janet's contribution to the study of the regular canons in medieval Wales has already been mentioned. But she has also worked on the regular canons in the British Isles more widely. Undeservedly, the regular canons had long been neglected by monastic scholars. In his monumental work on *The Monastic Order in England*, comprising over 750 pages, David Knowles dedicated to this important religious group little more than a handful of pages, under the title 'Increase of the regular canons'.[59] Several decades ago, Stefan Weinfurter lamented the comparative neglect the regular canons in German lands had been experiencing from monastic historians.[60] The same held true for the British Isles at the time, despite such weighty classics as H. M. Colvin's *White Canons in England*, or the work of J. C. Dickinson.[61] Much has improved in terms of Augustinian historiography since the 1970s, however. In 1980 David Robinson published his fundamental *Geography of Augustinian Settlements in Medieval England and Wales*.[62] Just over a decade later, Janet's *Monastic and Religious Orders in Britain* devoted an entire chapter to the regular canons, seeing them as representing a central aspect of medieval monasticism.[63] And 2001 saw the publication of Joseph Gribbin's work on the Premonstratensians in late medieval England.[64]

More recently, Janet has pursued her interest in this most versatile of religious groups through a series of publications and by organising an international and interdisciplinary conference, with Karen Stöber, at the University of Wales hall of Gregynog in 2008. It was during the preparation of this conference that the organisers became aware of the immense interest in the regular canons and related scholarly activity that was already underway across the British Isles, albeit at that stage often unpublished, or in the shape of doctoral theses in progress. The results of the conference were later brought together and published by Brepols.[65] Janet's own chapter in this book looked at the role of the regular canons in diocesan reform in the diocese of Coventry and Lichfield.[66] Other contributions to the volume are dedicated to individual monasteries, to community life and social and cultural contexts of the regular canons in England, Scotland, Wales and Ireland. In recent years, then, the regular canons in the medieval British Isles have enjoyed rather more well-deserved attention, a trend that appears to be ongoing.[67]

NUNS

Another area that has benefitted greatly from Janet's research over the years relates to the study of medieval nuns.[68] From the very beginning of her academic career, Janet's interest in female religiosity and the role of women in monasticism has seen her present conference papers and publish articles on aspects of this once-neglected and recently blossoming subject. Her focus was initially on Yorkshire nunneries, and has throughout mostly been on Cistercian nuns.[69] Janet thereby directly involved herself in the ongoing debate concerning the Cistercian Order's attitude towards women, and the character of Cistercian nunneries.[70] While she has never abandoned her interest in the Yorkshire nunneries,[71] and has paid special attention to the nunnery of Swine,[72] her research has more recently extended to the Welsh nunneries, as mentioned above,[73] in particular to the two female Cistercian houses of Llanllŷr and Llanllugan. An interest in the prosopography of medieval nuns has also inspired Janet to 'look for medieval nuns' and explore the possibilities of identifying nuns and reconstructing their lives.[74] Janet is also co-editor of the book *Women in the Medieval Monastic World*, based on the proceedings of a conference held at the Monestir de les Avellanes in Catalonia in 2011, and published by Brepols in 2015, and has a chapter in the same volume on 'Medieval nunneries and male authority; female monasteries in England and Wales'.[75]

Janet has most certainly left an enduring and far-reaching mark on the study of medieval monasticism in the British Isles, transforming many aspects of the field. Moreover, thanks to her many and varied innovative initiatives – such as the *Journal of Medieval Monastic Studies* – her legacy will be continued through the work of others and impact on scholarship internationally.

This volume is divided into three sections dedicated to three of Janet's publications: 'Monastic and religious orders in Britain', 'Religious and laity' and 'Women in the medieval monastic world'. In the first section, which addresses the study of *Monastic and Religious Orders in Britain* (including Ireland), James Clark considers the late medieval Cistercians and their presence and participation in the social, economic and political world of their times. Clark discusses historical narratives of late medieval White Monks in England and the shaping of a corporate monastic identity. Martin Heale focuses on the role of the prior in Benedictine monasticism in late medieval England, looking in particular at their various activities and considering their relationships with their abbots, and contemporary conceptions of their place in the religious community. Colmán Ó Clabaigh takes us to late medieval Ireland to discuss a very special manuscript, Trinity College Dublin MS 97, and its role in the formation of novices training to become Victorine canons. The final chapter in this section is by David Austin who presents the important Welsh Cistercian abbey of Strata Florida and its place in Welsh culture, as well as its role in the formation of Welsh identity. He introduces the Strata Florida Project, outlining its aims and results to date, and emphasises the significance of interdisciplinarity, tying this work into a wider context of medieval monastic studies in Wales.

The six chapters that form the second section look at different types of interaction between monastic communities and the world outside, both religious and secular. Edel Bhreathnach examines a group of prominent Irish bishops and archbishops who were in religious orders and presided over great changes in Ireland during the tumultuous years of the twelfth and early thirteenth centuries. The following chapter, by Michael Carter, discusses the ongoing vitality of the Cistercian abbey of Rievaulx in Yorkshire during the later Middle Ages, reflected in the community's building programmes, its responses to changes in late medieval spirituality, theology and liturgy, and the relationship between the monks and their patrons. In her chapter on the Augustinian priory of Bridlington, Claire Cross assesses the activities of its priors in the last years leading up to the Dissolution. Her particular focus is on Prior William Wood, who joined the Pilgrimage of Grace and was consequently hanged for treason in 1537. Marsha Dutton considers Aelred of Rievaulx's xenophobic characterisation of the Galwegians in his narrative of the 1138 Battle of the Standard. Dutton seeks to understand how Aelred's brutal depiction of the Galwegians can be reconciled with the peace-loving author of spiritual treatises and suggests that Aelred was attempting to resolve the emotional conflict caused by his divided loyalties. In the following chapter, Philippa Hoskin looks at the figure of the thirteenth-century bishop of Lincoln, Robert Grosseteste, and his often difficult relationship with the religious houses in his diocese. Using Grosseteste's writings, in particular his sermons and philosophical works, Hoskin shows how the bishop did indeed integrate monks and nuns within his pastoral theory, a fact that influenced his treatment of them. Finally, Andrew Prescott provides an account of the involvement of religious communities in Norfolk in the Peasants' Revolt of 1381 and the impact this had on them. He focuses on the abbeys of St Benet of Holme and West Dereham and the priories at Carrow and Binham.

The role of women in medieval monasticism is the subject of the third section. Kimm Curran explores the challenges in writing the history of female religious, especially in Ireland, Scotland and Wales where source material is scant. She argues that by taking a more creative approach and using, for example, prosopography, we can build up a group biography of these women and learn more about their interactions with patrons and their localities. Brian Golding considers corrodies and explains that although they have had a bad press and could disrupt claustral life, corrodies constituted an important element in the nexus of relationships between benefactor and community. Golding examines the establishment, function, maintenance and regulation of corrodies provided for secular men as well as women in English nunneries. The final chapter in this section is by Veronica O'Mara who looks at visitation records for East Anglia to assess the range and extent of monastic preaching to nuns on the eve of the Reformation. O'Mara considers comparative aspects of preaching to men and women, namely, in terms of frequency, language, theme and preacher.

The chapters of this book present new and recent research by some of Janet's friends and colleagues and are a testimony to the profound impact she has made over the years, as a scholar and as a person. It will become clear from the *tabula gratulatoria* that this could have been a much, much bigger book. However we had to draw a line and sought in this collection above all to represent the various fields of Janet's research. We are all indebted to Janet's scholarship as well as her friendship. She has always been, and continues to be, extremely generous with her time and her knowledge, keen to share, to inspire and to encourage new research.

Notes

1. Janet Burton, *The Cartulary of the Treasurer of York Minster and related documents*, Borthwick Texts and Calendars (York, 1978); Janet Burton, 'Charters of Byland Abbey relating to the Grange of Bleatarn, Westmorland. Two Twelfth-Century Agreements made between Newburgh Priory and Byland Abbey', *Transactions of the Cumberland and Westmorland Antiquarian and Archaeological Society*, 79 (1979), 29–50; Janet Burton, 'A roll of charters for Lenton priory', *Borthwick Institute Bulletin*, 2, 1 (1979), 13–26; Janet Burton, 'A confraternity list from St. Mary's Abbey, York', *Revue Bénédictine*, 89 (1979), 325–33; Janet Burton, *The Yorkshire Nunneries in the twelfth and thirteenth centuries*, Borthwick Papers, no. 56 (York, 1979).

2. Janet Burton, 'The foundation of the British Cistercian houses', in Christopher Norton and David Park (eds), *Cistercian Art and Architecture in the British Isles* (Cambridge, 1986), pp. 24–39.

3. Janet Burton, 'Rievaulx Abbey: the Early Years', in Terryl N. Kinder (ed.), *Perspectives for an Architecture of Solitude: Essays on Cistercians, Art and Architecture in Honour of Peter Fergusson* (Turnhout, 2004), pp. 47–54.

4. Janet Burton, 'The monastic revival in Yorkshire: Whitby and St Mary's York', in David Rollason, Margaret Harvey and Michael Prestwich (eds), *Anglo-Norman Durham 1093–1193* (Woodbridge, 1994), pp. 41–51; Janet Burton, 'The Eremitical Tradition and

the Development of Post-Conquest Religious Life in Northern England', *Trivium*, 26 (1991), 18–39; Janet Burton, 'The Knights Templar in Yorkshire in the twelfth century: a reassessment', *Northern History*, 27 (1991), 26–40; Janet Burton, 'Monasteries and parish churches in eleventh- and twelfth-century Yorkshire', *Northern History*, 23 (1987), 39–50.

5. For example: Christopher Brooke, 'King David I of Scotland as a connoisseur of the religious orders', in Coloman Etienne Viola (ed.), *Mediaevalia christiana, XIe–XIIIe siècles: Hommage à Raymonde Foreville de ses amis, ses collègues et ses anciens élèves* (Paris, 1989), pp. 320–34; Christopher Brooke, 'Monk and canon: some patterns in the religious life of the twelfth century', *Studies in Church History*, 22 (1985) 109–29; Christopher Brooke, 'Princes and kings as patrons of monasteries', in *Il Monachesimo e la riforma ecclesiastica 1049–1122: Atti della quarta Settimana internazionale di studio Mendola, 23–29 agosto 1968* (Milan, 1971), pp. 125–52; Judith A. Green, *The aristocracy of Norman England* (Cambridge, 1997).

6. Brian Golding, 'Burials and benefactions: an aspect of monastic patronage in thirteenth-century England', in W. M. Ormrod (ed.), *England in the Thirteenth Century. Proceedings of the 1984 Harlaxton Symposium* (Grantham, 1985), pp. 64–75; Emma Mason, 'Timeo barones et donas ferentes', *Studies in Church History*, 15 (1978), 61–75; Benjamin Thompson, 'From "alms" to "spiritual services", the function and status of monastic property in medieval England', in Judith Loades (ed.), *Monastic Studies*, vol. 2 (Bangor, 1991), pp. 227–61; David Postles, 'Monastic burials of non-patronal lay benefactors', *Journal of Ecclesiastical History*, 47 (1996), 620–37.

7. Burton, *Monastic Order*, pp. 125–52.

8. *Monastic and Religious Orders in Britain, 1000–1300*, Cambridge Medieval Textbooks (Cambridge, 1994).

9. Burton, *Monastic Order*.

10. Emilia Jamroziak, *Rievaulx Abbey and its Social Context, 1132–1300: Memory, Locality and Networks* (Turnhout, 2005); Emilia Jamroziak, *Survival and Success on Medieval Borders: Cistercian Houses in Medieval Scotland and Pomerania from the Twelfth to Late Fourteenth Century* (Turnhout, 2011).

11. Janet Burton and Julie Kerr, *The Cistercians in the Middle Ages* (Woodbridge, 2011).

12. Janet Burton (ed.), *English Episcopal Acta V, York, 1070–1154* (Oxford, 1988); Janet Burton (ed.), *The Cartulary of Byland*, Surtees Society 2008 (Woodbridge, 2004); Janet Burton (ed.), *The Foundation History of the Abbeys of Byland and Jervaulx*, Borthwick Texts and Studies, 35 (York, 2006); Janet Burton with Lynda Lockyer (ed. and trans.), *Historia Selebiensis Monasterii, The History of the Monastery of Selby*, OMT (Oxford, 2013).

13. Glanmor Williams, *The Welsh Church from Conquest to Reformation* (Cardiff, 1976), p. 347. Note also Glanmor Williams's book on *Wales and the Reformation* (Cardiff, 1999), which pays considerable attention to the dissolution of the religious houses in Wales.

14. David Knowles and R. Neville Hadcock, *Medieval Religious Houses. England and Wales*, 2nd edn (Harlow, 1971), pp. 52–95; R. Cooper, *Abbeys and Priories of Wales* (Swansea, 1992).

15. Janet Burton and Karen Stöber, *Abbeys and Priories of Medieval Wales* (Cardiff, 2015, repr. 2015).

16. His list of publications on the Welsh Cistercians is too long to reproduce here, but see *www.monasticwales.org/browsedb.php?func=sourcelist*. Perhaps the most important of his many works on the Cistercians in Wales is David H. Williams, *The Welsh Cistercians* (Leominster, 2001).

17. David M. Robinson, *The Cistercians in Wales: Architecture and Archaeology 1130–1540* (London, 2006). David Robinson is moreover the author of many guidebooks on individual Welsh Cistercian abbeys, published by CADW , including *Cymer Abbey* (Cardiff, 1990; rev. 1995), *Neath Abbey* (Cardiff, 1989; rev. 1993, 1997), *Basingwerk Abbey* (Cardiff, 2006), *Tintern Abbey* (Cardiff, 4th edn 2002); and together with Colin Platt, *Strata Florida Abbey, Talley Abbey* (Cardiff, rev. edn, 1998).

18. Janet Burton, '*Homines sanctitatis eximiae, religionis consummatae*: The Cistercians in England and Wales', *Archaeologia Cambrensis*, 154 (for 2005), 27–49. In the same volume, note also Madeleine Gray's paper on the Cistercians in Wales: 'Preface to Cistercians in Wales and the west', *Archaeologia Cambrensis*, 154 (2005), 17–26.

19. Emilia Jamroziak, 'Clairvaux and the British Isles', in A. Baudin and A. Grélois (eds), *Le Temps Long de Clairvaux: Nouvelles Recherches, Nouvelles Perspectives (XIIᵉ–XXIᵉ siècle)* (Troyes, 2016), pp. 105–13.

20. *www.strataflorida.org.uk/*. Note also David Austin, 'The Archaeology of Monasteries in Wales and the Strata Florida Project', in J. Burton and K. Stöber (eds), *Monastic Wales: New Approaches* (Cardiff, 2013), pp. 3–20; and by the same author, 'Strata Florida and its Landscape', *Archaeologia Cambrensis*, 153 (2004), 192–201.

21. Jemma Bezant, 'The Medieval Grants to Strata Florida Abbey: Mapping the Agency of Lordship', in Burton and Stöber (eds), *Monastic Wales: New Approaches*, pp. 73–87. By the same author note also 'Revising the Monastic "Grange": Problems at the Edge of the Cistercian World', *The Journal of Medieval Monastic Studies*, 3 (2014), 51–70.

22. The project was entitled *A Survey of the Neath Abbey estates, 12th–17th Centuries*. Note especially the recent article by Rhianydd Biebrach, '"The Fairest Abbay of Al Wales": Neath Abbey and its Estates', *The Journal of Medieval Monastic Studies*, 3 (2014), 97–118.

23. On Neath Abbey note also Tony Hopkins, 'Cistercians and the urban community at Neath', *Archaeologia Cambrensis*, 154 (2005), 125–32.

24. Note for instance David Williams's work on Cistercian estates in *The Welsh Cistercians*.

25. David M. Robinson and Stuart Harrison, 'Cistercian Cloisters in England and Wales: Part I', *Journal of the British Archaeological Association*, 159 (2006), 131–207.

26. Ruth C. Easterling, 'The Friars in Wales', *Archaeologia Cambrensis*, Sixth Series, 14 (1914), 323–56.

27. Note for instance A. W. Clapham, 'The Architectural Remains of the Mendicant Orders in Wales', *Archaeological Journal*, 84 (1927), 88–104; or A. Jones, 'Property of the Welsh Friaries at the Dissolution', *Archaeologia Cambrensis*, 91 (1936), 47–9; or W. Rees,

'The suppression of the friaries in Glamorgan and Monmouthshire', in H. J. Randall and W. Rees (eds), *Miscellany*, 3 (Cardiff, 1954), pp. 7–19.

28. Frances Andrews, *The Other Friars: Carmelite, Augustinian, Sack and Pied Friars in the Middle Ages* (Woodbridge, 2006), pp. 69–172; David H. Williams, 'The Carmelites in Medieval Wales', in Iestyn Daniel (ed.), *Cofio John Fitzgerald, O. Carm.* (Pwllheli, 2010), pp. 100–7; Jens Röhrkasten, 'Monasteries and Urban Space in Medieval Welsh Towns', in Burton and Stöber (eds), *Monastic Wales: New Approaches*, pp. 55–70. Note also H. J. Randall and W. Rees (eds), 'The Houses of the Friars at Cardiff and Newport. First Financial Accounts after the Suppression', *Miscellany South Wales and Monmouth Record Society*, 4 (1957), 51–6.

29. Jane Cartwright, 'The Desire to Corrupt: Convents and Community in Medieval Wales', in D. Watt (ed.), *Medieval Women in their Communities* (Cardiff, 1997), pp. 20–48; *Y Forwyn Fair, Santesau a Lleianod: Agweddau ar Wyryfdod a Diweirdeb yng Nghymru'r Oesoedd Canol* (Cardiff, 1999); *Feminine Sanctity and Spirituality in Medieval Wales* (Cardiff, 2008), especially ch. 6, which is an updated version of her 1997 chapter 'The Desire to Corrupt: Convents and Community in Medieval Wales'. Note also her article 'Dead Virgins: feminine sanctity in medieval Wales', *Medium Aevum*, 72 (2002), 1–28.

30. Roberta Gilchrist, *Gender and Material Culture. The Archaeology of Religious Women* (London, 1994), pp. 39 (Llanllŷr), 66 (Llanllugan), 39, 61, 63, 64 (Usk).

31. Madeleine Gray and John Guy, '"A Better and Frugal Life": Llanllugan and the Cistercian Women's Houses in Wales', *Archaeologia Cambrensis*, 154 (2005), 97–114.

32. Richard Morgan, 'An Early Charter of Llanllugan Nunnery', *Montgomeryshire Collections*, 73 (1983), 116–18.

33. David H. Williams, 'Cistercian Nunneries in Medieval Wales', *Cîteaux: Commentarii Cistercienses*, 26 (1975), 155–74.

34. Note for example Madeleine Gray, 'Women of holiness and power: the cults of St Radegund and St Mary Magdalene at Usk', *The Monmouthshire Antiquary*, 18 (2002), 13–22. On the excavation work at the nunnery, see C. Maylan, 'Excavations at St. Mary's Priory, Usk, 1987', *Montgomeryshire Collections*, 9 (1993), 29–42; A. G. Mein, 'Usk Priory: an Unrecorded Excavation', *Monmouthshire Antiquary*, 9 (1993), 43–5; or David H. Williams, 'St. Mary's Priory, Usk: Excavation of 1998', *Monmouthshire Antiquary*, 16 (2000), 73–83.

35. See *https://monasticmatrix.osu.edu/monasticon/llanllugan*, *https://monasticmatrix.osu.edu/monasticon/llanllyr*, *https://monasticmatrix.osu.edu/monasticon/usk*; *www.coflein.gov.uk/en/site/20700/details/priory-house-usk-usk-priory-benedictine-nuns*, *www.coflein.gov.uk/en/site/400436/details/llanllyr-nunnery-talsarn*, and *www.coflein.gov.uk/en/site/400314/details/st-marys-church-llanllugan*.

36. Helen Fulton, 'Medieval Welsh poems to nuns', *Cambridge Medieval Celtic Studies*, 21 (1991), 87–112; Jane Cartwright, 'The Desire to Corrupt: Convents and Community in Medieval Wales', in *Feminine Sanctity and Spirituality in Medieval Wales*; and by the same

author, 'Abbess Annes and the Ape', in Burton and Stöber (eds), *Monastic Wales: New Approaches*, pp. 191–207.

37. Janet Burton, '*Moniales* and *Ordo Cisterciensis* in medieval England and Wales', in Gert Melville and Anne Müller (eds), *Female vita religiosa between Late Antiquity and the High Middle Ages: structures, developments and spatial contexts*, Vita Regularis, 47 (Berlin, 2011), pp. 375–89; 'Transition and Transformation: the Benedictine Houses', in Burton and Stöber (eds), *Monastic Wales: New Approaches*, pp. 21–37; Burton and Stöber, *Abbeys and Priories of Medieval Wales*.

38. Helen J. Nicholson, 'The Knights Hospitaller', in Burton and Stöber (eds), *Monastic Wales: New Approaches*, pp. 147–61 (p. 147).

39. J. Rogers Rees, *Slebech Commandery and the Knights of St John* (London, 1900); 'Slebech commandery and the Knights of St John', *Archaeologia Cambrensis*, Fifth Series, 14, 54 (1897), 85–107, 197–228, 261–84.

40. Knowles and Hadcock, *Medieval Religious Houses. England and Wales*, p. 306; F. G. Cowley, *The Monastic Order in South Wales 1066–1349* (Cardiff, 1977), pp. 277–8.

41. Kathryn Hurlock, *Wales and the Crusades, c.1095–1291* (Cardiff, 2011).

42. Williams, *The Welsh Church from Conquest to Reformation*.

43. Martin Heale, *The Dependent Priories of Medieval English Monasteries*, Studies in the History of Medieval Religion, 22 (Woodbridge, 2004). Note also M. M. Morgan, 'The Suppression of the Alien Priories', *History*, 26 (1941), 204–12.

44. Cowley, *The Monastic Order in South Wales 1066–1349*. Similarly, Siân Rees has looked at the southern Benedictine priories: Siân E. Rees, 'Benedictine Houses in South East Wales: Continuity and Conservation', *The Monmouthshire Antiquary*, 20 (2004), 83–94.

45. D. Walker, 'Brecon Priory in the Middle Ages', in O. W. Jones and D. Walker (eds), *Links with the Past: Swansea and Brecon Historical Essays* (Llandybïe, 1974), pp. 37–65; Ron Shoesmith, *Excavations at Chepstow 1973–1974*, Cambrian Archaeological Monograph, 4 (Cardiff, 1991); Ron Shoesmith, 'Chepstow Town, Priory and Port Wall', in Rick Turner and Andy Johnson (eds), *Chepstow Castle: its History and Buildings* (Almeley, 2006), pp. 199–212, 288–9; Malcolm Thurlby, 'The Romanesque Priory Church of St Michael at Ewenny', *Journal of the Society of Architectural Historians*, 47 (1988), 281–94; David H. Williams, 'Goldcliff Priory', *The Monmouthshire Antiquary*, 3 (1970–1), 37–54.

46. Janet Burton, 'Transition and Transformation: the Benedictine Houses', in Burton and Stöber (eds), *Monastic Wales: New Approaches*, pp. 21–37; note also her *Monastic and Religious Orders in Britain, 1000–1300*, especially pp. 33–4.

47. Janet Burton, 'Haverfordwest, prieuré de chanoines reguliers dans le comté de Pembroke', in R. Aubert (ed.), *Dictionnaire d'Histoire et de Géographie Ecclesiastiques*, fasc. 133–4, 615 (1988).

48. Karen Stöber, 'The Regular Canons in Wales', in J. Burton and K. Stöber, *The Regular Canons in the Medieval British Isles* (Turnhout, 2011), pp. 97–113.

49. David M. Robinson, *The Geography of Augustinian Settlement in Medieval England and Wales*, BAR British Series, 80, 2 vols (Oxford, 1980).

50. Gerald of Wales, *The Journey through Wales / The Description of Wales* (Harmondsworth, 1978), pp. 100–1. On Llanthony, see for example I. Gardner, 'Llanthony Prima', *Archaeologia Cambrensis*, 15 (1915), 343–76; Kirsty Bennett, 'The book collections of Llanthony Priory from foundation until dissolution (*c.*1100–1538)' (PhD thesis: University of Kent, 2006); C. M. Crampin, 'Llanthony Prima : An Assessment of Medieval Library Culture at Augustinian Houses in Wales' (MSc (Econ.) thesis: University of Wales, Aberystwyth, 2003); Arlene Hogan, *The Priory of Llanthony Prima and Secunda in Ireland, 1172–1541: Lands, Patronage and Politics* (Dublin, 2007); or David H. Williams, 'Llanthony Prima Priory', *The Monmouthshire Antiquary*, 25–6 (2009–10), 13–50. For Penmon Priory, note A. D. Carr, 'The priory of Penmon', *Journal of Welsh Ecclesiastical History*, 3 (1986), 18–31, Burton and Stöber, *Abbeys and Priories of Medieval Wales*, pp. 160–4. And on Beddgelert, see Burton and Stöber, *Abbeys and Priories of Medieval Wales*, pp. 53–6; despite its age, note also H. Longueville Jones, 'Beddgelert Priory', *Archaeologia Cambrensis*, 2, 6 (1847), 153–66.

51. Karen Stöber and David Austin, 'Culdees to Canons: the Augustinian Houses of North Wales', in Burton and Stöber (eds), *Monastic Wales: New Approaches*, pp. 39–54; Some discussion of the regular canons in Wales can be found in houses about the Order in England, as in Joseph A. Gribbin, *The Premonstratensian Order in Late Medieval England* (Woodbridge, 2001), pp. 8–9.

52. E.g. Dafydd Johnston, 'Monastic Patronage of Welsh Poetry', in Burton and Stöber (eds), *Monastic Wales: New Approaches*, pp. 177–90; Eurig Salisbury, *Ar Drywydd Guto'r Glyn ap Siancyn y Glyn* (Aberystwyth, 2007).

53. Daniel Huws, *Medieval Welsh Manuscripts* (Aberystwyth, 2000), p. 215; Th. Jones (ed.), *Brut y Tywysogyon or The Chronicle of the Princes. Red Book of Hergest Version* (Cardiff, 1955).

54. Ceridwen Lloyd-Morgan, 'Manuscripts and the Monasteries', in Burton and Stöber (eds), *Monastic Wales: New Approaches*, pp. 209–27.

55. Huw Pryce, 'Patrons and patronage among the Cistercians in Wales', *Archaeologia Cambrensis*, 154 (for 2005), 81–95; David Stephenson, 'The Rulers of Gwynedd and Powys', in Burton and Stöber (eds), *Monastic Wales: New Approaches*, pp. 89–102; Jemma Bezant, 'The Medieval Grants to Strata Florida Abbey: Mapping the Agency of Lordship', in Burton and Stöber (eds), *Monastic Wales: New Approaches*, pp. 73–87; Julie Kerr, 'Cistercian Hospitality in the Later Middle Ages', in J. Burton and K. Stöber (eds), *Monasteries and Society in the British Isles in the Later Middle Ages*, Studies in the History of Medieval Religion, 35 (Woodbridge, 2008), pp. 25–39; Karen Stöber, *Late Medieval Monasteries and their Patrons: England and Wales, c.1300–1540*, Studies in the History of Medieval Religion, 29 (Woodbridge, 2007), and 'The Social Networks of Late Medieval Welsh Monasteries', in Burton and Stöber (eds), *Monasteries and Society,*

pp. 12–24; Andrew Abram, 'Monastic Burial in Medieval Wales', in Burton and Stöber (eds), *Monastic Wales: New Approaches*, pp. 103–15.

56. *www.monasticwales.org/*. Note also Janet Burton and Karen Stöber, 'The Monastic Wales Project', *Imago Temporis, Medium Aevum*, 10 (2016), 339–55.

57. *www.monastic.ie/*.

58. Burton and Stöber, *Abbeys and Priories of Medieval Wales*.

59. David Knowles, *The Monastic Order in England: A History of its Development from the Times of St Dunstan to the Fourth Lateran Council, 940–1216*, 2nd edn (Cambridge, 1966), pp. 175–6.

60. Stefan Weinfurter, 'Neuere Forschungen zu den Regularkanonikern im Deutschen Reich des 11. und 12. Jahrhunderts', *Historische Zeitschrift*, 224 (1977), 379–97.

61. H. M. Colvin, *The White Canons in England* (Oxford, 1951); J. C. Dickinson, *The Origins of the Austin Canons and their Introduction into England* (London, 1950).

62. Robinson, *The Geography of Augustinian Settlement in Medieval England and Wales*.

63. Burton, *Monastic and Religious Orders in Britain*, pp. 43–62.

64. Gribbin, *The Premonstratensian Order in Late Medieval England*.

65. This large volume of papers, substantially revised and with the addition of a number of further chapters, was edited by Janet Burton and Karen Stöber and published under the title *The Regular Canons in the Medieval British Isles*.

66. Janet Burton, 'The regular canons and diocesan reform', in Burton and Stöber, *The Regular Canons in the Medieval British Isles*, pp. 41–57. Note also Janet Burton, 'Les chanoines reguliers en Grande-Bretagne', in M. Parisse (ed.), *Les Chanoines reguliers: émergence et expansion (xie–xiiie siècles)* (St Etienne, 2009), pp. 477–98.

67. Note for example Andrew Abram, *Norton Priory: An Augustinian Community and its Benefactors*, Trivium, Occasional Papers, No. 2 (2007), or 'The Augustinian Priory of Wombridge and its Benefactors in the Later Middle Ages', in Burton and Stöber (eds), *Monasteries and Society*, pp. 83–94; Terrie Colk, 'Twelfth-Century East Anglian Canons: a Monastic Life?', in C. Harper-Bill (ed.), *Medieval East Anglia* (Woodbridge, 2005), pp. 209–24; A. A. M. Duncan, 'The Foundation of St Andrews Cathedral Priory, 1140', *The Scottish Historical Review*, 84 (2005), 1–37; Allison D. Fizzard, 'Shoes, Boots, Leggings and Cloaks: the Augustinian Canons and Dress in Later Medieval England', *Journal of British Studies*, 46 (2007), 245–62, also 'The Incumbents of Benefices in the Gift of Plympton Priory, 1257–1369', *Medieval Prosopography*, 25 (2008), 75–100, and *Plympton Priory: A House of Augustinian Canons in South-Western England in the Later Middle Ages* (Leiden, 2008); Judy Frost, *The Foundation of Nostell Priory, 1109–1153*, Borthwick Paper 111 (York, 2007); Lionel Green, *A Priory Revealed, Using Materials Relating to Merton Priory* (Merton, 2005); Joseph A. Gribbin, 'La Vie de Richard Redman, Abbé de Shap, Vicaire Général de l'Abbé de Prémontré et Évêque (env. 1458–1505)', in D.-M. Dauzet and M. Plouvier (eds), *Abbatiat et Abbés Dans L'Ordre de Prémontré*, Bibliotheca Victorina, 17 (Turnhout, 2005), pp. 295–310; Julian Luxford, 'A Leiston Document from Glastonbury', *Proceedings of the Suffolk Institute of Archaeology and History*, 40 (2003), 278–88; Joshua Easterling,

'A Norbert for England: Holy Trinity and the Invention of Robert of Knaresborough', *JMMS*, 2 (2013), 75–107.

68. Burton, 'Women and the religious life', in *Monastic and Religious Orders in Britain*, pp. 85–108.

69. Janet's earliest publications on medieval nuns are 'The election of Joan Fletcher as prioress of Basedale, 1524', *Borthwick Institute Bulletin*, 1, 4 (1978), 145–53; and *The Yorkshire Nunneries in the Twelfth and Thirteenth Centuries*, 54.

70. Note especially Constance Hoffman Berman, 'Were there Twelfth-Century Cistercian Nuns?', in C. Hoffman Berman (ed.), *Medieval Religion: New Approaches* (London, 2005), pp. 217–48; Burton and Kerr, *The Cistercians in the Middle Ages*, note especially pp. 27–8; Emilia Jamroziak, 'Cistercian nuns: the role of women in the Order', *The Cistercian Order in Medieval Europe, 1090–1500* (London, 2013), pp. 124–55; Brigitte Degler-Spengler, 'The Incorporation of Cistercian Nuns into the Order in the Twelfth and Thirteenth Centuries', in *Hidden Springs: Cistercian Monastic Women*, 2 vols (Kalamazoo, MI, 1995), and in the same volume, Brian Patrick McGuire, 'The Cistercians and Friendship: an Opening to Women'; by the same author note also, *Friendship and Faith: Cistercian Men, Women, and their Stories, 1100–1250* (Aldershot, 2002); Elizabeth Freeman, 'Cistercian Nuns in Medieval England: Unofficial Meets Official', *Studies in Church History*, 42 (2006), 110–19.

71. Note her articles on 'Yorkshire Nunneries in the Later Middle Ages: recruitment and resources', in Paul Dalton and John Appleby (eds), *Government, Religion and Society in Northern England, 1000–1700* (Stroud, 1997), pp. 104–16; and 'Cloistered Women and Male Authority: power and authority in Yorkshire nunneries in the later Middle Ages', in Michael Prestwich, Richard Britnell and Robin Frame (eds), *Thirteenth Century England*, 10 (Woodbridge, 2005), pp. 155–65.

72. Janet Burton, 'The Chariot of Aminadab and the Yorkshire nunnery of Swine', in R. Horrox and S. Rees Jones (eds), *Pragmatic Utopias: Ideals and Communities 1200–1630* (Cambridge, 2001), pp. 26–42.

73. Burton, '*Moniales* and *Ordo Cisterciensis* in medieval England and Wales'.

74. Janet Burton, 'Constructing the lives of medieval nuns', in Julia Boffey and Virginia Davies (eds), *Recording Medieval Lives*, Proceedings of the 2005 Harlaxton Symposium (Stamford, 2009), pp. 14–24; 'Looking for medieval nuns: prosopographical possibilities', in Burton and Stöber, *Monasteries and Society*, pp. 113–23.

75. Janet Burton and Karen Stöber (eds), *Women in the Medieval Monastic World* (Turnhout, 2015), pp. 123–43.

PART I

Monastic and religious orders in Britain

I

Cistercian histories in late medieval England, and beyond

James G. Clark

The Cistercian abbey at Forde, in the valley of the River Axe, arose from three particular moments in time. The first was when Richard Fitz Baldwin (d.1137), hereditary sheriff of Devon, persuaded a delegation of White Monks from Waverley, the early hub of the English colony, to settle in the lee of his new fortification rising above the River Ock at Okehampton, the defensive centre of his baronial domain. The second followed five years later: Richard died leaving no direct heir and expatriate monks without an incumbent lord at the outer reaches of the Anglo-Norman polity, a condition, as the monks remembered it 'of such poverty and want, horribly barren of foodstuffs' (pre inopia et pre dira sterilitate victualiumque penuria). They buried their prospective founder and were 'compelled to return to their original home' (amplius morari non potuissent ad domum suam pristinam ... redire sunt compulsi). The final moment came only days later and by chance. As the procession of monks made its way down the eastern slopes of the Blackdown Hills, the two brothers in front bearing the cross were spied by the Lady Adeliz (d.1142), sole surviving sibling of Sheriff Richard. She recognised them as her brother's brethren and, identifying herself as his heir, with the obligation to settle his debts, she offered them her manor of Thorncombe, which, by contrast with Brightley, was 'fertile and wooded' (fertile satis et nemorosum). The first two moments represented at once the power and the contingency of temporal lordship – a persistent trope in chronicle narratives – but the last, decisive event was dramatised by another staple of remembered history, a wonder, worthy of inspiring devotion, when the monks' crucifix carried them to the very doorstep of their hereditary founder who was ready with an infallible recall of their whole story.[1]

England's Cistercians were created by historical narratives of this kind. Their asceticism and the conditions of lordship in the regions they entered combined to make their first steps towards colonisation tentative, divergent and frequently interrupted. The plantation of their communities was not an act, despite the creation of a charter which expressed this aspiration; more typically it was an experience, shared and endured over a passage of time, the full consequences of which were often intelligible only at a distance, even for those able to remember them at first hand. It was by the recall, in memory, and then on the manuscript page that, as Janet Burton has written of Byland and Jervaulx, the identities of these monastic communities were first established.[2]

These histories captured and connected the impulses that made a Cistercian *conventus*: the organic, even contingent sense of *communitas*, defined more by the rhythms of its shared story than by any one event in time; the seigniorial contract that stayed, if not always immediately settled them; the sudden and supernatural demonstrations of divine agency, the crucifix that guided the monks over the hill and down the genealogical tree to their hereditary founder – or, indeed, the 'small white birds without number, like sparrows of a radiance that cannot be imagined' that led the brethren from Byland to Jervalux[3] – which was a bright spark of spiritual inspiration and, duly narrated took on a commemorative use that was almost liturgical.

The distinctive character of the Cistercians' histories has been recognised only in the research of recent years. Janet Burton's recovery of the foundation history of Byland and Jervaulx has highlighted the principal reason for its previous neglect, the late, patchy, sometimes post-medieval transcripts, often first appearing in private archives and book collections, that offer the main witness to many of these texts.

Elizabeth Freeman has also shown that a lively critical appreciation of the Cistercians' monastic values has inadvertently diminished aspects of their intellectual culture and an understanding of its place in their formation as communities and networks.[4] The Order arose at a time when the centres of gravity, and genres, of learned and literary activity were shifting but historians have been swayed too far by the rhetoric of Bernard of Clairvaux to recognise the Cistercian presence in the creative mainstream. This is especially true of historical discourse, the study of which at any rate has been distorted by the long dominance of a Benedictine model of monastic historiography which was the (re)construction of post-medieval readers. The editors of the Rolls Series framed the handful of Cistercian narratives to which they gave a place in the series with judgements founded on the features of the more familiar Benedictine discourse, reminding readers of the separation of the White Monks, their cultural austerity and 'denial of the practice or enjoyment of the ... arts'.[5] In fact, as Freeman has urged, the case may be made for a measurable Cistercian contribution to the richest period of historical writing in post-Conquest England. The narratives composed in their first century can be seen sharply to focus, and to shape, some of the major cultural and intellectual transformations of these years, the transfer of power from remembered authority to its embodiment in record; the resolution of the demands of scripture and the canons with the claims of human society, steering a course between revelation and lived experience and, in discovering and responding to the world visible and invisible, between the allegorical and the literal.

These perspectives have encouraged a new, capacious definition of Cistercian historiography, recognising the variety of genres, liturgy, hagiography, homiletic, scriptural commentary even, in which the monks were 'thinking about history, finding out about history and talking about history'.[6] It has also challenged the hierarchical outlook that has always marked the approach to Benedictine historical culture, highlighting the creative activity at the outer reaches of the network beyond the south-east or the North Riding. Yet this new interest in their narratives has been chronologically contained, and it would seem intentionally so. Cistercian history has been drawn out of the shadows primarily as a discourse of formation, in which narrative served as a vehicle for monastic colonisation, determining the location and patronal relationship of the convent and defining its mode of observant life. Freeman has acknowledged that its special properties were still demanded, and deployed, after the passing of that first, heroic age, just as Janet Burton has shown in the case of Byland.[7] But the waves of growing pains had generally passed by the centenary of the Order's coming into England and Freeman at least has represented the mid-thirteenth century as the 'end of an era'.[8]

There can be no doubt that later Cistercian life in England was marked by different dynamics: a developing society and a depressed economy extinguished the dual presence in the precinct and pressed the monastic experience into new moulds. That the old discourse was unsuited to these changing rhythms might explain the meagre manuscript traces of history, many of them damaged or discarded even before the Dissolution. Thomas Burton's *vox clamantis* from Meaux, that so many ancient membranes and parchments (*nonnullas cedulas antiquas et membranas neglectas*) were so long neglected, left out in the rain or consigned to the flames (*alias imbribus expositas alias igni deputatas*), might be quoted in support of this view.[9] Beyond Burton's own compendium, there has been passing attention only for those fragments of contemporary history which commented on national crises – the revolts of 1381 (Kirkstall), the Ricardian depositions, apparent (1387) and real (1399: Dieulacres), and the Ricardian rebellions against his usurper (Dieulacres, Whalley) – and these have been found wanting by comparison with the Benedictines and the growing number of seculars writing history.[10] 'The White Monks were not great book men', wrote Maud V. Clarke of the Kirkstall chronicle, 'the management of their estates left them little time for literary pursuits'.[11] Antonia Gransden agreed with her, judging these three 'north country' narratives to be limited in 'scope and literary quality'; and there has been no challenge from the most recent survey: the White Monks viewed the world as from the wrong end of a telescope, 'useful' observations only 'occasionally' breaking through their litany of 'land, livestock and leases'.[12]

Yet it would be wrong to equate the Cistercians' changing environment with the displacement of the personal, confessional, communal and corporate impulses that made a monastic community. The dominant themes of the early narratives, for what, how, and by whom the monastery, its people (*conventus*) and its presence (*domus*) were made still resonated for those that came two centuries after them. Of course, it is a defining feature of the monastic life that each new generation confronts the challenges of withdrawal from the world, formation and stability as if for the first time. But as we understand better the challenges of their later years, it is possible to see that their formative history held up to them not only an idea of the Cistercian profession but also a useable resource of information for their present concerns. The transformations of the later period were more than structural and material. At the end of Elizabeth Freeman's 'era', *c*.1250, the intellectual culture of the White Monks was already absorbing the new currents from the secular schools. The literal turn in scholastic exegesis which reached its fullest expression in the postils of Nicholas de Lyra (d.1349) surely made as great an impression on the historicism of England's Cistercians as it did on the Benedictines, perhaps more so given the pervasive influence of the Fordean school of Baldwin and John. The heightened historical colours of vernacular Romance also appeared on their horizons. It remains an open question whether Guy de Beauchamp's remarkable Romance library was accepted by the monks of Bordesley to whom he bequeathed it in 1315; if they did, the French *Alexandre* and *Artu* now entered their line of sight.[13] If the curious Anglo-Norman annal and genealogy of the West-Country Mohun family can be connected with Newenham, and it is at least plausible, then it shows that even a modest, rural convent was aware of the historical imagination that animated a secular household.[14]

The continuing evolution of their cultural life extended to the making and keeping of many 'membranes and parchments', despite Thomas Burton's lament. Of course, surviving catalogues and inventories, and the highly selective notes of John Leland can be used to support any argument but the mix of authors and texts old – foundational even – and new which they document do show a continuing turnover of textual material. Among the survivors there are many signs of 'thinking, finding out about and writing history'. This reached beyond the reproduction of the earliest histories and the recovery of the oldest charters, as Burton set himself to do. Across the network there were traces of new writing, still a mix of narrative and documents, and some continuing to turn over the matter of their origins but more of it digesting the testimony of more recent times, to establish order over, and some authority in, the past just passing out of living memory. The years between the accession of Edward I and the deposition of his son were especially active. Houses of the first phase of Cistercian settlement, for example, Pipewell (1143) and Stanley (1151), which had not known any earlier historical enterprise now confronted their past.[15] Forde, a beacon of learned Biblicism in its first century took to history with the same energy which earlier had been applied to the sacred page. Now the story of the Lady Adeliz was written up and shared with a wider audience.[16] Foundations scarcely a generation old such as Newenham (1247) began what seems to have been a whole programme of record-keeping, at the centre of which was a miraculous history of the (recent) death of their founder, Reginald de Mohun (d.1258).[17] Some reached beyond the most familiar forms of history to try narrative responses to the increasingly frequent challenges to their lordship, post-Mortmain disputes over property (Croxden, Robertsbridge) and the persistent disturbances of an aspirant tenantry (Pipewell).[18]

The raw materials of this later historical culture were diverse. The evolution of the Cistercians' provision of library books is not as well documented as the Benedictines or the Regular Canons but a handful of catalogues – for example, Rievaulx – show history recognised as a discrete component of the collection, with volumes arranged as a shelf-group. The anchor-hold at Rievaulx, and probably elsewhere, were the staple authorities of English, imperial and papal history, William of Malmesbury, Henry of Huntington, Martin of Poland.[19] Their standing is apparent in almost all the new compilations of these years: the monks of Stanley (Wiltshire) met William in the post-Conquest portion of their annal.[20] Henry was the mainstay of the narrative presented in the Dieulacres manuscript ahead of the annal of Richard II's reign.[21] Thomas Burton made them the pillars of his post-Conquest history, Henry for England's civil war, and Martin for the election of the Order's first pontiff, Eugenius III.[22] Generally, these most read, most referenced histories, were underpinned by the canonical authorities of a more distant past, sacred and legendary. The White Monks that 'thought about history' in the later period were surely aware of Bede, Eusebius, Orosius and although Geoffrey of Monmouth is recorded in only one inventory (Rievaulx again) his press on their historical imagination was apparent even just from the opening leaves of the Stanley Chronicle and Orosius.[23]

But the history shelf did not remain static. New authorities joined the Anglo-Normans: Nicholas Trevet's *Annales*; the chronicle attributed to John

Pike (at Kingswood); Ranulf Higden's *Polychronicon* (at Fountains, Furness and Meaux) and the anonymous chronicle of pre- and post-Conquest England (down to 1199) known (from John Bale's misattribution) as 'John of Brompton' (at Jervaulx).[24] Some also had a sharp eye for a real rarity: at Long Bennington (Lincolnshire) someone caught hold of disbound fragments which included a portion of Robert of Torigni's Norman history.[25]

Despite the different beginnings of their devotional culture, there was now a rich seam of history rising from their hagiographical collections which in the years after 1300 seem to have been as large and varied as the Benedictines. The legacy of Aelred's affiliation of the English congregation with the national cult was a sharp awareness of England's sacred history. Leland, searching especially for texts of this kind, saw multiple lives of Edward the Confessor together with those of David of Scotland and Ninian at Rievaulx; lives of Alban, Edward and Thomas Becket are witnessed in other inventories.[26] It seems likely that a surviving anthology of saints' lives which contains Aelred's *Vita Edwardi* and a life of St Bernard of Clairvaux was compiled by an English Cistercian, perhaps an Oxford monk given the presence at the end of the codex of the sermons of John Felton, fifteenth-century vicar of St Mary Magdalen.[27] A calendar which has been identified as Cistercian contains entries for no fewer than 198 obits of celebrated and canonised churchmen with cross-references (in the form of an alphanumerical key) to the narratives of their lives to be found (presumably) in the conventual book-collection; quite a number are figures of comparative recent English history, among them Gundulf of Rochester (d.1108), Godric of Finchale (d.1170), Thomas Becket (d.1170) and Edmund Rich (d.1247).[28] The progression of thought from England's host of holy men to the history and legend of the patrimony as a whole is apparent in an early fifteenth-century book from Bordesley Abbey, used, if not compiled, by a named monk, John Northwode. After a sequence of prayers on Thomas Becket, Edmund of Abingdon and others, there follows a folio of historical notes on the parishes and knights' fees of England.[29] For an unnamed monk of Kirkstead who was using an early fourteenth-century psalter for private devotion in the fifteenth century, such meditations framed by the festal calendar led the train of their thought to the house's own patrimony and they added a map of Kirkstead's domain, a note of those of its principal properties which had been disputed and a description of three neighbouring baronies.[30]

These calendars remind us that the formal, communal obligations of observance themselves generated and guided 'thinking about history'. The Kirkstead calendar records that the festal celebration of the dedication of the abbey church on 12 September was marked as a major feast of no fewer than twelve readings.[31] The marking of the date itself might be said to have prompted the historical imagination of the monastic community but it is possible that the readings or even the hymns and prayers performed at these commemorations carried a narrative passage from the foundation history. Certainly the chronology and principal events in the making of a Cistercian house seem to have had a wide reach across the textual environment of the monastery, and not simply because they made multiple copies of their original or principal history but also because selected material itself, for example the dated record of the first or second site of the colony, the dedication of its church, was carried over and added to, or assimilated into another context, a text, or a whole anthology of texts. The passage of the past from the church to the bookshelf, and the symmetry to be found between calendar and chronicle is neatly signalled in the Stanley annal, where death notices, of kings and prelates, were marked with an O capital, highlighted in red, just as they might have been in the calendar.[32]

For the history of pre-Christian antiquity, there was at least one point-of-contact familiar to almost any Latin reader in the later Middle Ages, the *Bellum Troianae* attributed to Dares Phrygius.[33] This was an historical taste strengthening in bookish Benedictine houses from the fourteenth century, fuelled perhaps by a greater reception of Romance literature.[34] Generally the Cistercians' holdings did not reach so far beyond their immediate horizons but there may have been exceptions. The Courtenay compendium, a fourteenth-century anthology of history ancient and modern, which brings together Dares, the *Gesta Cnutonis regis*, Geoffrey of Monmouth's *Historia regum Britanniae*, and the histories of the Muslim East of Pierre Tudebode and William of Tripoli, bears no *ex libris*, *ex dono* or personal inscription and remains unprovenanced but its presence in the library of the Courtenay earls of Devon might connect it with Forde, which they patronised and made their mausoleum.[35]

The Courtenay connection highlights the possible role of their lay affinities in sustaining, and resourcing, the Cistercians' historical culture. Abbot John Brompton's procurement of the manuscript containing an anonymous chronicle was surely in some way connected with the abbey's hereditary founders the Fitzhughs, whose arms feature in the initial capital on the first leaf of the main text.[36] Both the content and cultural influences — Romance in general, Wace in particular — of the Mohun Chronicle would strongly suggest that along the axis between the abbey (Newenham) and hereditary founder the traffic passed both ways; the relationship here seems reminiscent of the Gloucestershire Berkeleys and their hereditary canon house of St Augustine's Abbey, Bristol.[37] It seems these channels were also open at an individual level. A Sibton monk Richard Muttforde was given a copy of Higden's history to keep at his pleasure (*ad placitum habeat*) for his lifetime (with reversion to the conventual collection) by Thomas Crofts, gentleman (*armiger*), perhaps a kins-man or (and) patron.[38]

The remains of their book-collections are too meagre to gauge priorities as has been done for the greater Benedictine abbeys and cathedral priories which after 1300 were 'stocked' to supply university students and to support their subsequent obligations as preachers and pastors. Yet from the faint out-lines it may be said that history was not a central concern for the conventual purse and the needs of education and formation weighed just as heavily as they did elsewhere. Perhaps the books presented to the new house at Newenham by its inaugural abbot in 1243 may stand for a preferred syllabus for the sec-ond century of the English network, with John Beleth's manual *Summa de ecclesiasticis officiis* and William of Auxerre's Sentence commentary the standout authorities among the reference works.[39] The injunctions that Meaux's Abbot Roger of Driffield (1286–1310) issued (even) to his outlying colony of brethren at Ottringham chantry – as described by Thomas Burton – may give a fair indication of the formal position, that the monks should apply themselves to the study of theology so that the catholic faith might be surrounded with an impregnable wall of preachers (fides catholica muro inexpugnabili praedicta-torum sit circumcincta).[40]

The call to a clerical curriculum – which anticipated the reforms of Pope Benedict XII (1338) – may have weakened the impulse to pass historical material through the network. There is only glancing common ground between Thomas Burton at Meaux and one manuscript of the Kirkstall chronicle in the coverage of Edward II's reign, which, from the dates of their compilation would demand an almost immediate transmission. More noticeable are the differences between the narratives of the same years (1399–1413) found at Dieulacres and Whalley. Here the ties that can be traced through each text like a seam are quite distinct from one another, one to the economic and social centre point of the region (Chester), the other to the principal patronal fam-ily (the Percies). If there was any deliberate exchange of texts it was under local horizons.[41]

Perhaps the greater traffic in texts of historical interest in these houses after 1300 was not in the conventual collection at all but in the chambers and chanceries (where they had them) of the monastery's senior officers. Certainly their early historical writing had been sustained by a level of chancerial activity and archival organisation which somewhat belied their continuing institutional vulnerability. Other than the narratives themselves, the scope of this can only begin to be glimpsed in sources dating from the end of this first era. The earliest surviving cartularies from Fountains Abbey, first compiled in the third quarter of the thirteenth century, record with each charter copied a shelf mark corresponding to a storage chest and a bundle number where the original would be found, suggesting the formation of a principal (if not the only) conventual archive.[42] A mid-thirteenth-century cartulary roll from Flaxley reveals in its cross-references the distribution of charters in discrete collections held by the principal obedientiaries (for example, cellarer, sacristan).[43] The indications of manuscripts from the following century point to these early examples marking a transition, as the documentary turnover of these houses expanded steadily, giving rise to a greater variety of forms and a greater number of parallel repositories. After 1300 the rising managerial pressures – administrative, fiscal, legal – to produce new documents and to (re)appraise old holdings gave rise to targeted projects for the creation of new compilations.

The surviving examples suggest that these impulses were especially strong in the office of the abbot. The most complete cartularies – or perhaps more precisely, anthologies of documents – reveal the hand of their respective abbot. William de Lalleford of Pipewell (Northamptonshire) prepared for himself a digest of the royal, papal and seigniorial grants secured by the house, drawing on what was, to judge from what still survives, an already sizeable shelf-group of cartularies, and, apparently acknowledging that it was a personal conspectus of what was already written elsewhere he named it his 'Speculum'.[44] The so-called 'Coucher book' of Whalley Abbey was first put together under the direction of Abbot John de Lindley (1342–77).[45] At Rufford a pre-existing cartulary was pressed into the more particular service of Abbot John Lyle who added two quires of recent documents and framed the whole with the statement that it would now serve as his register.[46] The creation of a personal *speculum cartarum* might be inferred from Abbot Thomas de Lancasore's performance before the earl of Arundel in November 1400, when he was recorded to have sought the earl's confirmation of the abbey's privileges and read to him the terms of the foundation charter of *c.*1200.[47]

These later creations are marked by their (each) very different principles of selection and organisation, by not infrequent repetition – grants or privileges which are written out more than once in the same collection – and their retention of miscellaneous notes, many of which in origin were no more formal than a hastily composed memorandum or aide memoire. Yet it does seem that this shuffling and reshuffling of the monastery's documentary residue acted as another prompt for historical research. The making of a documentary collection had always represented a contribution to the historical discourse of a monastery but in the manuscripts of the later period it becomes palpable. According to Roger Dodsworth's transcripts, the Whalley register extended to the sketching of summary *gesta abbatum*.[48] After copying charters confirming a claim on the advowsons of churches for reference in a dispute, an unidentified obedientiary at Dunkeswell Abbey wrote out, on the same parchment sheet, a genealogy descending from the founder, William de Brewer.[49]

The concentration of creative activity among the officers aligns later Cistercian history with the conventual hierarchy. It was not only cartularies but many of the most developed narrative texts and most of the original writing that emanated from the office of the superior. Often this work was undertaken directly at the abbot's initiative. Thomas Burton made his historical compendium a defining contribution of his abbacy, an act of patronage for the restoration of the house, for its archival rather than its architectural fabric, offered as definitive statement, founded only on documentary or verbal authority ('nisi quod aut scriptum in aliorum opusculis et memorandis diversis inveni, aut ex fidedignorum relatione saepius audivi').[50] Apparently Whalley's Abbot Paslew embarked on a similar programme for his brethren in 1507, instructing and funding the making of a new *libellus* capturing the past distinctions of the house for future notice ('per cuius praeceptum et voluntatem huius compilationis ... sumpsit exordium').[51]

These were grand gestures but more generally later Cistercian heads seem to have found in narrative forms an effective means of accounting for their record in office. The fragment of an annal from Sibton is titled quite simply 'Notable things undertaken in the courts of the abbot at various times'.[52] Clearly this was not only a matter of marshalling the facts of their various causes but also taking control over them, drawing on the capacity of narrative to fix them and their interpretation. The Robertsbridge annal was written up either as formal record for Abbot John de Lamberhurst or as memoir of one of his household.[53] The narrator was surely with Abbot John on his progress from the courts to the king and back again because he recalled the words spoken to him by the official of Canterbury when he met with him in his private chamber; his stopover at Stratford to celebrate morning mass; and the fact that when finally installed at Hastings, he sat on the right-hand side of the choir.[54] In a similar fashion over a longer time span, the continuation of Forde's foundation history is formed of short narratives which summarise the causes of a number of abbots between 1270 and 1340 which are framed in respects of the 'good' and the 'evils' they confronted during their terms, culminating in the 'three evils' which Hugh de Courtenay wrought ('tria mala, que idem dominus Hugo fecerat in exheredationem monasterii') during the abbacy of William (1319–30).[55] These abbots not only turned to narrative to reinforce their rule in retrospect but also deployed it as an active instrument of their office. The enshrinement of the Holy Blood Relic at Hailes in 1277 was sealed in an annal whose close observation of the events that attended it and judicious commendation of the relic's royal patron, Edmund of Cornwall, point to its commission and compilation under the supervision of Abbot Hugh.[56] The account of the death of the founder of Newenham Abbey (Devon), Reginald [II] de Mohun in 1258, the centrepiece of which is the story of a wondrous vision of a Cistercian father that appeared to Lord Reginald on his deathbed, was surely prepared by Abbot Geoffrey (de Blancheville, 1252–62) to secure the burial for his house, founded scarcely ten years before and then still under the shadow of two older and wealthier Cistercian foundations at Forde and Torre Abbey, where Reginald had died.[57]

The close association of the Cistercian annals with the leadership of the house might modify our reading of the longest of the later annals, from Stanley, Dieulacres, Kirkstall and Meaux. If they are understood to have been oriented largely on an abbatial axis it is possible to see greater coherence and consistency in their coverage. Regarding external affairs, their purpose was not to provide a comprehensive account of Crown, prelacy and lordship but rather to describe those particular moments, and points-of-contact, which especially challenged them. The Stanley chronicler(s) expands, outspokenly, on the fiscal demands of the Crown before 1215, in 1254 and 1258, but passes briskly, and with terse detachment over other events of national moment, not least the second Barons' war and the battles of Lewes and Evesham.[58] Dieulacres and Kirkstall pause over the Peasants' Revolt but otherwise disengage from the difficult course of Richard II's reign until the descent (from 1397) towards his deposition.[59] A gesture towards a national annal at Croxden was made with even greater concision, the events from the birth of Christ to the death of Edward III filling only two and a half folios.[60] Naturally, at Meaux Thomas Burton's line of sight led northwards and he is at his most expansive – and most engaged with external documentary sources – in tracing English campaigns and Scots' incursions across the northern border.[61] The intersection of topics of less overtly political interest which are nonetheless treated at length, for example, the translation of the relics of Thomas Becket at Westminster, the (re)translation of the relics of Wulfstan at Worcester (Stanley), the coming of the cult of John Thweng at Bridlington (Kirkstall), also reflect the perspectives of the abbacy or, if broader, the conventual hierarchy.[62] It was to be expected that such pivotal moments in the making of a national cult would leave their mark on any monastic institution. Written at the time that the White Monks' interest in and assimilation of the English martyrology was deepening, and their own pattern of worship moving more into alignment with the churches of the orders (Benedictine, Regular Canons) which were the custodians of these shrines, in fact it might be suggested that the attention given in these narratives represented a conscious steering of the conventual discourse. Here the similarity of approach between Stanley, where the work was interrupted early in the 1270s, and Dieulacres and Kirkstall written up more than a century later, should be emphasised. The two later narratives have tended to be read (when they have been read at all) as northern chronicles of the revolution, measured alongside other Ricardian narratives of presumed monastic origin.[63] If, rather, they are placed on a continuum with the Stanley narrative, they may be recast as consistent in coverage and tone with the outlook of the Cistercian leadership as it unfolded between the restoration of royal authority under Edward I and its collapse under his great-great grandson.

The capacity for narratives of the past to aid the negotiation, even the resolution, of present conventual business now guided their handling of history in all of its forms. It decided the level of attention they gave to events outside their locality, and steadily shifted the priority attached to keeping a record of the nation's past. It might explain why the impulse to continue Higden's *Polychronion* – a national narrative ripe for re-framing for a domestic readership – did not pass through the Cistercian network as it did the Benedictines'.[64] It would be wrong to interpret this as the waning of any proper historical sensitivity. If they fixed their gaze ever more on their immediate situation it was not simply to sift and systematise their great residue of deeds, or to reassert the original terms of their foundation but to frame and formulate them differently; in short, to historicise them. At the same time, they returned to the early narratives, to restore and reproduce them and also to extend and elaborate them with touches of biography, topography, genealogy and even visualisation. Thomas Burton established a template which he used to sketch two centuries of history, with the abbot positioned in the foreground, surrounded by a sequence of property transactions and other *acta*, culminating always with contributions to the physical presence of the abbey, with the dramas of the national or international scene, beginning always with the papacy, bringing colour and points of detail to the background.[65] The visual emphasis of the Forde genealogy, and, especially, the detailed knowledge of arms when their use was still in flux at the turn of the fourteenth century was uncommon and may explain its transmission outside the Cistercian network.[66]

In style, tone and theme, these fresh narratives intensified the features that were distinctive in early Cistercian discourse. The narrator spoke not as an individual but as the voice of the convent. The Stanley annalist referred only to '*abbatiam*' and '*conventus*' which become the subjects of those sentences which refer to the fortunes of the house.[67] In the Robertsbridge annal the *acta* of the legal dispute were themselves made *dramatis personnae*. When a settlement is reached over the Hastings chapel, the next scene, of Abbot John de Wormdale's installation, is introduced by the written authority that enabled it, 'And so letters patent under the great seal for the installation of the abbot for himself and his successors, among other royal charters for the future being sent back' ('Et insuper litteras patentes sub magno sigillo pro installando abbatem pro se et successoribus suis inter alias cartas regias pro futuris reponendas'). The annalist's attention to the materiality of the patent letter heightens the presence of a corporate identity.[68]

The temporal framework was ever more closely aligned to the liturgical calendar, even to specific observant events particular to the house. Towards the end of the extant portion of the Waverley annal (down to 1291), the compiler marked the passage of time for the monastery only by the major acts witnessed in the monastic church, the reception of living patrons, the burial of those that have died, and the re-dedication of the church.[69] The difference of their approach can be clearly focused if the Robertsbridge annal, recounting the protracted dispute over the convent's claim to the Hastings chapel, is set alongside a section of the St Albans *Gesta abbatum*, also relating to a dispute over rights over temporal and spiritual properties, recorded in the same period, the second quarter of the fourteenth century. The St Albans narrative took its chronology from the court documents generated by the case. By contrast, Abbot John of Lamberhurst's progress is mapped across the festive calendar at Robertsbridge, and even, as it nears its climax, by Abbot John's own personal schedule of masses.[70]

The weight of their own conventual identity and its local customs did not diminish their corporate outlook. There remained an identification with a Cistercian '*ordo*'; indeed at times it seems stronger than the narratives written two centuries before. Recalling the assaults of King John, the Stanley compiler's lamentation was not for his own '*abbatiam*' but for the 'Cistercian Order, sorely afflicted for his own interest' ('ordinem quoque Cisterciensem interim valde afflixit pro voluntate sua').[71] His temper steadily rose and before he recorded the king's obit he observed that the Order in England had been 'stayed' ('Johannes rex anglie extorsit omnem tercimam decimam ... quietus tamen fuit ab hec exactione ordo Cisterciensis').[72] As he warmed to the theme he expressed outrage for his monastic order ('unde plurime abbathie destructe sunt et monachi atque conversi per totam provinciam dispersi sunt').[73]

The status of the Order in England and, implicitly at least, its claim to spiritual pre-eminence, was made the central theme of the Newenham narrative of the death of the founder, Reginald de Mohun. The opening glances at rivalry between the regular orders, as the dying baron calls upon the confessional service of a Franciscan, Henry, then 'at Oxford he reigned in the school of theology' (apud Oxonias regebat scolam theologiae).[74] The first vision that Reginald recounted in confession conjures up the figure of spiritual austerity, an aged pilgrim (venerabilem personam in habitu pelegrini);

in the second vision witnessed by Henry himself the confessor, the figure is clothed as a Cistercian brother (venerabilem in albo habitu).[75] Also for a polemical purpose, the Pipewell annalist described an image of a Cistercian ideal, not of monastic austerity but of a pastoral purity, the 'beautiful glade' in which his house grew up. Here the Cistercian ethic was articulated as much for his own brethren as for their patrons as the annalist condemns successive superiors who had actively robbed the forest of its timber, 'just as cook will pluck a bird for the pot' ('quae nunc velut quercus defluentibus foliis sicut avis ad coquinam quae deplumata') in the pursuit of profit. His bold image of an original paradise of nature was impressed on his brethren as a symbol of their own disciplinary decline.[76] The bond between house and order is a strong seam also in the continuations of foundation histories. A Kirkstall narrative of the Lacys role as patrons of the house was at pains to trace the progress of the family from supporters of unreformed, Benedictine monasticism to patrons of a new order. In the same way, the compiler of the later recension of the Forde history trod carefully to demonstrate the priority of the Fitz Baldwin Cistercian foundations – Brightley, Forde, Quarr – in the face of the family's support for the Regular Canons at Breamore and Christchurch as well as their interest in the Norman Benedictines.[77]

These narratives leave the abbot as the sole actor of the history, the very embodiment of the experience of the monastery over the whole course of its past. This was not a turn towards biography to the extent witnessed in Benedictine *gesta abbatum* of the same period. The Cistercian annalists were concerned to describe moral and spiritual attributes. The conduct of the Pipewell abbots who ruined the abbey's original woodland is traced less as a series of commercial transactions but more as a passage of decline. Although narrated with sufficient detail to locate it in place and time, the long struggle of Abbot John Lamberhurst of Robertsbridge for recognition of the claim to the Hastings chapel was represented largely as a spiritual trial for a superior known to be close to death. Here seems the annalist had in mind nothing less than to create an exemplum. Abbot John's circuit across England in search of justice became a pilgrimage punctuated by acts of observance at churches passed *en route* and its denouement is not in the recognition of his claim (which is awarded to his successor) but the onset of his final illness and in his model 'monastic' death. The annalist offered vignettes not far removed from the trials of a saint: John summoned remarkable energy (*in maximo ardore*) to press his case despite the physical toll ('infirmitate debilitatus ut praedicitur variis undique angustiis vallatus') of the protracted dispute. When, inevitably, he dies, still on the road, there is an almost devotional image of his body borne uneasily on his own palfrey (cum magna tamen difficultate delatum) back home.[78]

At the same time the annalists amplified the place of the secular patron in the convent's representation of its history. In fact the main focus of the amendments and additions to their earliest foundation narratives was to capture the record of their hereditary founder(s). Now at a distance of a century and a half, and more, from their first charter, there was a general concern to navigate the routes by which the house, its property and patronage had been carried into the present age. The scale and scope of this research might suggest that genealogy had become a scholarly end in itself. In the earliest extant medieval copy of the Forde genealogies of the Devon barons that made Brightley and Forde itself, the descent of the founders is visualised as a tree with a bright green stem and a wide span of branches running to rich red roundels to form the crane's foot of the archetypal '*pied de grue*' (see figure 1).[79] If this reflects the original made at Forde then it would seem to connect the foundation history with the historical imagination that might be found among the secular books of the library. Yet this sustained quarrying of their patrons' past also represented a further search to clarify their own place in time. It is significant that in each case the research did not stop at the founder but reached beyond them to a remoter, and generally undocumented past, and to their progenitors at the Norman Conquest '[qui] venit in Anglia cum conquestore' (Sawley Abbey).[80] The intention, not without a polemical edge, was surely to anchor the house, with England's past and the origins of its present lordship and authority, tacitly at least confronting the (often) older and (always) louder claims of other orders to early royal and noble foundation. Tracing the reach of their founders appears also to have reawakened the exchanges between houses of the network. The genealogical framework of the Fitz Baldwins, Redvers, Vernons and Courtenays built by the compilers at Forde were made available to their confrères miles away at Newenham, and from the date of their respective cartularies, the transmission took place in the same generation.[81] These narratives also recorded details that were more than genealogical, giving particular attention to the benefactions of each passing generation, their place of burial, and even, as at Stanley, Newenham and Robertsbridge, their funerary obsequies. Just as in their representation of their own superiors, here these later annals seem consciously to model the figure of the monastic patron, the hereditary patron, their lifetime contribution as benefactor and protector, their pious death and their post-mortem presence as a permanent proof of their bond with the house.

Such an exemplum spoke to the brethren themselves of their place in the world, past, present and future, but it is possible also that it was understood to offer something of value now to the patron themselves. While in many ways these later annals represent a concentration of the characteristics of the

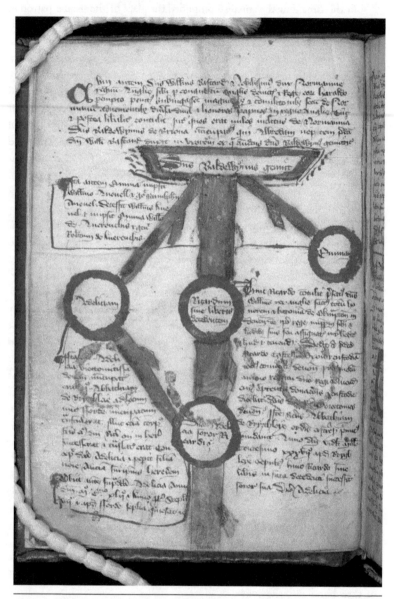

FIGURE 1: The foundation history of Forde Abbey as preserved in the early fifteenth-century genealogy of the Courtenay earls of Devon, now held at Powderham Castle (fol. 5v). © Powderham Estate and Exeter Digital Humanities.

early tradition, in one respect they do appear to have taken a new direction, since these texts passed out of the monastery to another readership. The latest version of the Forde history was copied in a cartulary of the Courtenay family around 1425; it was copied again by a related family, the Strodes of Somerset, in the second quarter of the sixteenth century, perhaps just prior to the suppression of the house.[82] There are signs of secular transmission elsewhere. The genealogy incorporated in the Pipewell annal is reproduced in a manuscript of *c*.1500 which would appear to be an anthology made for a secular household since it contains records principally concerning the succession in seigniorial titles. Interestingly, just like the Forde history as it passed through the hands of the Courtenays and their affinity, this manuscript shows continuous use over three generations between the reign of Henry VII and Elizabeth I, again pointing to the reception of Cistercian history across the Dissolution divide.[83]

The making of the Cistercian network in England was, at one level at least, the achievement of their historical enterprise. As Janet Burton has shown, it was their annalists that established ideological clarity, cultural community and the investment of a committed secular affinity in the pioneering decades of their settlement, so that, in the words of the Byland chronicler 'in a short time they ... [might] attain such a way of life on earth that they will never suffer hardship but will always grow and increase in every worldly good'.[84] From the same post-Reformation transcripts and other late fragments that have revealed this endeavour at the beginning of their history, it is possible to recover an impression of a continuing effort to document and deploy their past in the very different, often difficult environment of the later Middle Ages. In many ways the distinctive character of their work never faded, their established ways of tracing the passage of time and understanding their part endured in the face of novel cultural and intellectual currents. Indeed the impress of a communal identity, an idea of *conventus* and *ordo* only deepened. Where for the early pioneers this discourse acted to clarify their vocation, for the later generations, now it furnished exempla to refresh – and evidently sometimes to rebuke – contemporary practice. Like their forbears, the record of the past was still recognised for its currency in their wider world. The extension of their original foundation histories gave them, at least in their own minds, a greater integrity to the disparate, frequently interrupted lines of secular affiliation with which nearly two centuries of suffrage had surrounded them. It also verified and visualised, in pedigree trees and blazons of arms, a spiritual community which the early pioneers had perceived only on the far horizon, of monks and men sharing in the same inspiration of divine grace and serving God.[85] In this, it might be said that they saw small success of their own, as these texts were taken up by some hereditary founders and carried across the Reformation into their own, dynastic sense of a past.

Notes

1. The narrative of the moments that made the monastery of Forde is preserved in at least four versions closely related not only textually but also in date and provenance. It was printed by George Oliver in his *Monasticon dioecesis Exoniensis, being a collection of records and instruments illustrating the ancient conventual, collegiate and eleemosynary foundations in the counties of Cornwall and Devon, with historical notices* (London, 1846), pp. 341–6, from the bi-folium surviving from the now burnt manuscript, BL, MS Cotton Julius B X, which was separated from the codex and is now Bodl., MS Dodsworth 20. The text is also found in the cartulary of the hospital of St John at Exeter and in two manuscripts in the archive of the Courtenay family at Powderham Castle, a cartulary of the principal manors that formed the barony of Okehampton, held by the Courtenay earls of Devon, compiled between *c.*1350 and *c.*1425, and a genealogical history of the Courtenay family, known from its colophon as 'Liber tractans de origine, dignitatis et nominis de Courtenay in Anglia', fols 1r–11v, which on its first leaf (1r) is dated 1549. I am grateful to Lord Devon for permission to consult and cite this manuscript.

2. J. Burton (ed. and trans.), *The Foundation History of the Abbeys of Byland and Jervaulx*, Borthwick Texts and Studies, 35 (York, 2006), p. xxxvi.

3. Burton, *Foundation History*, p. 59.

4. E. Freeman, *Narratives of a new order: Cistercian Historical writing in England, c.1150–1220*, Medieval Church Studies, 2 (Turnhout, 2002), p. 94.

5. *Chron. Melsa*, I, p. xii; 'According to the usual custom of such establishments': J. Stevenson (ed.), *Radulphi de Coggeshall Chronicon Anglicanum*, RS, 66 (1875), p. x.

6. Freeman, *Narratives of a new order*, p. 94.

7. Burton, *Foundation History*, p. ix; Freeman, *Narratives of a new order*, p. 94.

8. Freeman, *Narratives of a new order*, p. 215.

9. *Chron. Melsa*, I, pp. 71–2 (71).

10. M. V. Clarke and N. Denholm-Young, 'The Kirkstall Chronicle, 1355–1400', *The Bulletin of the John Rylands Library*, 15, 1 (1931), 100–37; M. V. Clarke and V. H. Galbraith, 'The Deposition of Richard II', *Bulletin of the John Rylands Library*, 14, 1 (1930), 121–81; C. L. Kingsford, 'A Northern Chronicle', in C. L. Kingsford, *English Historical Literature in the fifteenth century* (Oxford, 1913), pp. 279–91.

11. Clarke wondered if the emotion caused by the papal schism and the 'long drama' of Richard II's reign had interrupted the Cistercian torpor: Clarke and Denholm-Young, 'Kirkstall Chronicle', 100. The unique manuscript copy of the Dieulacres chronicle was among the books of the abbey but apparently a lone 'literary curiosity': Clarke and Galbraith, 'Deposition of Richard II', 121–81 (125–6, 130). Clarke's verdict guided Antonia Gransden in her survey, and she passed briskly over the whole corpus as 'not

a very strong series of chronicles': *Historical writing in England. II. c.1307 to the early sixteenth century* (London, 1982), II, pp. 3–4, n. 13.

12. Gransden, *Historical writing*, pp. 158–9; C. Given-Wilson, *Chronicles. The writing of history in medieval England* (London, 2004), p. 94.

13. D. N. Bell (ed.), *The Libraries of the Cistercians, Gilbertines and Premonstratensians*, Corpus of British Medieval Library Catalogues, 3 (1992), Z2. 22; 25, pp. 8–9.

14. J. Spence, 'The Mohun Chronicle. An introduction, edition and translation', *Nottingham Medieval Studies*, 55 (2011), 149–215 (168).

15. The Pipewell annal is preserved uniquely in the later of two surviving abbey (abbatial?) registers copied at intervals in the century from *c.*1330 to 1444 now forming part of BL, MS Cotton Otho B XIV, at fols 150r–61r. It was transcribed in *Mon. Ang.*, V, pp. 434–6; G. R. C. Davis, *Medieval cartularies of Great Britain. A short catalogue* (London, 1958), pp. 88–9. The sole witness to the Stanley annal, whose corrections suggest it is a working copy, survives in a late thirteenth-century segment of the composite manuscript, Bodl., MS Digby 11, fols 149r–87r.

16. The surviving witnesses to historical narrative at Forde do point to a particular phase of new writing in the second quarter of the fourteenth century. The final scene in the extended foundation history is the funeral of Hugh II de Courtenay in 1340.

17. The text is witnessed in a seventeenth-century transcript bound with many others in Bodl., MS Dodsworth 20, fols 80r–1v. It was not known to George Oliver who transcribed narrative extracts and charters from two extant registers of the abbey which also attest to phases of record keeping after 1300: *Monasticon dioecesis Exoniensis*, pp. 357–71.

18. An annal recounting Abbot John of Lamberhurst's search for confirmation of the advowsons granted to Robertsbridge by its founder is bound with transcripts of documents relating to the abbey in BL, MS Add. 28805, fols 1r–6v. The opening of the text is missing and it breaks off with a cross reference, '*residuum quare ad illud signum* +' (6v) to a further portion which is now lost.

19. Bell (ed.), *Libraries of the Cistercians*, Z19. 116–121, pp. 106–7.

20. 'Iustae fuit staturae immensae corpulentiae facie fera fronte capillis nuda …': *Gesta regum Anglorum*, III. 279: Bodl., MS Digby 11, fol. 167r.

21. Clarke and Galbraith, 'Deposition of Richard II', 126–7.

22. Burton also displays knowledge of another authority near contemporary to these, Roger Howden: *Chron. Melsa*, I, pp. 111, 119–30, 135; C. Given-Wilson, *Chronicles of the Revolution, 1397–1400: the Reign of Richard II* (Manchester, 1993), pp. 93–4.

23. Bell (ed.), *Libraries of the Cistercians*, Z14. 184, p. 160; Z19. 116, 219; Z22. 1, p. 141. A surviving manuscript of Bede's *Historia Ecclesiastica* remained in use at Newminster (Northumberland) in the second quarter of the fourteenth century since dated inscriptions were made in the margin below the *ex libris*: BL, MS Add. 25014, fol. 2v. For the opening of the Stanley chronicle see Bodl., MS Digby 11, fols 149r–87r.

24. BL, MS Arundel 220, a manuscript bearing the *ex libris* of Kingswood Abbey contains Trevet, Pike and Martin of Poland. Bodl., MS Laud Misc. 619 is a fifteenth-century manuscript of Higden's *Polychronicon*, carrying the Fountains *ex libris* at fol. 1r; Cambridge, Corpus Christi College, MS 96, fol. 237v: 'Liber monasterii Joreuallis ex procuracione domini Johannis Bromton abbatis eiusdem loci'. Burton drew points of detail especially on the people and dramas on the European mainland, such as the celebrity of Hugh of St Victor at the time of his death, the drowning of Emperor Frederick, Henry II's death at Chinon, the vision of archbishop Richard of Dover: *Chron. Melsa*, I, pp. 111, 198, 202, 238, 241.

25. BL, MS Cotton Domitian A III, fol. 71r.

26. Bell (ed.), *Libraries of the Cistercians*, Z2. 23 (Bordesley); Z14. 120b, 121i, 13b2, 267–69, 271, pp. 8, 50, 52, 69–70 (Meaux); Z21. 13–15, pp. 138–40 (Rievaulx).

27. BL, MS Arundel 63.

28. Bodl., MS Rawlinson C 440. For this manuscript see also J. Proud, 'Collections of Saints' Lives in the thirteenth and fourteenth centuries: interpreting the manuscript evidence' in R. Myers, M. Harris and G. Mandelbrote (eds), *Collections of Saints' Lives in the Thirteenth and Fourteenth Centuries: Interpreting the Manuscript Evidence* (London, 2002), pp. 1–21; R. W. Pfaff, *The Liturgy in Medieval England: A History* (Cambridge, 2009), pp. 258–9.

29. BL, MS Add. 37787, fol. 181v.

30. BL, MS Add. 88905, fols 3r–v, 4v, 5r–6r.

31. BL, MS Add. 88905, fol. 12r.

32. Bodl., MS Digby 11, fols 178r, 180v.

33. Bell (ed.), *Libraries of the Cistercians*, Z19. 221, p. 106.

34. The surviving catalogues and book-lists of the later Benedictines map the strength of their holdings in historical writing, if such can be taken as a proxy for interest. The mid-fourteenth-century catalogue from Ramsey Abbey (Cambridgeshire) is notable for the mix of chronicles and Romance history, which are clustered as shelf-groups, an indication perhaps of their demand: R. Sharpe, J. P. Carley, K. Friis-Jensen and A. G. Watson (eds), *English Benedictine Libraries the shorter catalogues*, Corpus of British Medieval Library Catalogues, 4 (1996), B68. 21, 57, 215, 219–20, 228–9, 414, 491, pp. 350–415 (353, 357, 373–5, 395, 402). The library of St Augustine's Canterbury was unusually rich in Romance histories: B. Barker-Benfield (ed.), *Libraries of St Augustine's Abbey, Canterbury*, 3 vols, Corpus of British Medieval Library Catalogues, 13 (2008), BA1. 1515–30, Part II, pp. 1429–38. See also J. G. Clark, *A Monastic Renaissance at St Albans. Thomas Walsingham and his Circle, c.1350–c.1440* (Oxford, 2004), pp. 154–8.

35. The Courtenay Compendium is now Copenhagen, Royal Library MS Acc. 2011/5. A large codex, made from (originally) well-bleached parchment, written by a single scribe using a very cursive but neat book-hand of a style reminiscent of later medieval university books, with rubrics and colophons highlighted in red, it seems typical of a manuscript made in and for a clerical institution rather than the product of a

professional workshop. For a complete digital copy see: *www.kb.dk/en/nb/materialer/ haandskrifter/HA/e-mss/mdr.html* (accessed 7 July 2017).

36. Cambridge, Corpus Christi College, MS 96, fol. 1r.

37. I. H. Jeayes, 'Abbot Newland's Roll', *Transactions of Bristol & Gloucestershire Archaeological Society*, xix (1889–90), 117–30.

38. Bodl., MS Laud Misc. 545, fol. 8r: 'Hunc librum Thomas Crofftis de Drosthale armiger ob sinceram deuocionem dedit deo et beate Marie virginis et monasterio de Sybeton ita quod dominus Ricardus Muttforde monachus dicti monasterii de Sybeton istum librum ad placitum habeat in vsum et occupacionem tempore vite sue et tandem remancipteur monasterio beate Marie de Sybeton'.

39. J. W. Davidson, *The history of Newenham Abbey in the county of Devon* (London, 1843), pp. 14–15.

40. *Chron. Melsa*, II, p. 199.

41. Clarke and Galbraith, 'Deposition of Richard II', 175–81; Kingsford, 'Northern Chronicle', pp. 280–1.

42. A sequence of three manuscripts, parts of which were executed by the same scribe, represent this early archival activity, BL, MS Egerton 3053, the shelf marks at fols 9r, 18v, 20r, together with Bodl., MS Rawlinson B 449 and Oxford, University College, MS 170; Davis, *Medieval cartularies of Great Britain*, p. 47.

43. BL, MS Add. 49996; Davis, *Medieval cartularies of Great Britain*, p. 47.

44. BL, MS Cotton Otho B XIV, fols 150r–61r; *Mon. Ang.*, V, pp. 434–8; Davis, *Medieval cartularies of Great Britain*, pp. 88–9.

45. BL, MS Egerton 3126. The reference to Abbot Lindley is at fol. 30v; Davis, *Medieval cartularies of Great Britain*, p. 118.

46. BL, MS Add. 82958, fols 1r–16v; Davis, *Medieval cartularies of Great Britain*, p. 94, where it is identified with an earlier shelf mark as a loan.

47. Leicester Record Office, DE3214/10075.

48. Bodl., MS Dodsworth 59, pp. 134–9.

49. Exeter Cathedral Archives, D&C 3498/2. In the 1414 cartulary of Sibton Abbey the compiler, John de Gislingham does the same, tracing the descent from the founder alongside a note on the abbey's right to the appropriation of the church at Cransford: BL, MS Add. 34560, fol. 30r; *Mon. Ang.*, V, pp. 559–60.

50. *Chron. Melsa*, I, p. 72.

51. Bodl., MS Dodsworth 59, p. 135.

52. BL, MS Add. 34560, fols 33r–46v (33r).

53. BL, MS Add. 28550, 1r–6v.

54. The Robertsbridge annal survives incomplete in the opening number folios of BL, MS Add. 28550. For these reports see fols 2r–v, 6r.

55. Powderham Castle, 'Liber tractans de origine, dignitatis et nominis de Courtenay in Anglia', fols 1r–11v (8r); Oliver, *Monasticon dioecesis Exoniensis*, pp. 341–6 (345).

56. N. Vincent, *The Holy Blood. Henry III and the Westminster blood relic* (Cambridge, 2001), pp. 206–8; D. M. Smith and V. C. M. London (eds), *The Heads of Religious Houses in England and Wales 2, 1216–1377* (Cambridge, 2001), p. 284.

57. Bodl., MS Dodsworth 20, fols 80r–1v. The vision was somewhat loosely paraphrased by James Davidson in 1843 with the disapproving preface that 'it presents a lamentable but instructive picture of the extent to which the doctrines of Christianity were corrupted in that age': *Newenham Abbey*, pp. 211–14.

58. Bodl., MS Digby 11, fol. 185v ('*bellum gravissimum apud Lewes*'), 186r–v ('bellum crudelissimum apud Evesham … plures magnate capti sunt … fugit [the younger de Montfort] cum magna tristicia').

59. The Dieulacres narrative passes from 1381 to 1397 in scarcely two folios of text: Clarke and Galbraith, 'Deposition of Richard II', 164, 166. The Lords Appellant catch some small attention at Kirkstall but it is again fixed on the nation's fortunes only from 1396–7: Clarke and Denholm-Young, 'Kirkstall Chronicle', 128–9.

60. BL, MS Cotton Faustina B VI (Part I), fols 66r–8r.

61. *Chron. Melsa*, I, p. 119; II, pp. 332–7, 346, 361–78, 385 395; III, pp. 60, 87.

62. Clarke and Denholm-Young, 'Kirkstall Chronicle', 122–3.

63. The interest of the Kirkstall account has been represented as its 'first-hand account of [Bolingbroke's] moving around Yorkshire', and that of Dieulacres as an authority of events 'in and around Chester': Given-Wilson, *Chronicles of the Revolution*, pp. 132, 153.

64. It is worth noting that the interim (AB) version of Higden's *Polychronicon* included, among many others, an interpolation recounting the coming of the Cistercians from William of Malmesbury's *Gesta regum Anglorum*, but this was made at Chester by Higden himself. Although the successive continuations of the fourteenth century cannot all be assigned to a specific monastic context, there is a notable Benedictine affiliation to most of these versions: J. Taylor, *The Universal Chronicle of Ranulf Higden* (Oxford, 1966), pp. 98, 110–33, 176.

65. *Chron. Melsa*, for example, I, pp. 159–213 (Philip), pp. 159–79, transactions, building programme, etc.; pp. 179–213, wider horizons, beginning with papacy; II, pp. 183–281 (Roger of Driffield), pp. 183–238, transactions; pp. 238–40, regional events; pp. 241–81, wider horizons.

66. The extent of this is hinted at in the Courtenay manuscript which was derived from a Forde original and which illustrates the genealogy with a sequence of nineteen coats of arms: Powderham Castle, Courtenay cartulary, fols 13v–19r.

67. Bodl., MS Digby 11, fols 176v, 178r, 184r.

68. BL, MS Add. 28055, fol. 6r; Smith and London (eds), *Heads of Religious Houses 2*, p. 304.

69. H. R. Luard (ed.), *Annales monastici. II. Annales monasterii de Waverleia, AD 1–1291*, RS (1865), pp. 390–411.

70. BL, MS Add. 28055, fols 3v–4r. For the St Albans *Gesta abbatum*, see *Gesta abbatum monasterii sancti Albani*, ed. H. T. Riley, RS 28/4 (1867–9), II, pp. 331–4, 335–8; J. G. Clark and D. Preest, *The Deeds of the abbots of St Albans* (Woodbridge, 2018).

71. Bodl., MS Digby 11, fol. 176v.
72. Bodl., MS Digby 11, fol. 175r.
73. Bodl., MS Digby 11, fol. 176v.
74. Bodl., MS Dodsworth, fol. 80r.
75. Bodl., MS Dodsworth, fol. 80v.
76. *Mon. Ang.*, V, p. 435.
77. Courtenay cartulary, fol. 7r; Oliver, *Monastic dioecesis Exoniensis*, pp. 341–6 (345). In the same way, the founders' genealogy traced at Tintern took in their investment in houses of other orders, e.g. the Benedictine abbey at Colchester: *Mon. Ang.*, V, p. 269.
78. BL, MS Add. 28550, fols 3r–4r.
79. The genealogical tree was unfinished, the final three roundels were drawn but left unfilled: Courtenay cartulary, fols 5v–10r.
80. The Sawley genealogy opens with the Percies's forebears at the Conquest before turning to a detailed documentation of the succession of grants and gifts: *Mon. Ang.*, V, pp. 515–16. The genealogies integrated in the Forde history reached around and behind the Fitz Baldwins as far the two Norman conquerors they counted as their forebears, Baldwin and Richard de Redvers: Courtenay cartulary, fol. 5r; Oliver, *Monasticon dioecesis Exoniensis*, pp. 341–6. In the opening pages of his history Thomas Burton digressed from his account of the first abbot, Adam, to trace the origin of the founding Albermarles: *Chron. Melsa*, I, p. 89.
81. BL, MS Arundel 17, fol. 59v.
82. Powderham Castle, 'Liber tractans de origine, dignitatis et nominis de Courtenay in Anglia', fols 1r–11v. The first leaf (1r) of the manuscript bears the signature of William Strode and the date 1549; however, the style of the script and the illustrations might place the booklet as much as a generation earlier.
83. BL, Cotton MS Faustina E II, fols 216r–20v.
84. Burton, *Monastic Order*, pp. 287–8; *Foundation History*, p. 60.
85. *Foundation History*, p. 36.

2

'Like a mother between father and sons.' The role of the prior in later medieval English monasteries

Martin Heale

[He] ought to occupy a position midway between the Prelate and the convent, and, that he may provide them with sweet milk, ought to have as it were the breasts of a mother. Therefore, provided the Order suffer no harm, he ought to be prodigal towards them of consolation and friendship, sweetness and goodwill; he should temper the strictness of their father, and intervene between him and them, so that everything that is necessary for them may be properly supplied. Besides, he ought, as far as possible, to direct the hearts of all the brethren to love of the Prelate, to discountenance those who slander him or murmur against him, to cultivate more closely those who show him greater honour, and to the Prelate himself always to suggest a favourable opinion of those under his authority. By carefully acting in this manner he will be able to keep peace and tranquillity between the Prelate and the brethren, like a mother between father and sons; he will be able, on each day, by the grace of the Holy Spirit, to close the Chapter in the peace of Christ; and the brethren, in their turn, will enjoy tranquillity among themselves, and bear the easy yoke of the Lord with lightness of heart.[1]

Thus the late thirteenth-century observances of Barnwell Priory explain the role of the subprior, the monastic superior's deputy, who held the title 'prior' in abbeys.[2] The customary adopts the common analogy of the monastery as a family, overseen by its paterfamilias (the abbot), and with the prior occupying a feminine function as mother of the community. The prior was to nurture the brethren lovingly, as a mother provides breast milk for her children. And like a mother (or a queen in the body politic), he was to act as an intermediary and peacemaker between the abbot and the community, interceding for the latter while also encouraging the brethren to honour their superior. This gendered language closely echoes twelfth-century Cistercian depictions of the abbot as mother, fruitfully explored and contextualised by Caroline Walker Bynum. In such instances, maternal imagery was generally used to emphasise the nurturing and nourishing role of the monastic superior towards his charges, likened to the breastfeeding of infants.[3]

The conception of the prior as mother of the community raises a number of interesting questions about gendered roles and stereotypes in medieval monasteries, a topic on which the writings of Janet Burton have cast considerable light. The purpose of this chapter, however, is to address some more basic issues about the prior in late medieval English monasteries. What functions was he expected to fulfil, and how was his role evolving over the later Middle Ages? To what extent does the notion of the prior as an intermediary between the abbot and convent encapsulate his position within the monastic community, and what kind (and degree) of power and status did this office confer? These are questions that have received relatively little attention from historians of the later medieval religious orders. Indeed, aside from a collection of essays edited by Jean-Loup Lemaître – which focus primarily on priories and daughter houses – there have been few in-depth studies of the role of the prior.[4] It will be possible in this short chapter only to draw attention to certain notable features and developments regarding this important monastic office. My focus will be primarily on the great (and no doubt atypical) Benedictine houses of late medieval England, for which the extant evidence is richest. Further studies will be needed to bring out the range and variety of the prior's functions across monasteries of different orders and sizes.

Although the Barnwell observances' depiction of the prior as the mother of the community was not widely adopted in monastic customaries, their emphasis on nurture and mediation reflected some common assumptions about his office. The prior was required to assist the brethren in realising their monastic vocation, monitoring and guiding them in their everyday observance. To carry out this role effectually, he was expected to be gentle and supportive with his charges and wholly scrupulous in his own life.[5] In the words of the Abingdon customary, the prior 'ought to be humble, merciful, a pattern of religious observance, excellent in everything, conformable in all things. He should be first among the first, and last among the last.'[6] The foregrounding of the prior's role as mediator, moreover, draws on long-standing anxieties that he should not come to undermine or rival his superior. This concern was forcefully articulated in chapter 65 of the Benedictine Rule, which addressed the danger that the priors might become 'puffed up by an evil spirit of pride' and 'regard themselves as equal to the abbot'. In order to prevent this eventuality, Benedict of Nursia stipulated that the head of house should appoint the prior himself (having taken the advice of his brethren) and retain the right to depose his deputy should this prove necessary.[7] The importance of a close working relationship between abbot and prior, with the latter a loyal subject of his superior, was therefore axiomatic in many monastic writings.

The successful prosecution of the prior's role was crucial for the well-being of any religious community, on which it was agreed – in the words of the provincial chapter of the English Benedictines – 'the peace or disturbance of a house chiefly hangs'.[8] The day-to-day activities of the prior, as understood in late medieval English monasteries, were outlined in numerous customaries and visitation injunctions. His primary function was pastoral and disciplinary, overseeing the daily observances and occupations of the community with a small team of assistants: the *custodes ordinis*, consisting of the subprior, third and sometimes fourth prior. He heard the monks' confessions regularly, attended to sick brethren and oversaw the behaviour of the monastery's servants.[9] He also performed an important liturgical function, occupying the first stall on the opposite side of the choir to the abbot; and he often presided over the funerary services of deceased monks.[10] Moreover, whenever the abbot was absent or unwell, the prior would be called upon to deputise for him. In such circumstances, he presided over daily chapter meetings, punishing offences as appropriate but reserving more serious cases for the abbot's judgement; and when necessary he would fulfil the abbot's ritual role on major feast days.[11] This deputising was normally assumed on an ad hoc basis, but might be formalised whenever the abbot undertook a lengthy journey or was too infirm to fulfil his office adequately.[12] The prior was also, of course, a crucial figure during abbatial vacancies, taking temporary charge of the monastery's affairs and directing the preparations for the election of the new head.[13]

The functions of the prior, however, did not remain constant over the medieval period. Instead, as the role of the abbot gradually evolved so too did the position of his second-in-command. The head of house was increasingly drawn away from the daily life of the community, dwelling in a separate residence, relieved from many liturgical duties, and frequently absent from the monastery on business. By default, therefore, the prior came to discharge more and more of the pastoral functions associated with the abbot in the Benedictine Rule. Indeed, the extent to which the prior absorbed the pastoral role of the superior in large monasteries can be viewed in the thirteenth- and early fourteenth-century customaries of Westminster and St Augustine's Canterbury, which applied to the prior many of the Rule's pronouncements about the head of house. He was to be like a father to the community, meriting obedience from all, an example to the brethren in his life and 'a doctor of souls'; he should strive to be loved rather than feared; and he was reminded that he would have to give an account of his stewardship before God.[14]

By the thirteenth century, therefore, the prior was coming to be regarded in some respects as a substitute for the abbot – a state of affairs that challenged the notion of the prior as mediator between the superior and his community. Moreover, further contemporary developments served to undermine the traditional prohibition that priors should not become a rival source of power to the house's head. In those major Benedictine monasteries where there developed a formal division between the property of abbot and convent, the prior came to be viewed as the head of the latter establishment.[15] In this capacity, he was expected to act as the guardian and champion of conventual 'liberties', overseeing their portion of the monastery's endowment; and wherever the superior was deemed to be encroaching on those rights, it was considered the duty of the prior to lead the resistance. Thus when Richard of Wallingford, abbot of St Albans (1327–36), made unaccustomed demands on the convent's food and clothing, it was the house's prior, Nicholas de Flamstede, who voiced the conventual protestations.[16] This state of affairs raised the prospect of acrimonious disputes between abbot and prior, such as the notorious clash between Walter of Wenlock and Reginald de Hadham at Westminster Abbey in 1305–7. Following disagreements between Abbot Wenlock and his convent, Prior Hadham denounced his superior for disregarding the monastery's previous compositions, 'to the peril of his soul, to the grievous loss and injury of the portion allotted to the Prior and Convent, and to the pernicious leading astray of future Abbots'.[17] He then appealed against his superior to both the pope and king. Wenlock responded by deposing and imprisoning Hadham, thereby provoking further conventual appeals to Rome, and it was only the abbot's death in December 1307 that restored an uneasy peace.[18] A similarly bitter dispute between Abbot John de Sutton of Abingdon and his convent in 1320–2 also resulted in the physical detention of the house's prior by his superior.[19]

This understanding of the prior as the formal head of the convent also raised a number of constitutional questions about the office, not least how priors should be appointed and removed. As we have seen, the Benedictine Rule stipulated that the appointment of the prior should ultimately be the preserve of the abbot alone, but this approach did not sit comfortably with notions of the prior as a bulwark against abbatial tyranny. One of the aims of the 'democratic' movements which developed in certain major Benedictine monasteries in twelfth- and thirteenth-century England, therefore, was to establish the principle of elective priors. As a result, the late medieval priors of Abingdon, St Augustine's Canterbury and Westminster were all elected, most commonly using a system whereby the convent selected a pool of approved candidates from which the abbot would appoint his favoured nominee.[20] The convent of Bury St Edmunds, meanwhile, enjoyed the right of formally approving the abbot's choice of prior, and a similar system seems to have obtained at late medieval St Albans.[21] The practice at monasteries that had no formal division between the revenues of abbot and convent is less clear, but the election of priors was by no means unknown in such houses.[22]

The abbot's right to remove priors from office also came under challenge in some large Benedictine monasteries. The 1225 composition between Abbot Richard de Berking of Westminster and his convent implied that the prior should not be removable at the abbot's will, but this provision was omitted in a subsequent agreement of 1252 and thereafter remained a matter of contention in the monastery.[23] In a number of instances, individual priors are known to have obtained papal indults stipulating that they should not be removed from office without canonical cause (i.e. as perpetual priors). This privilege was sought and acquired by the prior of Reading in 1402, the prior of St Augustine's Canterbury in 1448 and the prior of St Albans in 1456.[24] Nevertheless, such attempts to retain their office for life could prove controversial. When during the abbacy of William de Scarborough of Meaux (1372–96), an unnamed monk of the house secured a grant of the prior's office in perpetuity from the cardinal abbot of Cîteaux, the clamour within his monastery was so great that he was compelled to renounce his indult and opted to move to another abbey.[25]

These attempts to enhance the freedom of priors from abbatial control, however, gradually lost momentum over the later Middle Ages, as monastic superiors successfully re-asserted exclusive rights over the appointment and removal of their deputy. The provincial chapter of the Benedictine Order, itself an assembly of superiors and their delegates, supported this abbatial endeavour. Thus its 1363 statutes, making reference to chapter 65 of the Rule, ordained that all priors of the Order should be removable at the will of their superior (with the advice of his brethren), *except* in monasteries which had received a papal indult specifying that its prior should be perpetual.[26] Monastic superiors, moreover, increasingly found that fifteenth-century popes – embroiled in their own struggles with conciliarism – could be receptive to arguments in favour of untrammelled abbatial authority. For example in 1406, at the petition of Abbot Richard Salford of Abingdon, Pope Innocent VII annulled an earlier (papally sanctioned) agreement between the abbot and convent of the house which had laid down that its priors could be removed from office only with the agreement of the whole community. Citing the insubordination of the monastery's priors, and also the canons and institutes of the

Order, the pope ordained that henceforward the prior should be removed at the sole pleasure of the abbot.[27] Similarly, in 1478 Pope Sixtus IV sided with Abbot William Upton of Evesham in overturning an oath imposed on him immediately after his election the previous year, guaranteeing amongst other things that the monastery's prior should hold his office for life.[28]

But if conventual attempts at certain major Benedictine monasteries to set up the prior as a rival source of authority to the superior gradually faded over the fourteenth and fifteenth centuries, the office of prior retained considerable status. It was not infrequently a stepping stone to the permanent headship of the house.[29] Monastic customaries, moreover, emphasised the reverence which ought to be paid to the prior, who 'should be honoured above the other servants of God's house'; whereas the Cistercian general chapter laid down in 1286 that no monk with a birth defect should be promoted as prior.[30] We also find the honorific designation 'lord prior' used relatively frequently in the larger monasteries of late medieval England.[31] The holder of the office was generally allocated a sizeable annual cash allowance from the monastery's central receiving officer, as was the practice at late medieval Bury St Edmunds, Reading, Selby and Worcester;[32] and this sum was augmented by liveries of food and drink, and by payments and pittances received on notable anniversaries.[33] At some large houses, the prior's office even came with its own independent landed endowment. Thus the late medieval priors of Westminster held the manor of Belsize in Hampstead, the rectory of St Martin in the fields in Westminster and various local tenements and at St Augustine's Canterbury the church of Frittenden was permanently attached to the prior's office in 1398, to help cover his hospitality expenses.[34]

As the dignity of the abbatial office steadily grew over the later Middle Ages,[35] we can observe a knock-on effect on the status of the priorate. In the first place, the priors of major Benedictine houses were routinely allocated their own commodious residence in the precinct. Thus in c.1316 the prior of Gloucester took over the house of the abbot in the west range of the cloister when the latter was accorded a new residence, and he soon afterwards made arrangements for it to be enlarged.[36] The prior's house at Bury was sufficiently impressive to serve for a time as accommodation for King Henry VI during his extended stay in the monastery in 1433–4, whereas the equivalent lodgings at Glastonbury and Westminster comprised a hall, chapel, buttery, two chambers, a kitchen and a bakehouse.[37] Even in middling monasteries, the prior might be assigned quite spacious private quarters. In 1459, the abbot and convent of Haughmond issued an ordinance permanently assigning a chamber under the dormitory, a garden and a dovecote for the 'recreations' of the house's prior. This chamber had been in the use of the current prior of Haughmond,

William Shrewsbury, who had recently financed its renovation.[38] Benedict XII's 1335 ordinances for the Cistercian Order, meanwhile, made provision for priors to be accorded a private cell in the dormitory.[39]

Alongside these residences, the priors of larger monasteries were afforded a personal servant or servants, although the particular amenities to which they were entitled might become a matter for debate. In 1277, the Benedictine provincial chapter legislated that priors should not have their own esquires or horses, but this injunction was overturned two years later in a statute which also clarified that they might receive their own chamber and servants.[40] The number of attendants maintained by late medieval priors seems to have varied considerably. The late medieval priors of St Augustine's Bristol, Fountains and Selby had a single servant (of yeoman rank, judging from the attendants' annual stipends of 13s. 4d to 20s.); while in 1402, the prior of Reading was being served by a yeoman, a groom and a page.[41] At the exceptionally wealthy Westminster Abbey, however, the staff of Prior William Walsh in 1443/4 comprised an esquire (or gentleman), his own father, a butler, a cook and two further servants; and there are several references to the 'prior's gentleman' in fifteenth-century accounts from Westminster.[42] The priors of Westminster were also afforded their own monk-chaplain, a perk found at other major Benedictine monasteries such as St Augustine's Canterbury and Bury St Edmunds.[43]

There can have been very few priors in late medieval England, however, who enjoyed the generous amenities of the monks holding that office at Westminster Abbey. As well as their sizeable house in the cloister, the priors of Westminster enjoyed possession of a manor house at Belsize – an apparently irregular arrangement, since the 1363 statues of the Benedictine chapter stipulated that priors should reside within the cloister.[44] From their surviving account books, it is clear that they spent a significant amount of time in their manorial residence. During the summer of 1511, Prior William Mane was often based at Belsize during much of the week, returning to Westminster for the weekend services.[45] Presumably the prior's pastoral functions were delegated to the subprior or third prior during these absences from the cloister. Prior Mane also not infrequently entertained visitors at his table, including 'the wives of the town', a range of mid-ranking ecclesiastical dignitaries (suffragan bishops, visiting heads of local priories and a canon of Windsor) and – most intriguingly – on 5 July 1511 'Skalton the poet'.[46] Moreover, on leaving office the priors of Westminster could expect generous provision for their retirement. Thus Prior Walsh received on his resignation an annual pension of £12, a monk-chaplain, a chamber in the infirmary, a parcel of ground and a weekly corrody of food, drink and fuel.[47]

There are signs that priors enjoyed high status outside the cloister, too. When monastic prayers were sought in wills, some testators saw fit to assign a higher sum for the attendance at their funeral of not only the house's superior but also his deputy.[48] More than one prior/subprior in late medieval England, moreover, was sufficiently renowned to be elected directly to a bishopric – as was the career trajectory of Robert de Greystanes of Durham (bishop of Durham, 1333; election overturned) and Nicholas Ashby of Westminster (bishop of Llandaff, 1441–58).[49] Priors might also be appointed to external commissions by the ecclesiastical or secular authorities. Thus Nicholas Selman, subprior of Plympton, and Simon, subprior of Launceston, were among Bishop Lacy of Exeter's chosen penitentiaries for the archdeaconry of Exeter in February 1421.[50] These kinds of activities, when added to instances where priors fulfilled exterior roles on behalf of, or alongside, their abbots – for example, serving as visitors of monasteries of their order, attending provincial chapter meetings, conducting junior brethren to their ordination ceremonies, or accompanying their heads on ecclesiastical or secular business[51] – could potentially draw them away from their internal duties for considerable stretches of time.

The rising status of the prior might therefore increase the distance between him and the monastic community, in exactly the same way that this occurred for heads of houses. The centralisation of monastic administration in the fifteenth and early sixteenth centuries, as superiors strove to bring the house's finances more tightly under their control, accentuated this trend. As well as taking conventual obediences into their own hands, several abbots are known to have appointed their second-in-command to important administrative offices: a practice traditionally frowned upon by monastic authorities and visitors.[52] Thus under the centralising rule of Abbot John Newland of St Augustine's Bristol (1481–1515), both Prior John Martyn (in 1491/2) and Prior Robert Elyot (in 1511/12) can be found holding three further conventual obediences. The late fifteenth- and early sixteenth-century priors of Selby likewise frequently held one or two additional offices, such as pittancer, sacrist or fabric keeper; and more than one prior of Bury St Edmunds occupied the office of conventual treasurer in these same years.[53] This tactic may have allowed the superior to concentrate important offices in a few (loyal) hands, but the result must often have been to distract the prior from his primary function as the guardian of the monastery's daily observance.[54]

In various ways and for various reasons, therefore, the separation between the prior and his convent in major English monasteries was growing by the early sixteenth century. The regularity with which priors were physically present in the cloister cannot be fully established, but at great houses like Westminster

Abbey they appear to have been relatively remote figures. Even at lesser monasteries, the accessibility of the second-in-command could not be taken for granted. Thus at a visitation of the modest Taunton Priory in 1451, Bishop Bekynton of Bath and Wells required the subprior to eat in the refectory with the canons at least three times a week, unless he had a reasonable excuse to absent himself.[55]

The role of the prior in English monasteries thus evolved notably over the medieval period in ways that challenged traditional interpretations of the office. The growing detachment of monastic superiors from the life of the cloister required the prior to assume a number of pastoral and disciplinary roles that had previously been associated with the abbot. Furthermore, during the thirteenth and early fourteenth centuries, internal 'democratic' movements heightened the potential for conflict between abbot and prior, at least in the great Benedictine houses of the realm. These familial tensions, however, seem to have relaxed by the later fifteenth century, when the dominance of the superior over internal affairs was successfully re-asserted. The later Middle Ages also witnessed the rising status of the prior, apparently a by-product of the growing dignity of the abbatial office. As the status of priors was increasingly emphasised – through comfortable residences, personal servants, internal office-holding, and external occupations and recognition – it is likely that they themselves became more distanced from their community. In short, the idealised equilibrium promoted in the Barnwell observances, whereby the prior both nurtured the brethren and supported his abbot – like a mother between father and sons – proved tantalisingly difficult to maintain in the monasteries of late medieval England.

Notes

1. J. Clark (ed.), *The Observances in Use at the Augustinian Priory of S. Giles and S. Andrew at Barnwell, Cambridgeshire* (Cambridge, 1897), pp. 146–7.

2. For ease of reference, this chapter will use the shorthand 'prior' to refer to the superior's deputy, rather than the technically accurate 'prior or subprior'. The title 'claustral prior' is sometimes used by historians to denote this monastic officer, but is best avoided in the light of its assignation to the prior's own deputy in several medieval English customaries: e.g. Lanfranc, *The Monastic Constitutions of Lanfranc*, ed. D. Knowles (London, 1951), pp. 76–7.

3. C. Walker Bynum, 'Jesus as Mother and Abbot as Mother: some Themes in Twelfth-Century Cistercian Writing', in C. Walker Bynum, *Jesus as Mother: Studies in the Spirituality of the High Middle Ages* (Berkeley and Los Angeles, 1982), pp. 110–69. For the mediating role of medieval queens, see inter alia A.-B. Fitch, 'Maternal Mediators: Saintly Ideals and Secular Realities in Late Medieval Scotland', *Innes Review*, 57 (2006),

1–35; and J. Carmi Parsons, 'The Queen's Intercession in Thirteenth-Century England', in J. Carpenter and S.-B. MacLean (eds), *Power of the Weak. Studies on Medieval Women* (Urbana, 1995), pp. 147–77.

4. J.-L. Lemaître (ed.), *Prieurs et prieurés dans l'occident médiéval*, Hautes études médiévales et modernes 60 (Geneva, 1987). See, in particular, Colomon Viola's article in this volume: 'Un célèbre prieur du XIᵉ siècle: Saint Anselme. Contribution à l'histoire de la notion et de la fonction de prieur', pp. 29–45.

5. Cf. *The Rule of St Benedict in Latin and English*, ed. J. McCann (London, 1952), ch. 65.

6. J. Stevenson (ed.), *Chronicon Monasterii de Abingdon*, RS, 2, 2 vols (1858), II, pp. 355–6.

7. *Rule of St Benedict*, ch. 65.

8. W. A. Pantin (ed.), *Documents Illustrating the Activities of the General and Provincial Chapters of the English Black Monks 1215–1540*, Camden Society, Third Series, 3 vols, 45, 47, 54 (1931–7; hereafter *CBM*), II, p. 209.

9. E.g. *CBM*, II, pp. 44, 48–9; F. M. Powicke and C. Cheney (eds), *Councils and Synods with Other Documents relating to the English Church, II, AD 1205–1313*, 2 parts (Oxford, 1964), II, p. 787; E. M. Thompson (ed.), *Customary of the Benedictine Monasteries of Saint Augustine, Canterbury, and Saint Peter, Westminster*, 2 vols (London, 1902–4), I, pp. 76–7, II, p. 11; *The Chronicle of St Mary's Abbey, York*, ed. H. Craster and M. Thornton, Surtees Society, 148 (1934), pp. 82–3.

10. E.g. Thompson (ed.), *Customary of Saint Augustine, Canterbury, and Saint Peter, Westminster*, I, pp. 78–9; A. Gransden (ed.), *Consuetudines Burienses*, Henry Bradshaw Society, 99 (1966), pp. 7–10; J. Greatrex, *The English Benedictine Cathedral Priories: Rule and Practice, c.1270–c.1420* (Oxford, 2011), p. 306.

11. E.g. Clark (ed.), *Barnwell Observances*, pp. 144–5.

12. E.g. H. Maxwell-Lyte (ed.), *The Registers of Oliver King, Bishop of Bath & Wells 1496–1503, and Hadrian de Castello, Bishop of Bath & Wells 1503–1518*, Somerset Record Society, 54 (1939), p. 25; H. Riley (ed.), *Annales Monasterii S. Albani a Johanne Amundesham, monacho, ut videtur, conscripti (A.D. 1421–1440)*, RS, 28.5, 2 vols (1870–1), I, pp. 118–26; H. Maxwell-Lyte et al. (eds), *Calendar of Patent Rolls, AD 1216–1582*, 74 vols (London, 1901–; hereafter *CPR*), *1354–1358*, p. 97. Cf. Viola, 'Un célèbre prieur du XIᵉ siècle', pp. 39–40.

13. For a summary of the practical arrangements surrounding an abbatial election, see M. Heale, *The Abbots and Priors of Late Medieval and Reformation England* (Oxford, 2016), pp. 15–27.

14. Thompson (ed.), *Customary of Saint Augustine, Canterbury, and Saint Peter, Westminster*, I, pp. 75–80, II, pp. 9–16. Cf. *Rule of St Benedict*, chs 2, 27–8, 64.

15. For a fuller discussion of this state of affairs, see D. Knowles, *The Monastic Order in England. A History of its Development from the Times of St Dunstan to the Fourth Lateran Council, 940–1216*, 2nd edn (Cambridge, 1966), pp. 411–17; Heale, *Abbots and Priors*, pp. 115–22; A. Gransden, 'A Democratic Movement in the Abbey of Bury St Edmunds in the

Late Twelfth and Early Thirteenth Centuries', *Journal of Ecclesiastical History*, 26 (1975), 25–39.

16. H. Riley (ed.), *Gesta Abbatum Monasterii Sancti Albani*, RS, 28.4, 3 vols (1867–9; hereafter GASA), II, pp. 209–12. See also Riley (ed.), *Amundesham*, II, pp. 211–12; A. H. Thompson (ed.), *Visitations in the Diocese of Lincoln 1517–1531*, Lincoln Record Society, 3 vols, 33, 35, 37 (1940–7), III, pp. 84, 87.

17. E. Pearce, *Walter de Wenlok, Abbot of Westminster* (London, 1920), pp. 170–1.

18. For this episode and its wider context, see B. Harvey (ed.), *Documents Illustrating the Rule of Walter de Wenlok, Abbot of Westminster, 1283–1307*, Camden, Fourth Series, 2 (1965), pp. 17–24; Pearce, *Walter de Wenlok*, pp. 167–204.

19. H. Salter, 'A Chronicle Roll of the Abbots of Abingdon', *English Historical Review*, 26 (1911), 727–38; *CPR, 1317–21*, pp. 498, 526–7; *Cal. Close Rolls, 1318–23*, pp. 350–1; C. Elrington (ed.), *The Registers of Roger Martival, Bishop of Salisbury, 1315–1330*, Canterbury and York Society, 55, 57–9, 68, 4 vols in 5 parts (1959–75), II (ii), pp. 385–6.

20. Stevenson (ed.), *Chronicon Monasterii de Abingdon*, II, pp. 355–6; *Cal. Papal Registers*, VIII, pp. 587–8, X, p. 416; Thompson (ed.), *Customary of Saint Augustine, Canterbury, and Saint Peter, Westminster*, I, pp. 73–4; Westminster Abbey Muniments (hereafter WAM) 9501. For the range of electoral systems used at late medieval Westminster, see B. Harvey, *The Obedientiaries of Westminster Abbey and their Financial Records c.1275–1540* (Woodbridge, 2002), p. xxvii.

21. See, for example, Gransden (ed.), *Consuetudines Burienses*, pp. xix–xx; H. Riley (ed.), *Registrum Abbathiae Johannis Whethamstede, Abbatis Monasterii Sancti Albani*, RS, 28.6, 2 vols (1872–3), II, p. 50.

22. E.g. A. Jessopp (ed.), *Visitations of the Diocese of Norwich, A.D. 1492–1532*, Camden Society, New Series, 43 (1888), pp. 101–6 (Westacre); A. H. Thompson (ed.), *Visitations of Religious Houses in the Diocese of Lincoln, 1420–1449*, Canterbury and York Society, 3 vols, 17, 24, 33 (1915–27; hereafter *VRH*), III, pp. 231–9 (Newnham).

23. Harvey, *Obedientiaries of Westminster*, p. xxviii.

24. *Cal. Papal Registers*, V, p. 550, X, p. 416, XI, pp. 88–9.

25. *Chron. Melsa*, III, p. 191.

26. *CBM*, II, pp. 73–4.

27. *Cal. Papal Registers*, VI, p. 81.

28. *Cal. Papal Registers*, XIII (ii), p. 635.

29. See Heale, *Abbots and Priors*, pp. 48–9; and cf. F. Garnier, 'Discipulus – Prior – Abbas – Depositus d'après un manuscrit de la *Rota vere religionis* et de la *Rota simulationis* de Hugues de Saint-Victor', in Lemaître (ed.), *Prieurs et prieurés*, pp. 23–8.

30. Knowles (ed.), *Monastic Constitutions of Lanfranc*, p. 75; Thompson (ed.), *Customary of Saint Augustine, Canterbury, and Saint Peter, Westminster*, I, pp. 75–6, II, pp. 9–11; J. M. Canivez (ed.), *Statuta Capitulorum Generalium Ordinis Cisterciensis 1116–1786*, 8 vols (Louvain, 1933–41), III, p. 235.

31. E.g. San Marino, Huntington Library, BA 139, 142, 144; J. Tillotson, *Monastery and Society in the Late Middle Ages. Selected Account Rolls from Selby Abbey, Yorkshire, 1398–1537* (Woodbridge, 1988), pp. 54, 99, 111; *GASA*, II, p. 210; *Mon. Ang.*, VI, p. 112.

32. TNA, SC 6/HENVII/1693, SC 6/HENVIII/3395; *Cal. Papal Registers*, V, p. 550; Tillotson, *Monastery and Society*, p. 111; J. Wilson (ed.), *Accounts of the Priory of Worcester for the year 13–14 Henry VIII, AD 1521–2*, Worcestershire Historical Society, 44 (1907), pp. 17–20.

33. See WAM 33288, fols 20r–22v.

34. Harvey, *Obedientiaries of Westminster*, pp. 16–17; *Cal. Papal Registers*, V, p. 193.

35. See Heale, *Abbots and Priors*, ch. 4.

36. A. Emery, *Greater Medieval Houses of England and Wales, 1300–1500, Volume III. Southern England* (Cambridge, 2006), pp. 101–2.

37. J. Elston, 'William Curteys, Abbot of Bury St Edmunds 1429–1446' (unpublished PhD thesis, University of California, Berkeley, 1979), 22, 59, 82; *Mon. Ang.*, I, p. 8; J. A. Robinson, *The Abbot's House at Westminster* (Cambridge, 1911), pp. 41–4.

38. *Mon. Ang.*, VI, p. 112. Certain modest rents and pensions were also allocated to the prior's office at this time.

39. L. and A. Cherubini, A. Auda and J. Paulus (eds), *Magnum Bullarium Romanum, a Beato Leone Magno usque ad S. D. N. Benedictum XIII. Tome primus, ad A. B. Leone Magno ad Paulum IV* (Luxemburg, 1727), p. 214.

40. *CBM*, I, pp. 66, 103. This latter judgement was re-stated in 1343: *CBM*, I, p. 36.

41. G. Beachcroft and A. Sabin (eds), *Two Compotus Rolls of Saint Augustine's Abbey, Bristol. For 1491–2 and 1511–12*, Bristol Record Society, 9 (1938), pp. 170–3; J. Walbran and J. Fowler (ed.), *Memorials of the Abbey of St Mary of Fountains*, Surtees Society, 3 vols, 42, 67, 130 (1863–1918), III, pp. 32–3, 74–5; Hull History Centre, U DDLO/20/1–2, 13; *Cal. Papal Registers*, V, p. 550.

42. WAM 33288, fol. 24v; e.g. WAM 33289, fol. 19r.

43. See, for example, Thompson (ed.), *Customary of Saint Augustine, Canterbury, and Saint Peter, Westminster*, II, p. 97, I, p. 315; TNA, SC 6/HENVIII/3395.

44. Harvey, *Obedientiaries of Westminster*, p. 16; *CBM*, II, p. 74.

45. Harvey, *Obedientiaries of Westminster*, pp. xxxviii–xxxix; WAM 3325, fols 5r–33r.

46. WAM 3325, fols 5r–33r, 36v–70r.

47. *Cal. Papal Registers*, X, pp. 590–1. Cf. WAM 30180, for the provision made for Prior Richard Excestre of Westminster in 1382/3, summarised in E. Pearce, *The Monks of Westminster* (Cambridge, 1916), pp. 101–2.

48. E.g. F. Weaver (ed.), *Somerset Medieval Wills*, Somerset Record Society, 3 vols, 16, 19, 21 (1901–5), II, pp. 19, 171, III, pp. 31, 36.

49. J. Raine (ed.), *Historiae Dunelmensis scriptores tres*, Surtees Society, 9 (1839), pp. 120–1; E. F. Jacob (ed.), *The Register of Henry Chichele, Archbishop of Canterbury 1414–1443*, Canterbury and York Society, 4 vols, 42, 45–7 (1938–47), I, pp. 125–6.

50. G. Dunstan (ed.), *The Register of Edmund Lacy, Bishop of Exeter, 1420–55*, Canterbury and York Society, 5 vols, 60–3, 66, (1963), I, pp. 21–4.

51. E.g. Durham Cathedral Muniments, Registrum II, fols 195v–6r; *CBM*, II, p. 188, III, pp. 248–53; Pearce, *Monks of Westminster*, p. 122; Beachcroft and Sabin (eds), *Compotus Rolls of Saint Augustine's Abbey, Bristol*, pp. 263–5. See also San Marino, Huntington Library, BA 139, 144 and TNA, DL 29/158/18.

52. E.g. *CBM*, II, p. 84; *VRH*, I, p. 106, II, p. 58; A. Bannister (ed.), *Registrum Thome Spofford, Episcopi Herefordensis, AD 1422–1448*, Canterbury and York Society, 23 (1919), pp. 216–17. Such appointments might prove unavoidable in smaller monasteries, however, as the Benedictine provincial chapter recognised. Thus that body applied its prohibition of priors holding external monastic offices only to houses with over twenty inmates: *CBM*, I, p. 67, II, pp. 36, 194.

53. Beachcroft and Sabin (eds), *Compotus Rolls of Saint Augustine's Abbey, Bristol*, p. 10; Hull History Centre, U DDLO 20/29, 31, 36, 38, 40, 49; TNA, SC 6/HENVII/1693, SC 6/HENVIII/3395.

54. For a rather different instance of a prior accumulating conventual offices, see J. Brewer, J. Gairdner and R. Brodie (eds), *Calendar of the Letters and Papers, Foreign and Domestic, of the Reign of Henry VII*, 22 vols (London, 1864–1932), VIII, pp. 324–5.

55. H. Maxwell-Lyte and M. Dawes (eds), *The Register of Thomas Bekynton, Bishop of Bath and Wells, 1443–1465*, Somerset Record Society, 2 vols, 49–50 (1934–5), I, pp. 162–4.

3

Formed by word and example: the training of novices in fourteenth-century Dublin

Colmán Ó Clabaigh

This chapter examines the context and contents of Trinity College Dublin MS 97, a late thirteenth-/early fourteenth-century codex from the Victorine Abbey of St Thomas the Martyr on the outskirts of Dublin. It argues that this compendium of ascetical, legislative, literary and monastic texts helped forge an *esprit de corps* in the community and provided the resources for training candidates in the novitiate stage of formation as Victorine Canons. It is offered with gratitude and affection to Janet Burton for her *sans pareil* dedication as a scholar, mentor and friend.

Ireland in the late eleventh and twelfth centuries witnessed radical changes that transformed all aspects of society. The emergence of an indigenous reform movement and increased contacts with an aggrandising papacy wrought significant changes in Irish ecclesiastical life.[1] Diocesan and metropolitan structures were established by the synods of Ráith Bressail (1111) and Kells/Mellifont (1152) and new religious orders like the Regular Canons and Canonesses, and the Cistercian monks transformed Irish monasticism. The Anglo-Norman incursion in 1169 likewise impacted church affairs as the newcomers took control of ecclesiastical appointments and established religious houses to further the process of colonisation. The Augustinian Canons, with their combination of monastic observance, intercessory prayer and pastoral activity, were particularly favoured by both Gaelic and Anglo-Norman patrons as able agents for erecting parishes, running hospitals and staffing centres of pilgrimage. Approximately 120 foundations were established by the canons and the canonesses by the early thirteenth century, several of which adopted the customs of continental congregations, most notably those of St Nicholas of Arrouaise, Premontré and St Victor in Paris.[2]

One of the most significant of these foundations, the Abbey of St Thomas the Martyr near Dublin owed its origins and dedication to an act of reparation by Henry II for his involvement in the murder of Thomas Becket, archbishop of Canterbury (d.1170).[3] The initial royal endowment in

March 1177 was relatively modest, consisting of approximately 120 acres of land in the city's southern suburb of Donore, but the community subsequently received an annual grant of royal alms from the Dublin exchequer that continued until its dissolution in 1538. It remained the Crown's principal religious foundation in Ireland and in 1240 Henry III ordered the archbishop of Dublin to preside in person at the liturgy on St Thomas's feast day (29 December) and supplied 800 wax tapers for the occasion. Further royal grants meant that the canons enjoyed extensive fishing rights on the River Liffey, controlled the city's main watercourse and received a 'tollboll' or tithe of beer from every batch brewed for sale in Dublin. Despite the royal patronage these privileges were resented and occasioned long-running litigation between the canons and the city.[4] Devotion to the martyred archbishop was strong among the Anglo-Norman *conquistadores* and the abbey received extensive temporal and spiritual endowments in their newly conquered territories, eventually becoming one of the wealthiest monasteries in Ireland.[5] By 1192 the community had adopted the customary of St Victor and it became the principal house of the Victorine foundations in Ireland.

The community played a significant role in both civic and colonial affairs. The abbot was a parliamentary lord and the precinct at Thomas Court included a suite of buildings known as the 'king's lodgings' that routinely accommodated senior officials engaged in Crown service. The abbey also had a crucial role in the development of Dublin's southern suburb and constituted an ecclesiastical 'liberty' that enjoyed immunity from the authority of the mayor and the sheriff of Dublin. Although the only aboveground evidence of its existence comes from the street names Thomas Street and Thomas Court in modern Dublin's inner city, archaeological and documentary evidence indicate that it was one of the most extensive monastic complexes in Ireland. Its construction corresponded with the thirteenth-century rebuilding of many of Dublin's premier churches and it probably resembled elements of the surviving Early English Gothic architecture of the nearby Christ Church and St Patrick's cathedrals.[6]

CONTENTS AND CONTEXT

For those, like the Regular Canons, who looked to the great theologian and exegete Augustine of Hippo (d.430) as a role model, reading and study were central to their identities. As new forms of canonical life emerged in the eleventh and twelfth centuries, canons of varying hues were at the forefront of theological investigation, liturgical innovation, scriptural exegesis and mystical writing. The work of the scholars associated with the abbey of St Victor on the outskirts of Paris was of particular significance. Established as a hermitage in 1108 by William of Champeaux (d.1121) the community soon adapted the lifestyle of Canons Regular and combined an ascetic monastic observance with rigorous intellectual activity. Several of its early members such as Adam, Achard and Richard of St Victor were at the forefront of European intellectual life and the abbey and its school attracted students and recruits from all over Europe.[7] The most significant figure to emerge however was the Saxon canon Hugh of St Victor (d.1141) whose wide-ranging interests influenced all aspects of theology and whose writings on the religious life provided the fundamental texts for the formation and training of novices for the rest of the Middle Ages. Although the evidence for contact between the Irish Victorines and their Parisian confreres is slight, the codex under consideration shows they were well aware of their intellectual work and of its significance.

Trinity College MS 97 is a composite manuscript of 297 vellum leaves containing texts transcribed by different hands in the latter part of the thirteenth century with some additional material added in the early fourteenth century.[8] One of the final folios bears the signature of Canon Henry Duff, the last abbot of St Thomas's, who surrendered the monastery in 1538. At a later stage the codex belonged to the scholarly archbishop of Armagh, James Ussher, who noted its St Thomas's provenance. In 1661, with the rest of the archbishop's manuscripts, it passed to the library of Trinity College, Dublin.

The first text (fols 1–4v) is a calendar listing the various feast days of the liturgical year. The rank of each holy day is indicated by the use of black, blue or red ink for the entries. The text is incomplete and ends with the feast days for the month of August. The calendar also contains marginal entries from the thirteenth, fifteenth and sixteenth centuries recording the obits of canons and their relatives and a memorandum from 1478 relating to an arrangement concerning a transfer of property between St Thomas's Abbey and the Cistercian community at St Mary's Abbey on the north side of the River Liffey. The liturgical calendar consisted of both fixed and moveable elements. Of the latter category the feast of Easter was the most important as its date determined when the other moveable celebrations occurred. These permutations impacted the fixed elements of the calendar, forcing them to give precedence to the higher-ranking moveable festivities. The complex astronomical and mathematical equations used to determine these changes were known as *computus*, proficiency in which was a basic requirement of clerical education. It is appropriate that the next texts to appear in the volume are both compustistical works: the *Doctrina Tabularum* (fols 5–6v) attributed to the English friar-philosopher Roger Bacon (d.1292) and the *Massa Compoti* (fols 7–32) of the French Franciscan mathematician Alexander of Villedieu (d.1240).[9]

The latter text was composed in verse to facilitate memorisation and was one of the most widely consulted works in the field.

These works are followed by various prayers for recitation throughout the monastic day (fol. 33rv). They include collects recited on entering the church for the Divine Office, for protection against the 'terrors of the night' as well as instructions on how the reader was to behave at the daily chapter meeting. This devotional material is followed by short introductory texts relating to the martyrology (fols 33rv–6), the listing of feast days and liturgical celebrations whose recitation formed an integral part of the daily chapter meeting in medieval religious communities. The version of the martyrology (fols 36v–72v) used by the canons of St Thomas was an adaptation of that compiled in the mid-ninth century at the abbey of St-Germain-des-Prés in Paris by the Benedictine monk Usuard (d.877).[10] This was the most popular of the medieval martyrologies and its influence in Ireland is evident from the late twelfth century when Máel Muire Ua Gormáin, abbot of the community of Augustinian Canons at Knock, Co. Louth, used it when compiling his vernacular, versified martyrology between 1168 and 1170.[11] The text was adapted for use at St Thomas's sometime after 1253 as it includes an entry for the Dominican martyr Peter of Vercelli who was canonised in that year. Unlike their Gaelic confreres who were keen hagiographers, the Anglo-Irish canons of St Thomas seemingly had little interest in native Irish saints as the text contains only five additional commemorations beyond the six already listed by Usuard. The five were Sts Brendan of Clonfert (16 May), Kevin of Glendalough (3 June), Moling of St Mullins, Co. Carlow (17 June), Aidan of Lindisfarne (31 August) and Laurence O'Toole of Dublin (14 November). Of these the commemorations of Sts Kevin and Laurence O'Toole were to be expected in the united dioceses of Dublin and Glendalough. The monastery's dedication to St Thomas Becket accounts for the lengthy entries commemorating his martyrdom (29 December) and the translation of his relics in Canterbury in 1220 (7 July). The community's devotion to St Augustine is evident in the commemoration of his feast day (28 August) along with that of the translation of his relics (11 October). The presence of twenty commemorations of English and Welsh saints in addition to the ten already included by Usuard led Aubrey Gwynn to propose that the exemplar for the St Thomas martyrology might have come from the Victorine foundation of St Augustine's Abbey in Bristol.[12] In contrast Pádraig Ó Riain notes the close correspondence between the St Thomas text and the standard Dominican martyrology and suggests that it might have derived instead from an exemplar borrowed from the Dominican priory of St Saviour in Dublin. He suggests that the inclusion of several Welsh saints, which Gwynn used to advance his

Bristol hypothesis, was because the prior of St Thomas at the time of the martyrology's compilation was William the Welshman.[13]

The next section of the codex consists of texts relating to the rule of St Augustine and aspects of Victorine observance. The first of these is the *Expositio in Regulam S. Augustini* (fols 73–95) a pseudonymous work attributed to Hugh of St Victor. The text of the rule is divided into twelve sections, written in a large, clear script while the commentary takes the form of marginal notes written in a smaller script.[14] This is followed by the only known copy of the *De Quaestionibus Regulae S. Augustini* (fols 95–102) by Richard of St Victor (d.1173), who served as subprior of St Victor from 1159 to 1162 and then as prior from 1162 to 1173. The commentary takes the form of responses to twenty practical questions on Augustinian life and observance posed by a Brother Simon.[15] The questions addressed included the reasons why a canon could legitimately withdraw from the monastery of his profession, what elements of the Rule of Augustine were universally binding, what the commitment to living without personal property entailed, how the canons were to conduct the liturgy and what obligations they had regarding fasting and abstinence. Other issues addressed include how they were to safeguard chastity, engage in spiritual reading and an instruction that they travel in pairs when engaged in business outside the monastery.

The commentary is followed by the *Liber Ordinis S. Victoris* (fols 102–47).[16] This is the customary of St Victor in Paris and was normative for houses that adopted the Victorine reform. Divided into ninety chapters, it supplemented the *Rule of St Augustine* and gave detailed instruction on the practical aspects of coenobitic life, including an elaborate system of sign language.[17] The Dublin text is an early witness to the customary and was used by Jocqué and Milis in their 1984 critical edition of the text.

The text of the *Liber ordinis* is followed by some short miscellaneous monastic regulations (fols 147v–52v), concerning topics such as the reception of guests, the conduct of laybrothers, the treatment of apostates and a prohibition on abbots exacting payments from their daughter houses. Some of the decrees related to the Dublin community, including instructions that no servile labour was to be done on the feast days of St Thomas Becket and prohibiting the canons from providing accommodation for female guests because of the availability of appropriate lodgings in the city. The section concludes with a lengthy, unpublished treatise detailing the correct manner of celebrating Mass (fols 150v–2v). There then follows a list of epistles and gospel readings that were read in the course of the liturgical year beginning with the first Sunday of Advent (fols 153–65). The practice of reading the scriptural texts that would be used during that day's celebration of the liturgy was a feature of the chapter office and these often formed the basis of a sermon to the community by the superior or his delegate.

The next section consists of copies of monastic rules and legislation from other monastic traditions. The first text, the *Regula S. Benedicti* (fols 166–78), is of particular interest as it is the oldest surviving copy of the *Rule of St Benedict* in Ireland.[18] It contains marginalia in various sections commenting on the status of the abbot, warning against sloth and negligence and reiterating the superior's obligations towards sick brethren, pilgrims and guests. It also provides the formula for monastic profession with a commentary on its significance. In his study of the formation of English Benedictine novices James Clarke noted that these marginal commentaries on core chapters were used to instruct newcomers on the obligations of their vocation.[19]

The 1224 *Regula Secunda* or *Rule of the Friars Minor* (fols 178–9v) then follows. This is the earliest copy to survive in Ireland and is accompanied by two of the three authoritative papal interpretations of the Franciscan Rule: the 1230 bull *Quo elongati* of Gregory IX and the 1279 bull *Exiit qui seminat* of Nicholas III (fols 179v–86v). The fact that it does not include the third document, the 1312 bull *Exivi de paradiso* of Clement V, is significant for establishing the *terminus ad quem* for the compilation of the manuscript. The inclusion of this material may indicate a close connection between the canons and the nearby Franciscan friary in St Nicholas Street. The Dublin friary was one of the order's principal houses in Ireland and, like the Victorines, the Franciscans and the Dominicans also benefitted from an annual grant of alms from the royal exchequer.[20] The friary lay within the boundaries of the liberty of St Thomas and in 1315 Abbot Ralph cited them to appear before his ecclesiastical court. As an exempt religious order subject only to papal jurisdiction, the friars vigorously contested this and Trinity College Dublin, MS 250, a fifteenth-century Franciscan codex, contains a copy of their public refutation of the abbot's citation delivered to him and the chapter of St Thomas and later repeated before the prior, clergy and congregation of Holy Trinity cathedral.[21]

The next two texts relate to the anchoritic life (fols 187–91). Of these the first, the *Ordo Anchoritalis Vitae* is a unique text probably dating to the twelfth century but related to two other anchorites' rules that circulated in England and the diocese of Armagh. The second text is a letter addressed to a certain Robert about how to conduct himself as an anchorite. Whereas little evidence for anchorites in medieval Ireland survives, it is sufficiently widespread to indicate that they were common in both Gaelic and Anglo-Irish church contexts. Both of the St Thomas's texts legislate for anchorites who were living independently but it was not uncommon for religious communities either to support solitaries or to occasionally allow some of their own members to pursue the eremitical vocation. One of the earliest accounts of the pilgrimage to St Patrick's purgatory in Lough Derg records an Augustinian Canon living as a hermit there. There is also a 1508 reference to Richard Grace, a deceased anchorite formerly attached to the Cistercian community at Dublin's St Mary's Abbey.[22]

The next items are a selection of excerpts from Patristic writers (fols 192–7v). The works cited include the letters of St Jerome, the *Pastoral Care* of St Gregory the Great and St Isidore's *De Ecclesiasticis Officiis*. These are followed by miscellaneous spiritual admonitions (fols 198–203) that include texts by Sts Augustine, Bede, Gregory the Great and Jerome. There then follows the *Synonyma* or *Book of Lamentations* of Isidore of Seville (fols 203v–5v). This takes the form of a dialogue between man and reason in which man bewails his lot on account of his sinfulness and receives assurance from reason he may still attain happiness.

The following two texts consist of a version of the *Speculum Monachorum* by the French Cistercian Arnulf De Boeriis (d.1149) (fol. 206rv) and an anonymous exhortation on monastic conduct. The former work was influential because of its attribution to Bernard of Clairvaux. These are followed by Prosper of Aquitaine's *Sententiae ex Operibus S. Augustini* (fols 207–18v), a compilation of spiritual maxims drawn from the work of Augustine by his fifth-century disciple.

The next text, Hugh of St Victor's *De Institutione Nouiciorum* (fols 219–27), was one of the most influential of his works and enjoyed widespread circulation throughout the Middle Ages. Compiled in the early decades of the twelfth century it gave a comprehensive and at times humorous account of how a religious should behave laying particular emphasis on deportment and external gestures.[23] The work was extensively quarried by later writers in the mendicant tradition and also influenced the compilers of secular courtesy books designed for the education of squires. Humour and parody are also much in evidence in the following treatise, an anonymous text *Contra Religionis Simulatores* (fols 227v–38v). This unique text takes the form of a dialogue between Gregory and Romanus, a negligent monk who believed himself to be a paragon of monastic observance.[24] The work has echoes of another monastic classic, the *Dialogues* of Gregory the Great, while its use of satire and parody is reminiscent of Bernard of Clairvaux's commentary on false religious in the treatise *The Steps of Humility and Pride*.

Another reality of the religious life is illustrated by the later addition to the compilation of Benedict XII's 1335 constitution, *Super apostatis revocandis* (fols 239–40). Issued in June 1335, it gave instruction on how to deal with those who abandoned the religious life. Because of the public and perpetual nature of monastic vows such apostasy had wider social implications. In addition to risking the wrath of God for their actions, fugitives could be arrested by the local sheriff and forcibly returned to their monasteries. The punishment for apostasy ranged from penitential fasting through corporal punishment administered in the chapter to lifelong imprisonment in the monastery prison. The canons of St Thomas had practical experience of the problem. In 1311, Brother Roger of Corbaly had abandoned his habit, shaved his head to disguise his tonsure and then broken into the coffers of the abbey and mutilated various documents before stealing £60 worth of silver.[25]

The next text in the codex, the *De Miseria Humane Conditionis* (fols 241–52) was one of the most influential works of medieval ascetic theology. Compiled between 1194 and 1195 by Cardinal Lothar of Segni, later Pope Innocent III (d.1216), it enjoyed widespread circulation with over 670 medieval copies of the Latin text surviving, including one in Trinity College Dublin, MS 667, a codex associated with a Franciscan house in Co. Clare. It was translated into Irish in 1443 and a copy of this translation is found in a manuscript written in the Franciscan friary at Kilcrea in 1475.[26] As the title suggests, its perception of the human condition was bleak.

The remaining documents seem slightly incongruous in a chapter book as they were designed primarily for a secular audience. The first of these, the short poem *Facetus* (fols 253–4) was composed in the twelfth century and was a staple of the English school curriculum by the fourteenth century. It was loosely modelled both in form and content on the third-century *Distichs of Cato* and gave advice on courtly conduct in a wide range of social situations including conversation, interaction with social superiors and table manners.[27]

The next work *Urbanus Magnus* (fols 254–72v) is the earliest English courtesy book to survive and was composed at the beginning of the thirteenth century by Daniel of Beccles, a courtier in the service of Henry II.[28] It consists of 2,835 lines of Latin verse presented in the form of an instruction from a father to his son. Its intended audience was junior members of aristocratic households who had to interact appropriately with both social superiors and inferiors. The range of situations covered is both comprehensive and unflinching. Thus, the instructions on how to behave at the table also included sections on the polite manner of farting, belching and nose clearing. While some of these social skills were undoubtedly applicable in a monastic context, instructions on how to murder one's enemy, deflect unwanted sexual advances from your master's wife or visit a prostitute hopefully were not. Nevertheless, the text is heavily annotated and was obviously being read carefully by someone.

The final items in the volume (fols 272v–5v) consist of a collection of proverbs by Serlo of Wilton (d.1181) and some verses concerning proper behaviour in church. The former text was a very popular collection by a twelfth-century English poet who after studying in Paris became first a Cluniac monk before transferring to the Cistercians and spending the last decade of his life as the abbot of L'Aumône abbey in France.

DISCUSSION

Although most of the individual works in Trinity College Dublin, MS 97 have received scholarly attention, the volume's overall significance as an intentional compilation has escaped notice. Viewed synoptically, the texts provide a comprehensive and, in an Irish context, almost unique insight into the *mentalité* of a late medieval monastic community. The texts helped forge the canons' sense of corporate identity and facilitated its transmission to newcomers to the monastery. The forum in which this took place was the daily meeting of the conventual chapter. Although not prescribed in the daily cursus outlined by St Benedict in his rule, the chapter meeting had become a standard feature of monastic life by the ninth century and followed an established format. It normally took place immediately after the cycle of private Masses that followed the office of Prime, the first of the day hours of the Divine Office. The gathering took place in the chapter room, which was normally situated in the east range of the cloister. The importance of the chapter house was reflected in its architecture and although nothing survives from St Thomas's, the impressive remains of the chapter rooms at Dublin's Holy Trinity Priory and St Mary's Abbey give some impression of how it might have appeared. The texts used during the chapter meeting formed a distinct subset of a monastery's book collection known as 'chapter books', of which Trinity College Dublin, MS 97 is a good example.[29] These works characteristically included copies of the martyrology, patristic and scriptural texts, monastic rules with commentaries, customaries and the necrology, a list of deceased individuals whose anniversaries were commemorated. As novices often received instruction in the chapter room the chapter books often included devotional or ascetical material designed to inculcate the principles of religious life.

Attendance at the assembly was the prerogative of members of the community although outsiders might be admitted by invitation.[30] In addition to listening to the recitation of the daily reading from the martyrology and the Rule of St Augustine, the assembly also heard pericopes from scripture and patristic writers that elaborated on what they heard during the liturgy in the church. The commemoration of the dead was another important element and although the necrology for St Thomas's Abbey does not survive, that of the nearby Augustinian priory of Holy Trinity contains obituary notices of over 1,000 individuals. These included the canons, their relatives, benefactors and servants, as well as mayors of Dublin, leading members of the colonial administration and Anglo-Irish aristocrats.[31] Given its pre-eminence as a royal foundation the St Thomas's community was probably similarly well connected. Towards the end of the chapter meeting community members confessed their faults, charitably drew attention to the shortcomings of others and received appropriate penances for transgressions. As the chapter meeting was the forum in which the canons collectively interacted with outsiders such encounters took place once the religious elements of the assembly had concluded. Patrons and prominent benefactors might occasionally be admitted to confraternity or spiritual membership of the community and this ceremony also took place in the chapter room.

The monastic legislation helped consolidate the canons' identity as a religious community with a distinctive spiritual tradition that combined clerical and monastic elements.[32] Daily exposure to readings from the Rule of St Augustine and commentaries on it by Victorine writers re-enforced their self-perception as Regular Canons while the *Liber Ordinis*, with its detailed prescription of their lifestyle, gestures and conduct, consolidated their identity as Victorines. The presence of the Rules of Sts Benedict and Francis as well as the anchoritic material indicates openness to the insights of other religious traditions that was a characteristic of the Victorines. They in turn exercised a profound influence on how later religious, particularly the friars, inculcated in their novices the fundamental principles of the religious life. Likewise, the presence of devotional works such as Innocent III's *De Contemptu Mundi* situates them within the mainstream of medieval spirituality. The presence of secular courtesy literature initially seems incongruous but one of the features of the Victorine formation system as outlined in Hugh of St Victor's treatise on the formation of novices was how external gestures should reflect interior attitudes. The canon was to be gracious in all his actions and his dealings, both as an expression of self-control and as a means of edifying others. He was called to instruct both by word and example – *docere verbo et exemplo*. The contents of Trinity College Dublin, MS 97 allow us to see how the canons of St Thomas's Abbey understood and articulated that vocation to themselves and to their novices in early fourteenth-century Dublin.

Notes

1.   C. Ó Clabaigh, 'The Church, 1050–1460', in B. Smith (ed.), *Cambridge History of Ireland, vol. 1* (Cambridge, 2018), pp. 401–32.

2.   Aubrey Gwynn and R. Neville Hadcock, *Medieval Religious Houses: Ireland* (London, 1970), pp. 146–216; Marie Therese Flanagan, *The Transformation of the Irish Church in the Twelfth Century* (Woodbridge, 2010), pp. 118–68.

3.   M. Staunton and C. Ó Clabaigh, 'Thomas Becket and Ireland', in E. Mullins and D. Scully (eds), *Listen, You Islands unto me: Studies in Medieval Word and Image presented to Jennifer O'Reilly* (Cork, 2011), pp. 87–101.

4.   V. Davis, 'Relations between the Abbey of St Thomas the Martyr and the Municipality of Dublin, *c*.1176–1527', *Dublin Historical Record*, 40, 2 (1987), 57–65.

5.   Newport B. White, *Extents of Irish Monastic Possessions, 1540–1541* (Dublin, 1943), pp. 25–48; M. T. Flanagan, '*Conquestus* and *adquisicio*: some early Cork charters relating to St Thomas' Abbey', in E. Purcell, P. McCotter, J. Nyhan and J. Sheehan (eds), *Clerics, Kings and Vikings: Essays on Medieval Ireland in Honour of Donnchadh Ó Corráin* (Dublin, 2015), pp. 127–46.

6.   Áine Foley, *St Thomas's Abbey* (Dublin: n.p., 2018); C. Walsh, 'Archaeological Excavations at the Abbey of St Thomas the Martyr', in S. Duffy (ed.), *Medieval Dublin I* (Dublin, 2000), pp. 185–201.

7.   Jean Longère (ed.), *L'Abbaye Parisienne de Saint-Victor au Moyen Âge* (Turnhout, 1991).

8.   Unless otherwise stated the following analysis is based on Marvin L. Colker, *Trinity College Library: Descriptive Catalogue of the Medieval and Renaissance Latin Manuscripts* (Aldershot, 1991), I, pp. 183–95.

9.   Roger Bacon, *Opera Hactenus Inedita VI*, ed. R. Steele (Oxford, 1926), pp. 284–9, 268–89.

10. Jacques Dubois, *Le Martyrologe d'Usuard* (Brussels, 1965).

11. Pádraig Ó Riain, *Feastdays of the Saints: a History of Irish Martyrologies* (Brussels, 2006), pp. 247–66.

12. A. Gwynn, 'The Early History of St Thomas' Abbey, Dublin', *Journal of the Royal Society of the Antiquaries of Ireland*, 84, 1 (1954), 30.

13. Ó Riain, *Feastdays*, p. 253.

14. Hugo de S. Victore (?), 'Expositio in Regulam S. Augustini', PL, 176 (Paris, 1854), pp. 881–924.

15. M. L. Colker, 'Richard of St Victor and the Anonymous of Bridlington', *Traditio*, 18 (1962), 201–23. Colker suggests that this may be Abbot Simon of St Albans who corresponded with Richard and who had a great interest in the work of Hugh of St Victor.

16. Lucas Jocqué and Ludovicus Milis (eds), *Liber Ordinis Sancti Victoris Parisiensis* (Turnhout, 1984).

17. H. F. Berry, 'On the Use of Signs in the Ancient Monasteries, with Special Reference to a Code used by the Victorines Canons of St Thomas's Abbey, Dublin', *Journal of the Royal Society of Antiquaries of Ireland*, 2, 2 (1892), 107–25.

18. C. Ó Clabaigh, 'The Benedictines in Medieval and Early Modern Ireland', in M. Browne and C. Ó Clabaigh, *The Irish Benedictines: A History* (Dublin, 2005), pp. 79–121 (p. 83).

19. J. G. Clarke, 'Monastic Education in Late Medieval England', in Caroline M. Barron and Jenny Stratford (eds), Proceedings of the 1999 Harlaxton Symposium: *The Church*

and Learning in Later Medieval Society: Essays in Honour of R. B. Dobson, Harlaxton Medieval Studies XI, NS (Donington, 2002), pp. 25–40 (p. 28).

20. Colmán Ó Clabaigh, *The Friars in Ireland, 1224–1540* (Dublin, 2012), p. 90.

21. Trinity College Dublin, MS 250, fols 166v–7v; Colker, *Catalogue*, I, p. 449.

22. C. Ó Clabaigh, 'The Hermits and Anchorites of Medieval Dublin', in S. Duffy (ed.), *Medieval Dublin X* (Dublin, 2010), pp. 267–86.

23. Emmanuel Falque, 'La Geste et la Parole chez Hughes de Saint Victor: L'*Institution des Novices*', *Revue des Sciences Philosophiques et Théologiques*, 95 (2011), 383–412.

24. Marvin L. Colker (ed.), *Analecta Dublinensia: Three Medieval Latin Texts in the Library of Trinity College Dublin* (Cambridge, Mass., 1975), pp. 2–62.

25. Margaret G. Griffith, *Calendar of the Justiciary Rolls or Proceedings in the Court of the Justiciar of Ireland, I–VII years of Edward II* (Dublin, 1905), p. 212.

26. Georges Dottin, 'Le Manuscrit Irlandais de la Bibliothèque de Rennes', *Revue Celtique*, 15 (1894), 79–91.

27. Carl Schroeder (ed.), 'Facetus', *Palestra*, 86 (1911), 14–28.

28. Daniel of Beccles, *Urbanus Magnus Danielis Becclesiensis*, J. Gilbart Smyly (Dublin, 1939).

29. Jean-Loup Lemaître, '*Libri Capituli*: Le Livre du Chapitre, des origines au XVI siècle. L'exemple Français', in K. Schmid and J. Wollasch (eds), *Memoria: der geschichtliche Zeugniswert des liturgischen Gedenkens im Mittelalter* (Munich, 1984), pp. 625–48.

30. Jocqué and Milis, *Liber Ordinis*, pp. 153–63, gives a detailed description of how the chapter meeting was conducted in Victorine communities.

31. Colm Lennon, 'The Book of Obits of Christ Church Cathedral, Dublin', in R. Gillespie and R. Refaussé (eds), *The Medieval Manuscripts of Christ Church Cathedral, Dublin* (Dublin, 2006), pp. 163–82.

32. Caroline Walker Bynum, 'The Spirituality of Regular Canons in the Twelfth Century', in C. W. Bynum, *Jesus as Mother: Studies in the Spirituality of the High Middle Ages* (Berkeley, 1982), pp. 22–58.

4

Strata Florida: a former Welsh Cistercian Abbey and its future

David Austin

INTRODUCTION

Strata Florida is the site of a former Cistercian Abbey set in the heartlands of Wales on the western side of the Cambrian Mountains in Ceredigion.[1] It lies in a small and beautiful valley at the head of the Teifi river system and was, and remains, an iconic place in the historic identity of Wales, evoking strong sentiment and retaining a forceful sense of spiritual presence.[2] The site was excavated in the later nineteenth century by Stephen Williams, a railway engineer and entrepreneur, who wanted to develop it as a place for people to visit using the new train service from Carmarthen to Aberystwyth.[3] Today Cadw has guardianship of the foundations Williams revealed consisting largely of the abbey church and a portion of the cloister including the chapterhouse.[4] Since 1999, the Strata Florida Project has been conducting research and a programme of regeneration through heritage, at first under the auspices of the University of Wales Trinity Saint David and now under the direction of the Strata Florida Trust. This work builds on the extensive scholarship undertaken by others over the last forty years or so on the Cistercian Order in Wales, notably that of David Williams, David Robinson and Janet Burton herself, often in collaborative partnership, not least with the editors of this volume.[5]

Janet Burton, who has been a colleague of mine at Lampeter for more years than either of us care to acknowledge, has often stood with me among these consolidated remains and talked of its history and meaning. She has shown her characteristic patience and calm when I have, just as characteristically, been forcefully expounding some theory or other about its origin or architectural layout. Her impressively broad knowledge and profound understanding of medieval monasticism, the Cistercians especially, have been an important foil for me in adjusting and formulating my ideas about the place. The work she and her colleagues (including two of the editors of this volume) have done in constructing the excellent website on Monastic Wales is a clear example of scholarly rigour which has provided me with specific information.[6] My focus on the evidence of the particular and her narratives of the wider politics and practices of the Cistercian Order have encouraged, I think, an important synthesis of ideas in my mind which both challenge and strengthen some of the received wisdoms about how these monks set about adapting themselves and their ways to those parts of the world they had been given. I am eternally grateful for that and for her constant support.

STRATA FLORIDA

I now believe that although the abbey was first founded as a small entity on the lands controlled by a sub-infeudated knight of the Clare lordship of Ceredigion in 1164, its appropriation six months later by Rhys ap Gruffydd, prince of Deheubarth, was a critical moment in Welsh history. It had fallen his way when he drove out the Clares and added Ceredigion to his patrimonial lands in the Towy valley of Carmarthenshire to the south and east. This consolidated lordship, Deheubarth, was the rock on which he carved out a presence which stood both as opposition to, and feudal servant of, the ever-threatening kingdom and marcher lordships of England to the south and east, then in the relentless overlordship of Henry II. Famously Rhys reached an accommodation with this imperially minded man, becoming the king's justiciar over the southern Welsh princes and achieving some hegemony over the northern. For about two decades, Rhys was in his pomp and, I believe, harboured ideas of a Welsh state that might stand forever as the bulwark of his people. This cannot be found in the scant documents of his reign, but rather in his acts, one of the foremost of which was the effective re-foundation of Strata Florida in 1184 as a massive presence in the heart of Wales.

Called subsequently 'the Westminster Abbey of Wales', Strata Florida with its burials of some of Rhys's family members became a centre for an ideology of identity centred on Welsh language, history and culture. Here as well as in other major Cistercian abbeys in Wales, it can be argued, were gathered together oral traditions both mythical and historical. Embedded in poetry and prose alike, they became inscribed monuments in manuscripts enshrining the memory and meaning of the people. The *Brut y Twywosogion*, the history of Wales in Welsh, was probably created here as a continuation of what had been begun at the great pre-Norman bishop-house and monastic *clas* at Llanbadarn Fawr.[7] Less easy to prove, but highly likely was the production of books of the law as well as collections of works from the early bardic poetic and prose traditions.[8] This will all need further study, but the ambition that Strata Florida should be a key element in the resistant presence of an independent-minded

Wales was one that was recognised by political contemporaries and has resonated down the centuries until today.

All of this, academically, will need further research and justification, but Strata Florida is undoubtedly no ordinary place in Wales and has long deserved a better understanding and a celebration of its historic and cultural meaning and significance, especially at a time when Wales is politically resurgent, albeit made, as Rhys conceived, within a larger, island polity. What I want to rehearse here is not the specific history nor indeed the immense archaeology of Strata Florida, but rather lay out how this aspiration to celebrate may be achieved and what steps we are taking to bring this about.

First, we need a little topography. In figure 2 I have superimposed an outline of the 1184 abbey on a superb air photograph by Dr Toby Driver of the RCAHMW (see figure 2). The view is looking westwards from the Cambrian Mountains (just visible in the lower foreground) towards the Irish Sea, with Aberarth the coastal holding and effective port of the abbey in the far distance. The area around the abbey and in the middle part of the landscape was the abbey's demesne, farmed, probably, from the abbey's outer precinct. This consists of a series of specialist farms, each responsible for a different element of the abbey's supply needs, such as Dolebolion ('Meadow

FIGURE 2: The former monastery of Strata Florida (red shading) in its topography looking westwards towards the Irish Sea. With kind permission of the Royal Commission on Ancient and Historical Monuments of Wales.

of the Foals') for horses or Bron y Berllan ('Slope of the Orchard'), whose terraced south-facing lands provided fruit. Beyond is the demesne village of Pontrhydfendigaid and the vast expanse of Cors Caron (Tregaron Bog) today a National Nature Reserve and Ramsar site, but that was once a huge reserve of fuel and wildlife for the abbey. To the south lay the planted and managed woodland of the abbey, much of which still survives with traces of historic wood management and a stunning array of archaeological sites within it, surveyed for us by Louise Barker of the RCAHMW.

Within the circle on figure 2 is a complex of buildings which includes the Cadw monument with, to the north, the parish church and graveyard of St Mary's and, to the south, the farm of Mynachlog Fawr ('Great Abbey'). This is shown in more detail on figure 3. In August 2016 the Strata Florida Trust purchased the farm buildings and a field to the east. The farm buildings consist of the farmhouse itself (A), which had once been the mansion of the Stedman family (c.1560 to c.1780), which itself had been built out of part of the ruins of the abbey refectory. To the west are the buildings of various dates (B), which served as the working courtyard of the farm from the mid-nineteenth century and to the south of that is another courtyard (C). To the east is a field of extensive earthworks (D), which are the remains of a late sixteenth- or early seventeenth-century garden, but beneath which lie the archaeological remains of many stone buildings and open spaces of the former abbey, including the infirmary.

The Strata Florida Trust, a not-for-profit charitable company, was established in 2006 under my chairmanship with the expressed aim of conserving the five listed buildings of Mynachlog Fawr and developing them as a centre for visitors and scholars alike, celebrating the long cultural and landscape history not only of the abbey itself, but also its antecedents and modern successors. During a long process of research, carried out while I was still working at the University of Wales Trinity Saint David at Lampeter in which many students of my department were taught the basic skills of survey, excavation and heritage management, we revealed the true extent of the abbey and established that it survived intact if only as major archaeological remains.

We have been able to show the likely layout of the abbey (see figure 4) and this forms the core of one of the four key narratives that will drive the presentation of the site to the public and provide the focus for a range of activities which will take place to make the centre a sustainable element in the Welsh upland countryside. At approximately 126 acres (51 ha.) in size the precincts represent one of, if not the, largest Cistercian abbey in Britain by area. There are two large precincts: the inner, with three access gates shown on post-medieval estate maps, contains all the major stone buildings found by geophysics and tested, in part, by excavation. At the heart of this and in front

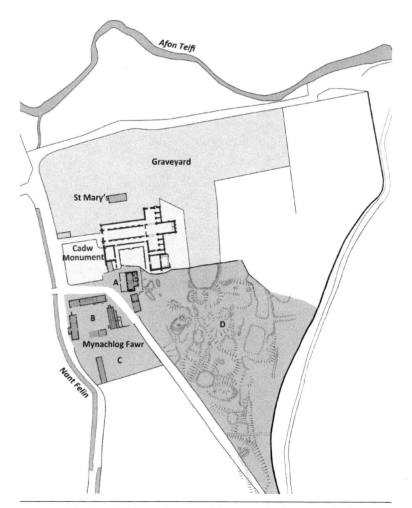

FIGURE 3: The Great Abbey site. Property of the Strata Florida Trust, in the darker shade of grey. © David Austin.

of the west end of the abbey was a vast open space, called the 'Great Court' by Leland in about 1536 when he visited it.[9] The function of this is hard to determine, but seems to have lain between the main gate and the church. The estate maps call it 'the Convent Green' and it may have been a space for gatherings and events perhaps linked to pilgrimage or displays of power. The outer precinct, by contrast, is much more likely to have contained timber buildings in the local vernacular tradition as well as farming and industrial enclosures which

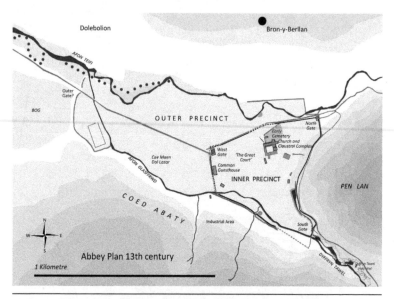

FIGURE 4: What is currently known of the abbey precinct as redesigned in 1184 and functioning at its height in the thirteenth century. © David Austin.

are harder to detect on the geophysics. The inner precinct was surrounded by a wall which replaced an earthen bank. On the outside of this curtilage, all the way round, was a road that allowed travellers to pass around the abbey's sacred space as they journeyed along the ancient routeway from England to Ireland, across which the monastery had been placed.

If you link all of this precinct size and layout with the vast endowment of land given by the Lord Rhys when re-founding the abbey in 1184, the project aspiration of this prince is transparent. It appears to match his great political intention of making Strata Florida central to a reconceived Welsh polity, that is before his sons effectively ripped the proposition apart after his death. This story of the land and the landscapes of Strata Florida is the second great narrative and it is a particularly Welsh account. Working within the frameworks of local custom and Welsh law the abbey organised the land and its revenues in a complex way and their management of the landholding has left an enormous legacy of preserved archaeological sites in the surrounding landscape. Although the components of this estate were later called granges, this seems rather to have been an administrative gloss put on a pattern of tenure which was essentially non-manorial and thus did not entirely fit the European model of Cistercian farming.[10] In reality they created a great central demesne of specialist farms focused around the abbey itself, intended to service the needs of this large house. This seems to have included the sheep farms which were clustered on the mountain edge just to the east of the precincts. This was because what they seem to have been given in the 1184 grant were two things: the first were the royal rights and holdings of bond settlements and grazing on the one hand; and on the other the renders to the prince (*gwestfa* and *commortha*) made by freeholders of various ranks which were commuted into rents. It was the latter only which seems to have been estimated at £118 in the *Valor Ecclesiasticus* of 1535, with the revenues from its own demesnes perhaps not included in this account.[11] This is a complex argument which will be made elsewhere, but it is just one of the ways in which the Cistercians of Strata Florida modified and adapted their ways to the context, both social and material, that they found themselves in.

This capacity to adapt their economic model to local circumstance was probably matched, and this brings us to the third great narrative for Strata Florida, by a more spiritual and religious syncretism drawing on a deep heritage of pre-Norman practice which drew together a uniquely 'Celtic' sentiment. Under the crossing tower and in front of the high altar was an earlier holy well deliberately set at the very heart of the church and the liturgy. The church appears to have been built around it: the holy well lies true east–west while the church was laid out on the alignment of sunrise and sunset on St David's Day 1184.[12] Of itself the latter is a powerful indicator of the 'national' intentions of the project, but the presence of a holy well in this position is another. Its rhetoric is that of the pre-Norman church in Wales and suggests that a holy cult of water may have been, for Strata Florida, the equivalent of a shrine. There are also at least three other holy wells up the course of the Afon Glasffrwd which provided the water supply for the abbey as well as a complex of early cross-marked stones on the hill above. It also seems clear that the present graveyard of St Mary's was not a post-Dissolution addition, but actually an earlier cemetery over part of which the Cistercian church was laid out. On the southern edge of this cemetery originally, therefore, sat the holy well, 'captured' by the plan of the abbey church and perhaps originally dedicated to a saint whose name was lost in the re-dedication to the Holy Virgin when the Cistercians established their monastery there. However, in a fifteenth-century ode to Abbot Rhys of Strata Florida by Guto'r Glyn there are these lines:

> Tai Gynfelyn, talm a'u gwelyn'
> Teimlai delyn, teml adeilad.
>
> [St Cynfelyn's houses, a host of people see them,
> he would play a harp, temple building.][13]

It is possible that these otherwise unexplained lines refer to the Welsh saint to whom a pre-existing monastery was dedicated and onto which the Cistercian abbey was deliberately placed to draw on all its associations with an earlier, Welsh church. These elements and others have been drawn together in one speculative plan of where a possible antecedent for the Cistercian abbey might lie (see figure 5).

A parallel for such a sequence beneath a later, reformed abbey, including a holy well, early saint and pre-Carolingian monastery, has recently been discovered at Landevennec beneath the remains of a later Benedictine house in Finistère in Brittany.[14] All of this layered meaning at Strata Florida may also have been deliberately signalled by the use of 'Celtic' art on the façade of the great west door of the church at the liminal point of entry to the sacred.

This great weight of meaning has come down to the present day and within the complex web of sentiment that is modern Welsh identity Strata Florida retains a significant place, one I feel that was deliberately designed into the fabric and plan of the abbey from the start. One measure of its success is its absorption into the Welsh narrative of resistance to the English. Soon after Strata Florida was open for business following its consecration in 1201, King John ordered it to be destroyed because it 'harbours out enemies'.[15] It

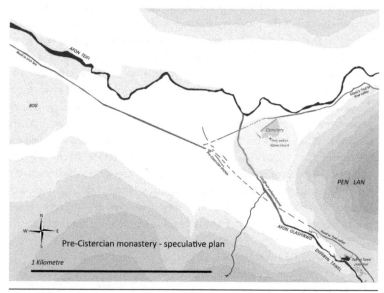

FIGURE 5: Speculative plan of a possible earlier monastery under Strata Florida Cistercian Abbey. © David Austin.

was here in 1238 that Llywelyn ab Iorwerth, who certainly had explicit concepts of an independent Welsh state, summoned the other princes of Wales under his hegemony to swear allegiance to his heir Dafydd.[16] This did not bear fruit and the oath was broken, but it is noteworthy that Llywelyn chose not one of his own great abbeys in Gwynedd but Strata Florida for this great political act of unity. The tide turned with the Edwardian wars and it may have been more than coincidence that in 1284, according to the English Chronicles that Strata Florida's church was 'struck by lightning and burned'.[17] Even worse, over a century later, the abbey, having backed the rising of Owain Glyndŵr, was systematically devastated by an English force on three separate occasions.[18]

It never fully recovered and it limped towards the Dissolution in 1539, despite the investment in rebuilding by two abbots in the fifteenth century. Here the fourth narrative truly begins. The abbey and its estates were acquired by permanent lease from the Crown by Sir Richard Devereux and were held by the earls of Essex until the earlier seventeenth century at which time much was acquired by older gentry families such as the Powells of Nanteos and the Vaughans of Trawscoed.[19] However, the abbey itself and surrounding land, called 'the Demesne', were sold, by 1560, to John Stedman, perhaps a 'live-in' official of the Devereux earls. This family quickly established itself by marrying into the local gentry and by 1600 were High Sheriffs of Cardiganshire. Although much more architectural and archaeological analysis is required, it is already clear that the Stedmans built their mansion out of the remains of the abbey's refectory and parts remain embedded in the fabric of the current farmhouse which was first depicted by the Buck brothers in 1741. When also the Powells acquired this estate through marriage in the mid-eighteenth century, they created a detailed map (dated 1765) which, together with our preliminary fieldwork, allows us to recreate a plan of the gentry layout established by the Stedmans from the later sixteenth century (figure 6).

Not long after the Powells had secured the title and succession to the Stedman estate, the former mansion and the demesne were made into a tenant farm. Throughout this early modern period the great estates maximised the returns from their tenant farms, especially in the boom years of the late eighteenth and nineteenth centuries, and exploited mineral rights, notably in lead and silver, despite incursions by Crown interests. Near to Strata Florida and exploiting lodes once dug by the Cistercians, Abbey Consol Mine was opened in 1849, and the small demesne village of Pontrhydfendigaid grew from its historic, agrarian core to become a sizeable mining settlement.

Not long after the Vaughans of Trawscoed acquired the Mynachlog Fawr estate in the mid-nineteenth century a long-term agricultural decline began, particularly impacting mountain farming, and the hills around Strata Florida

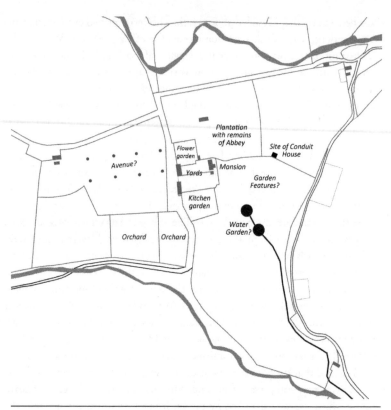

FIGURE 6: Strata Florida House and designed landscape in 1765. © David Austin.

are full of ruins from this era. As the world economy and globalisation continued to affect the upland communities of Europe, mining too began to fail. Slowly the great estates were wound down and the former tenants began to acquire the freehold of the land, although the going was tough. The Arch family who had been put into the farmhouse of Mynachlog Fawr as tenants by the Vaughans in 1875 eventually bought their freehold in the 1950s. It was from their descendants that the trust bought the farm buildings in 2016. The house they lived in contains strong material memories of their way of life, but there are also traces of the mansion it had once been. All of this will permit the telling of their story as the heirs and successors of the Cistercian tradition and way of life among the same hills.

So, how do we relate these four narratives and how do we create a sustainable centre out of it all? First we must conserve the buildings, both interiors and exteriors. This will be done to preserve the visual nature of their long-term presence in the landscape and let their narratives be seen. Then, as we prepare for this we must also design into them and their surrounding spaces the capacity to let them be used for the enjoyment of visitors as well as for the continuing study and revelation of their history and that of the surrounding landscapes once held by the Cistercians.

VALUE

All will depend on us convincing funders of all types that this is worth doing. We have begun this by identifying the complex array of values, opportunities and, indeed, responsibilities that this place represents. First and foremost is its heritage value to the Welsh nation in telling the story of the growth of its identity and its culture, particularly in the rural heartlands. Of all the medieval monuments in Wales it is the one that so patently shows the high aspirations of its people and the achievements of its very special culture. There is no doubt that the Cistercians of Strata Florida embraced both and did much to shape and form their representation. For this reason the World Monuments Fund (WMF) has recognised the international significance of this site and they will be supporting our work:

> Strata Florida is an extraordinary historic and archaeological site, of international importance as a centre of early Welsh cultural heritage. The WMF supports, among others, projects at the Mugjhal Gardens next to the Taj Mahal, Angkor Vat, the Nazca Lines and Coventry's medieval cathedral.[20]

So the story of the Strata Florida Cistercians will be told on a site where there will be continuing research as well as physical and heritage development. In addition to the current monument and in partnership with Cadw we will look to demonstrate the true extent of this large site. This will involve the capacity to walk around and see other surviving archaeological remains, to participate in the revelation and possible consolidation of new elements of the monastic plan and buildings, and to use computer generated and other imagery to visualise the whole monastery and the environment in which it sat.

This historic environment is already recognised by Cadw and the International Committee on Monuments and Sites as a Landscape of Outstanding Historic Interest,[21] but our discoveries over the last decade have uncovered a rich wealth of archaeology that demonstrates the abbey's sustainable exploitation of the natural resources, in itself a lesson for the future.

There are many Sites of Special Scientific Interest, not least Cors Caron, and the Cambrian Mountains once nearly became Wales's fourth national park. The whole represents an opportunity to reconstruct, for a number of different periods, the story of how the landscape was formed and used. This will include the antecedents of the abbey going back into a deep prehistory when some of the meanings of this landscape were being created. This includes a remarkable collection of Bronze Age monuments clustered around the source of the river down the course of which there were later holy wells culminating in the one enclosed by the abbey church.

As to the post-Dissolution era we shall be showing the material remains of how a great house and new estate were formed out of the wreckage of the abbey. Here there are buildings, their interiors and the remains of a complete Renaissance garden. These later became a working farm and an important element of our storytelling at Strata Florida will be the intangible heritage of a complete way of life born out of the monastic past. The last 200 years or so have seen the emergence of modern Wales. The story of its place in industrial history has, rightly, dominated because of its pre-eminent role in the development of the modern world system. There are many heritage locations celebrating and narrating that fantastic story. However, what happened in rural Wales in that time has had a more muted narration. In England and elsewhere in Europe a number of locations have been preserved and opened to the public that tell and re-enact the story of the countryside. In Wales this is more exceptional outside St Fagans which has done such an important job in preserving buildings and lifeways of the Welsh rural landscape, but not in situ. Strata Florida gives us a chance to use the stories of a farm and its people to show how the modern countryside and its Welsh culture have come into being and what changes are threatening them.

Within the Welsh culture of the local communities there is also a very important 'intangible' heritage of language and social tradition, as defined by the World Heritage Organisation. This is yet to be fully documented and researched, although it includes a book in Welsh by Charles Arch on his early life on the farm.[22] Strata Florida and its hinterlands include heritage elements that will permit the visitor to understand local communities and their heritage and which will enable local people to celebrate through memory the importance of Welsh culture in one of its principal heartlands.

In presenting Strata Florida to a wider audience we will have to take account also of other values than those simply of heritage and research. There is no doubt, for example, that Strata Florida has a special spiritual quality, partly because of its long history as a place of religious contemplation and practice which may have antecedents stretching back into prehistory, but partly also because of the great beauty of its surrounding landscape. In carrying out our work at this site this value will be recognised and built into the principles of conservation design and activity.

Strata Florida is a source of great historical pride for the communities roundabout and everyone has been there and knows something of its history, not least because they were taken there when they were children at school, an element that the project has consciously fostered. There is also a sentiment that this is a particularly Welsh monument, perhaps the Welsh monument, and this must be consciously recognised as a special national community value. The abbey and its successors have had a central role in the economic life of the region. Today the potential for economic regeneration of the area through heritage is high as the abbey site offers great potential for developing a much richer story than at present with many more things for the visitor to see and do, thus becoming a focus for cultural and environmental tourism. Sites of historic significance the world over are an important way for communities and local businesses to improve income generation.

Strata Florida too has had a long history of formal academic education, and there is highly likely to have been an abbey school which we have already reconstituted with local primary schools. The abbey would also have been training a skilled workforce for all the tasks a major institution of this kind would have needed. The site and its heritage development offer the location and opportunity for high quality and inspiring study and skills training in a wide variety of subjects, including not just archaeology and history, but also Welsh language and literature, religious history, the arts, conservation, land management, environmental studies and sustainability, and heritage and management.

The arts have been a key element of what Strata Florida has promoted and supported over the centuries, not consciously as a separate endeavour, but as part of the fabric of worship, prayer and work. A strong survival has been sculpture, not just in the styles of the high Middle Ages, but also in the antecedent traditions of Celtic motifs. We have already revived that long practice with two major international sculpture exhibitions and, more recently, by placing on the mountain skyline to the east of the monastic church a four-metre high sculpture of a *Pilgrim* by Glenn Morris. This has already become an icon of the Welsh landscape, appearing on the front cover of at least three books. Further in-situ pieces are intended for the future.

Finally, one of the key elements of the story of Strata Florida is the significance of water and its healing qualities. The unique existence of a holy well at the core of the abbey's religious space and liturgy was a distinctive presence and practice for this important part not just of Catholic, but also

Celtic tradition and teaching. The abbey also had a major infirmary and through its hospice system along the pilgrim and trade routes criss-crossing the area it would have provided a key source of healing in the region. The one object that symbolises all this deep tradition is the Nanteos Cup, a medieval mazer that has strong associations with Strata Florida and which, if water or wine was drunk from it, had healing powers.[23] Once a year this will be shown at Strata Florida where its ancient associations and significance will be celebrated.

CONCLUSION: THE DEVELOPMENT OF THE STRATA FLORIDA CENTRE

The Strata Florida Project will aim to create a centre predicated on Welsh history and culture, housed in a series of restored listed buildings. Even before all the doors are open in four to five years' time, we will take the opportunity to place before Wales and the rest of the world the immense importance of this place and its heritage. In doing so we will celebrate Strata Florida and share that celebration with others, while still retaining its essence as a very special Welsh place with particular qualities. In this way Strata Florida will become an attraction and amenity for visitors, reflecting the heritage and other values of the site's long history and cultural traditions. As such it will function all year round with its own staff, working with local businesses on a franchise or partnership basis, interacting with other regional tourism and cultural organisations and sites to create a 'networked offer' to draw visitors to stay longer. From the centre visitors will have informed access to the historic landscapes and special ecologies of the former abbey's hinterlands and espouse the principles of environmental sustainability and renewable energy as the Cistercians themselves had done.

To support and develop the key narratives we have identified, we will continue to develop programmes of research, including excavation, to extend the understanding and visibility of the site. We will also work with local communities to achieve higher levels of employment and wealth generation as well as improvement of amenities and infrastructures. This will include work with schools, colleges and universities to educate and inform students within their course structures about the heritage of the site with more informal programmes of learning notably as summer schools, such as a volunteer-based excavation. We will also work with the same institutions to develop local and regional capacities in the skills required for the modern heritage and conservation industry. And finally we will work with national and international artists and arts administrators to develop Strata Florida as a creative location and exhibition centre. Particular emphasis will be put on Welsh language and literature, music, sculpture and performance. In all these ways we seek to bring the abbey and all it means in historical terms back into the communities and landscapes it did so much to create.

Notes

1. D. H. Williams, 'The Cistercians in west Wales II: Ceredigion', *Archaeologia Cambrensis*, 159 (2010), 241–86; D. Austin, 'The Archaeology of Monasteries in Wales and the Strata Florida Project', in Janet Burton and Karen Stöber (eds), *Monastic Wales, New Approaches* (Cardiff, 2013), pp. 3–20. For more information see the website of the Strata Florida Trust: *www.strataflorida.org.uk* (accessed May 2017).

2. D. Austin, 'An aura of *hiraeth* – Strata Florida', in H. Bowen, *Buildings and Places in Welsh History* (Llandysul, 2013), pp. 51–8.

3. S. W. Williams, *The Cistercian Abbey of Strata Florida: its history, and an account of the recent excavations made on its site* (London, 1889).

4. D. M. Robinson and C. Platt, *Strata Florida [and] Talley Abbey*, 3rd edn (rev.) (Cardiff, 2007).

5. D. H. Williams, *Atlas of the Cistercian Lands in Wales* (Cardiff, 1990); D. H. Williams, *The Welsh Cistercians* (Leominster, 2001); D. M. Robinson, *The Cistercians in Wales, Architecture and Archaeology 1130–1540* (London, 2006); Burton and Stöber (eds), *Monastic Wales, New Approaches*.

6. *www.monasticwales.org.uk* (accessed July 2017).

7. T. Jones (ed.), *Brut y Tywyosogion or the Chronicle of the Princes. Peniarth MS. 20 Version* (Cardiff, 1952), p. xli.

8. D. Huws, *Medieval Welsh Manuscripts* (Cardiff, 2000).

9. L. Toulmin Smith, *The Itinerary in Wales of John Leland* (London, 1906), p. 56.

10. T. Jones Pierce, 'Strata Florida Abbey', *Ceredigion*, 1 (1950), 28–9; F. G. Cowley, *The Monastic Order in South Wales* (Cardiff, 1977), pp. 90–1.

11. J. Caley and J. Hunter (eds), *Valor Ecclesiasticus temp. Henr. VIII. Auctoritate regia institutus*, 6 vols (London, 1810–34), IV, p. 396.

12. O. Pritchard, 'Archaeoastronomy and the sacred landscape of the Strata Florida landscape: landscape, skyscape and structure from 2000 BC to AD 1200' (unpublished MA dissertation, University of Wales Trinity Saint David, 2014). P. Guigon, 'The archaeology of the so-called 'Celtic Church' in Brittany', in N. Edwards (ed.), *The Archaeology of the Early Medieval Celtic Churches*, Med. Arch. Monograph 29 (London, 2009), p. 176, fig. 9.2.

13. D. Johnston, *Poems of Guto'r Glyn* (online edition), 'No. 8 Ode in Praise of Abbot Rhys of Strata Florida', ll. 75–6 (*www.gutorglyn.net/gutorglyn/poem/?poem-selection=008*, accessed September 2017).

14. Annie Bardel, personal communication.

15. T. D. Hardy, *Rotuli Litterarum Clausarum I* (London, 1833), p. 122.

16. J. G. Edwards, *Calendar of Ancient Correspondence Concerning Wales* (Cardiff, 1935), p. 30.

17. R. C. Christie (ed.), *Annales Cestriensis; or Chronicle of the Abbey of St Werburg, at Chester* (London, 1887), pp. 114–17.

18. J. Riley, 'The military garrisons of Henry IV and Henry V at Strata Florida, 1407 and 1415–16', *Welsh History Review*, 27, 4 (2015), 645–71.

19. For the Powells and Vaughans, see G. Morgan, *Nanteos – A Welsh House and its Families* (Llandysul, 2001); and G. Morgan, *A Welsh House and its Family: the Vaughans of Trawsgoed* (Llandysul, 1999).

20. Quotation in e-mail (October 2016) from Professor John Darlington, director of the World Monuments Fund Britain; for the work of the WMF, see C. Fehrman, *World Monuments: 50 irreplaceable sites to discover, explore and champion; in celebration of the 50th anniversary of the World Monuments Fund* (New York, 2015).

21. Cadw and ICOMOS, *Register of Landscapes of Outstanding Historic Interest in Wales* (Cardiff, 1998).

22. C. Arch, *Byw dan y Bwa* (Caernarfon, 2005).

23. J. Wood, 'Nibbling pilgrims and the Nanteos Cup: a Cardiganshire legend', in G. Morgan (ed.), *Nanteos: A Welsh House and its Families* (Llandysul, 2001), pp. 202–53.

PART II

Religious and laity

5

The world of bishops in religious orders in medieval Ireland, 1050–1230*

Edel Bhreathnach

The renown of the early twelfth-century bishop of Limerick, Gillebertus (d.1145), who corresponded on familiar terms with St Anselm,[1] rests on his treatise *De statu ecclesiae* which outlines church hierarchies and their duties along with a parallel secular hierarchy.[2] While addressing in detail the duties of the priest in the parish, Gillebertus also deals with the responsibilities of bishops and archbishops (see figure 7):

> For lack of space, a small pyramid is placed on the top with notes to demonstrate that the bishop in his proper see in the Church has priests and six other grades together with three orders of the faithful as shown above under his care, which is evident from the number of points. And not only for that reason are the two churches as such subjected to the bishop but he can possess the two because he is shown to hold the parishes through one and the abbeys which he rules through the other. He protects, therefore, at a minimum ten churches and at a maximum a thousand ... The bishop governs the abbot, the abbess, the priest and the other six grades. The bishop uses, for purposes of dignity, a staff and a ring, gloves and a mitre, a belt, a dalmatic and sandals. He ought to have with him the Sacred Scripture and the tradition of the Fathers so that he may be able to settle individual cases justly and respond reasonably to those who question him on any subject.[3]

By laying down such prescriptions, Gillebertus, as one among many high-ranking clerics of his time throughout western Christendom, was providing a handbook for those charged with implementing canonical, liturgical and infrastructural changes in their church.[4] The many disputes that resulted from

* The research for this chapter was made possible by a Visiting Fellowship to All Souls College Oxford.

FIGURE 7: Bishop Gilbert of Limerick's *De statu ecclesiae*, Durham Cathedral Library, MS B.II.35, fol. 36v. © Durham Cathedral Library.

an intense period of change exposed the considerable pressures inflicted on the individuals involved. These disputes draw attention to the part played by familial and ecclesiastical affiliations, the tensions between competing authorities – kings, abbots, monastic orders and greater bishops – and the cultural and ecclesiastical realms that needed to be navigated by two generations of bishops involved in the upheavals of the eleventh, twelfth and thirteenth centuries. There is no clearer illustration of these pressures than the long-running tension between Anselm, an Italian-born Benedictine who had come from Bec in Normandy to Canterbury, and contemporary kings of England who resented his calling on papal authority above their own authority.[5] Indeed tensions often erupted between prelates as evidenced by Anselm's admonishing of Samuel Ua hAingli, bishop of Dublin *c.*1100–3, for dispersing books, vestments and religious vessels (*alia ornamenta ecclesiae*) that had been presented to his uncle, Donatus, also bishop of Dublin, by Lanfranc. Anselm rebuked Samuel for expelling the monks, possibly Benedictines like himself, from the church of Dublin (*monachos ecclesiae Dubliniae*) and for processing with a cross in front of him (*portari crucem ante te in via*), a practice only permitted to an archbishop who had received a pallium from Rome ('non pertinent nisi ad archepiscopum a Romano pontifice pallio confirmatum').[6]

This chapter considers the origins and careers of a specific group of highly influential bishops and archbishops who presided over great changes in Ireland during the twelfth and early thirteenth centuries, namely, men who were born in Ireland, belonged to monastic orders and who were appointed to lead the Irish church through a turbulent long century. A number of them, including Gillebertus, Lorcán Ua Tuathail, Áed Ua Cáellaide and Ailbe Ua Máel Muaid, have been the subject of much scholarship and while their careers will be alluded to, due to their significance, others who have not gained so much notice will also be taken into account.

I dedicate this chapter to Janet Burton who through her inspiring work and following many animated conversations has led me to a fresh understanding of the place of the medieval Irish church in the West and to the importance of delving into cross-cultural influences and tensions that are so often misinterpreted when viewed through the lens of a grand narrative rather than in the context of local and regional circumstances. Be it in Lampeter, Dublin or Oxford, these conversations enabled us to withdraw from the toils of our own worlds to reflect on the course of the medieval world.

During the eleventh century a number of Irish bishops, predominantly bishops of Dublin and also Waterford, were Benedictines who had trained either in England – in Canterbury, St Alban's and Winchester – or in Germany, and most likely in Cologne.[7] This Benedictine phase of the Irish episcopacy appears to have been initiated by Sitric, king of Dublin's pilgrimage to Rome in 1028. He returned through Cologne, gathering a set of foundation relics for Christ Church Cathedral, Dublin as part of his visit.[8] The establishment of a cathedral dedicated to the Holy Trinity or known as Christ Church close to a royal palace was not a phenomenon confined to Dublin. In the 1060s King Olaf Kyrre of Norway founded Christ Church cathedrals in Trondheim (Nidaros) and Bergen, and in the latter case transferred the relics of St Sunniva from the island of Selje to his new church.[9] Cologne, along with Metz, Trier and Gorze, centres of monastic restructuring since the late ninth century,[10] were places that had attracted Irishmen – there is no evidence of women – to them. St Pantaleon and Groß Sankt Martin in Cologne following a Benedictine rule were headed by an Irish abbot, Ailill (Elias) of Mucknoe (d.1042). A major problem in relation to this Irish presence on the Continent concerns the extent of any influence trickling back to Ireland and how that might be detected in the customs and liturgy of monastic communities there. At least the evidence of the Cologne relics returning to Dublin, and also that the content of medieval Irish martyrologies had their origins on the

Continent,[11] offers some proof that ideas, texts and objects filtered back. How continental religious culture was received can be even more difficult to discern, especially as so much of the textual evidence used for this period is dominated in general scholarship by the views and activities of major international figures such as Lanfranc, Anselm, Malachy, Bernard and Giraldus Cambrensis.[12] In recent decades, however, the prejudices of these sources have been scrutinised by scholars, particularly Marie Therese Flanagan, who has demonstrated that – as might be expected – the situation in Ireland was complex and not that different from elsewhere.[13] A review of the works of St Anselm, and particularly his letters, immediately shows that his – and Lanfranc's – admonishment of the Irish was not necessarily exceptional, and that far graver issues arose for him regarding his relations with English kings.[14] But these debates and tensions were arising throughout western Christendom. The difficulty with Ireland is that it is a challenge to detect how the various established religious communities in Ireland reacted to transformation as the responses to Lanfranc, Anselm and Bernard were mediated through the letters of like-minded individuals in Ireland or their representatives.

One possible means to understanding the mentality of the Irish church is to establish the background and follow the careers of those who come to the fore during the period of transformation from the late eleventh to early thirteenth centuries. This is a very extensive topic and hence the decision to examine a particular group of Irish born bishops who were in religious orders. Their choice to join communities of reformed or new orders implies that they were open to change and were in many cases active in re-structuring the Irish church, even if their familial and political connections were rooted in existing structures.

DIFFERENT ORIGINS

The Norse town of Dublin appears to have been the conduit through which changes that were being initiated in England, the Continent and Scandinavia filtered into Ireland. Little is known of the background and origins of the early bishops of Dublin. The likelihood is that they were all Benedictine monks but the evidence is scant.[15] It is noteworthy that two of them, Donngus (d.1095) and Samuel Ua hAingli (d.1121), were uncle and nephew.[16] Donngus (Donatus) is commemorated among the obituaries of Christ Church Canterbury: *Obiit Donatus episcopus Dublinie, et Kinsinus decanus, monaci nostre congregationis*, thus confirming that he had been a Benedictine in Canterbury.[17] According to Eadmer in his *Historia Novorum*, Samuel had been a monk in St Albans.[18] Unusually for Dublin bishops of the period their familial name, Ua hAingli(u), is recorded.

If they were from Dublin this name may be a corrupt form of a Norse name or perhaps, although unlikely, a hibernicised form of the common religious epithet *de Angeli* (although the genitive singular/plural *aingil/aingel* would be expected after *úa*). Otherwise their origins were elsewhere in Ireland. The form is rare, and should not be confused with the more widespread Ua hAinlige. It occurs in Roderick O'Flaherty's Iar Chonnacht tract in a section on the *bailte* of Uí Briúin Rátha (barony of Clare, Co. Galway) where he notes the family of *O h-Aingli o daire i Aingli cona baili* ('Ó hAingli from Daire Í Aingli with his *baile*').[19] This family is also included in Mac Fhirbhisigh's seventeenth-century genealogies.[20] How two members of a family in the West could have become Benedictines in English monasteries and what their attachment to Dublin before their appointment as bishops might have been leaves this origin open to question. Their royal supporters in Ireland were the kings of Munster and Ireland, Toirdelbach and his son Muiredach Ua Briain, who were also overlords of Dublin.[21] As the territory of Iar Chonnacht was intermittently subject to the Uí Briain in the late eleventh and early twelfth centuries, it is conceivable that Donngus and Samuel's family somehow had a connection with the Munster kings. One possible connection may have been through Toirdelbach's daughter Mór who married Ruaidrí na Saide Buí Ua Conchobair (d.1118) of the Uí Briúin dynasty of Iar Chonnacht, whose son was the powerful Toirdelbach Ua Conchobair, king of Ó Connacht and Ireland (d.1156).[22]

Not much more is known of the origins of Malchus (Máel Ísu Uí Ainmire), bishop of Waterford (from 1096) and possibly later archbishop of Cashel (d.1135), although this is not certain.[23] He was trained in Winchester under the keen eye of the energetic Walchelin, bishop of that city, and was consecrated bishop of Waterford by Anselm in the cathedral priory of St Swithun's, Winchester, in December 1096. His election to the see had been requested in a letter to Anselm from Muirchertach, king of Ireland, his brother Diarmait, governor of the Norse city of Waterford and four bishops Domnall Ua hÉnna (bishop of Killaloe and court bishop to Muirchertach), Máel Muire Ua Dunáin (bishop of Mide and later papal legate), Samuel Ua hAingli (the bishop of Dublin mentioned above) and Ferdomnach (bishop of the men of Leinster). The likelihood is that Malchus belonged to the Dál Cais family of Ua hAinmire whose lands north of Limerick city were granted to the Anglo-Norman Thomas FitzMaurice in the late twelfth century.[24] If this was the case, Malchus was from the heartland of his royal patron, Muirchertach Ua Briain's dynastic kingdom, probably known to the king prior to his move to England and even in correspondence with him about the ecclesiastical changes being wrought there. An alternative, and somewhat tentative, familial connection for Malchus could be read into the death in 1135 in Lismore – the same place and year of Malchus's death – of a certain Echmarcach Ua hAinmire.[25] Either this is a duplicate entry and Máel Ísu's secular name was Echmarcach or he had a brother also resident in Lismore. Is it possible that Malchus/Máel Ísu and Echmarcach, if they are not the same person, were descendants of (Mac) Bethad mac Ainmire, *prím ollam* and *ard brithem* ('chief poet and judge') of Armagh and Ireland who died in 1041?[26] The relocation of an illustrious family from Armagh to Lismore was a phenomenon in the eleventh century as witnessed by the death of the poet and scholar Máel Ísu Ua Brolcháin in Lismore in 1086. He belonged to an ecclesiastical family associated with Armagh and Derry.[27] Similarly Niall mac meic Áedacáin, bishop of Lismore (d.1113), whose name is inscribed on the Lismore crozier, may have been related to Ímar Ua hÁedacáin who caused a stone church dedicated to SS Peter and Paul to be built at Armagh in 1126. Ímar died in Rome in 1134.

This brings us to the question of the status of the foundation at Lismore in the eleventh and twelfth centuries which in terms of change in the church seems to have been another conduit, like Dublin, through which new ideas and influences filtered into Ireland. Apart from being an ecclesiastical settlement since the seventh century, Lismore was also the residence of kings, mainly if they were in need of shelter from internecine feuds, as was the case for Muirchertach Ua Briain (1116) and Cormac mac Cárthaig (1127), kings of Munster. Alliances and peace negotiations were conducted and broken there. The local king Ua Bric was killed by his nephew in the stone church of Lismore in 1051 while brothers Muirchertach and Diarmait Ua Briain agreed a truce to their feud in 1093 in Cashel and Lismore. There is also the oft-quoted passage from Bernard's Life of Malachy that tells of Malachy going to Lismore to study under Bishop Malchus and how Cormac Mac Cárthaig sought refuge with Malchus in Lismore.[28] Malchus appears to have adopted a role of teacher and counsellor similar to that of St Anselm in his dealings with religious and kings alike. One aspect of Lismore that may have contributed to its importance, and that has been somewhat overlooked, is that it may have been a wealthy monastery due to its control of the very lucrative fisheries of the Blackwater River. In a detailed study of these fisheries, Arthur Went has narrated the complex and often contentious history of their ownership, beginning with the attempts by the thirteenth-century Anglo-Norman Thomas FitzAnthony to seize them from the bishop of Lismore, requiring the king to intervene. The royal decision was in favour of the bishop 'the right which formerly belonged to the Abbot and monks of Lismore as custodians of the river Blackwater and the fisheries'.[29] One element of the case between FitzAnthony and the bishop involved rightful possession of the 'Thewd of Thaceth' in the Port of Lismore which had been granted originally to the abbot of Tewkesbury. An alternative form of this place-name is given as Uhachath in a mandate to the archbishop of Dublin, dated 16 November 1223.[30] The transfer of these lands (*terra quae vocatur Dungarvan in Lissemor*) into the possession of Henry Comyn, archbishop of Dublin, is recorded in the annals of Tewkesbury Abbey in 1224. The text notes that Lismore had been granted to that abbey by King John.[31] In 1233 the king's bailiffs in Bristol and Henry de Trubleville were commanded to deliver his ship which had been detained at Bristol to Griffin, bishop of Lismore.[32] Confirmation that Lismore had a navigable harbour at an earlier period is implied in an entry in the annals of Tigernach 1130, which tells of a man who had stolen the treasures of Clonmacnoise and had tried to escape by seeking to go overseas from Cork, Lismore or Waterford. Even the medieval life of Mochutu – the founder of Lismore – alludes to the importance of the river and its fish when the place was granted to him by the king, Máelochtair.[33] While the Norse town of Waterford was clearly emerging as an important trading centre by the eleventh century, it is possible that Lismore was as economically powerful for a considerable period before that, and that the tension between the two dioceses, which lasted into the late fourteenth century, originated with the rise of Waterford.[34] It could be surmised that one reason why Muirchertach Ua Briain had such an interest in Lismore, indeed resided there at times, is that its economic importance offered him another link to the outside world, as Dublin, Limerick and Waterford did. In that context, Malchus taking up residence in Lismore, an established monastic settlement, rather than in Waterford, was not altogether surprising, especially if it offered a lively intellectual milieu and was open to the world, as Bernard infers in his life of Malachy.[35]

CONFLICTING IDENTITIES

Conflicting identities and interests of Irish reform bishops were not confined to Benedictines: these conflicts must have often dominated all their lives. In many cases their association with the church did not begin with their joining a religious order. They often belonged to families who held immediate interests in existing churches or church networks. Conchobar mac Meic Conchaille, abbot of the Augustinian house of SS Peter and Paul in Armagh, appointed archbishop of Armagh *c.*1174, was a member of such a family.[36] Congalach mac Meic Conchaille died as *airchinnech* (lay abbot) of Derry in 1112 at an advanced age (Annals of the Four Masters (AFM)[37]), while rather remarkably in an Irish context, the annals record the death in 1134 (AFM) of Bébhinn daughter of Mac Conchaille, *banairchinnech* (female head) of Derry – a possible rare reference to a pre-Norman female foundation. And as with so many such families they held onto their interests in the church often well into the medieval period. Áedh Mac Conchaille died in 1247 as the Augustinian abbot of SS Peter and Paul in Clones, Co. Monaghan. It should also be noted that in the eleventh century the Uí Chonchaille held the kingship of Uí Nialláin, whose territory lay in the vicinity of the primatial city of Armagh. And yet the new circumstances prevailing in the twelfth-century Irish church is demonstrated by Conchobar mac Meic Conchaille's death. He died in 1175 on his return from collecting his pallium in Rome and was buried in the church of St-Pierre-de-Lémenc in Chambéry in Savoie where he is venerated as St Concors.[38]

The case of the Uí Chonchaille straddling between two systems of religious organisation was not exceptional. The ecclesiastical families of pre-Norman Ireland did not relinquish their power easily and often manipulated the transformation for their own benefit. Donnchadh Ó Corráin masterfully demonstrated how skilful various branches of the Dál Cais were in creating an ecclesiastical network that withstood the zeal of reforming kings and bishops. Notable among them were the Uí hÉnna and Uí Longargáin, and among them two Cistercians, Muirges (Matha) Ua hÉnna (d.1206), archbishop of Cashel and papal legate, and Donnchad Ua Longargáin (d.1236), also archbishop of Cashel whose kinsman had occupied the seat at Cashel between 1206 and 1216. Of such prelates, Ó Corráin mused: 'Is this reform in any of the many senses in which the term is used and abused, or is it agile professional adaptation to changing circumstances and new styles?'[39] In response, in her study of the twelfth-century transformation of the Irish church, Marie Therese Flanagan argued that it was 'not uniquely in Ireland that high-status ecclesiastics were drawn from royal and aristocratic families. Ties between the nobility and the upper clergy were the norm throughout Europe.'[40] It is useful to follow the career of Muirges Ua hÉnna as an illustration of the difficulties encountered by those attempting to combine existing practices with an increasingly centralised and probably bureaucratic church structure. If he was a Cistercian of Holy Cross Abbey, at least at the end of his life, Muirges was subject to a rule and particular lifestyle, while as an archbishop he was involved in ecclesiastical and secular politics during a period of considerable flux in Ireland on both fronts. Muirges was born into a family steeped in the church. Among his near relatives were the early reforming bishop, who corresponded with Lanfranc and Anselm, Domnall Ua hÉnna (d.1098), also Gilla Pátraic Ua hÉnna, bishop of Killaloe (Co. Clare) and head of the 'monastery' of Cork, Gilla na Náem Ua hÉnna, also associated with Killaloe (d.1095) and Conchobar Ua hÉnna, bishop of Killaloe (c.1195–1216).[41] Muirges's position as papal legate led him to settle disputes over church lands and as shown from his settlement between the archbishop of Dublin and St Mary's Abbey, Dublin involved him in legal matters and also in being part of an administration that recorded his judgements.[42] Giraldus Cambrensis's description of him as a 'learned and discreet man', and clearly an astute politician, is evident from his success in coming to an agreement with John, lord of Ireland c.1192/3 that confirmed the possessions of the see of Cashel and assured John's 'firm and stable peace to him and all his men, that they may build, plant and inhabit their lands'.[43] Despite these skills, his appointment as papal legate and his possible formation as a Cistercian, nevertheless he was put aside as legate and indeed excommunicated by 1201.[44] The primary reason for this fall from grace had to do with his refusal to consecrate certain bishops in his diocese and most pertinently to this study by his expulsion of Ua Conaing from the bishopric of Killaloe as part of his attempt to intrude Uí hÉnna kinsmen into the same bishopric.[45] Of course, Muirges was not alone in ensuring that his kinsmen held onto their offices and patrimonial churches. The remarkable register of Clogher, for example, includes many instances of families clinging to authority and lands in the church, sometimes disappearing from the records and re-appearing decades or even centuries later. A contemporary of Ua hÉnna, Máel Ísu Ua Máil Chiaráin (d.1197) was bishop of Clogher and abbot of Mellifont, the mother-house of the Cistercians in Ireland. His father is likely to have been Echthigern mac Máil Chiaráin, bishop of Clonard and learned elder of Ireland (*ardsenoir Erenn*, Annals of Loch Cé (ALC) 1191).[46] The Uí Mháil Chiaráin continue to turn up in various ecclesiastical offices – Dionysius Ó Maoilchiaráin died as *airchennach* of Ardcarne, Co. Roscommon in 1257 (AFM). As Katharine Simms has demonstrated in her work such ties remained strong until the Reformation and at times beyond then.[47] But what of the Cistercian affiliation of bishops such as Muirges Ua Ua hÉnna and Máel Ísu Ua Máil Chiaráin? Muirges witnessed Domhnall Mór Ua Briain's charter in favour of Holycross Abbey, Co. Tipperary (1182–6), and appears to have retired there in 1205 (AFM).[48] Ua Máil Chiaráin was even more involved as he was abbot of Mellifont before his appointment as bishop of Clogher. Can we foresee in such religious careers the divergent regional approaches to 'new' monasticism, as seen to be represented by the Cistercian Order, that led to Stephen of Lexington's constant irritation at how the Irish houses and monks were performing? Viewed from a different perspective, this was one of the many regional variations of the Cistercian world as the Order settled into the different cultures of Europe, a key aspect of its history as demonstrated by Emilia Jamroziak in her recent study.[49] Unfortunately for Ireland, Stephen, a powerful player in the Order, left the legacy of a partisan document that influenced the historiography of the Order on the island for a long time.[50]

THE RESISTANCE OF THE ESTABLISHMENT

Straddling between the existing practices and systems and the new Order – particularly the bureaucratic element of that new Order – was one option that Irish ecclesiastical families or churches could choose. What may not be as clear or as well documented is the resistance put up by those opposing change or those who feared loss of power and wealth as a result of new systems. Drawing on the lessons of examining conversion periods in many societies, including Ireland, such transitions can be lengthy and often disorderly. The twelfth and thirteenth centuries in Ireland have been tumultuous, and not just in the military arena. In the ecclesiastical sphere, new administrative systems were being introduced and with that new forms of records and correspondence – primarily in Latin – and lands and inheritance were being affected. An oft-cited case of resistance was the fierce rivalry that erupted in the north-eastern diocese of Down (Ulaid) involving the early foundation of St Finnian of Movilla and the Augustinian house of Saball (Saul, Co. Down) in 1170 and as described by the Annals of Ulster:

> A great, unbecoming deed was done by the monk, namely, by Amlaimh, son of the successor of [St] Finnian of Magh-bile and by Maghnus Mac Duinnsleibhe [Ua Eochadha], king of Ulidia, along with the chiefs of Ulidia and with the Ulidians besides, except the bishop, Mael-Isu and Gilla-Domanghairt Mac Cormaic, successor of [St] Comgall and Mael-Martain, successor of [St] Finnian, with their communities: that is, the Congregation of Canons Regular, with their abbot, whom Mael-Moedoic Ua Morgair, Legate of the successor of [St] Peter, instituted in Saball of [St] Patrick, were expelled out of the monastery they themselves built and were despoiled completely, both of books and furniture, cows and persons, horses and sheep and all things they had collected therein from the time of the Legate aforesaid to then, save the tunics and the capes which were upon them at that hour – through carnal jealousy and self-love and desire of honour for himself.[51]

Marie Therese Flanagan has dealt with this incident as a telling example of what was occurring on the ground, in this case when rival factions competed for the bishopric of Ulaid/Down, the abbacy of the old monastery of Movilla and involved the Augustinian foundations of Bangor and Saul.[52] The unreconstructed elements were supported by the local king Magnus Mac Duinn Sléibe who was killed a year later. Gilla Domangairt mac Cormaic, abbot of Bangor and a canon regular became embroiled in a tussle for the bishopric of Down/Ulaid with Amlaím, 'traditional' abbot of Movilla in 1175, and was supported by Amlaím's rival to control Movilla, Máel Martain. Neither man gained much as they both died in 1175, most likely unable to perform their duties as bishops. Some form of stability ensued when Malacy III (Echmilid), also successor of Finnian of Movilla, became bishop and with the support of the Anglo-Norman lord John de Courcy secured Downpatrick as the episcopal seat of the bishopric of Down. As Flanagan has noted the diocese of Down/Ulaid was not particularly wealthy, and hence the competition was probably as much to do with hereditary possession of lands as the dignity of the office. The incident may well have related also to the issue of who should be involved in the election of bishops, and especially the restriction of elections to *viri religiosi*, be they canons or monks affiliated to religious orders.[53] That these issues were not confined to the seat in Down can be extrapolated from Innocent III's letter to Cathal Croibhdhearg, king of Connacht, requesting him to ensure that bishops and abbots be elected by clergy and be free from interference, and to oppose those who sought to take hereditary possession of the Lord's sanctuaries (*sanctuarium Domini possidere*).[54] This letter must have been written at the behest of Felix Ua Ruanada, archbishop of Tuam, who had attended the Fourth Lateran Council in Rome in 1216. Felix had come to Tuam from the Augustinian house at Saul, where he had been prior, and no doubt had known of or even encountered the bitter rivalries in the diocese of Down. Indeed he may have belonged to a hereditary family himself as the Uí Ruanadha held a prebend in the diocese of Dromore in the fifteenth century and their name is preserved in the place-name Ballyroney, Co. Down.[55]

NEGOTIATING MULTIPLE ALLEGIANCES

The distinctiveness of Irish bishops in religious orders was characterised by their capacity to have multiple allegiances, be it to their own kin and traditions, to the international monasticism of their orders, and to secular rulers, local and provincial Irish kings, newly arrived Anglo-Norman adventurers, and the English Crown. This testing environment brought some remarkable men forth in the ranks of Irish bishops, among them, Áed Ua Cáellaide, bishop of Louth (d.1182) and Ailbe Ua Máel Muaid, bishop of Ferns (d.1223). In his obit, recorded not only in Irish annals but also in a marginal entry in the Benedictine monastery of San Savino in Piacenza, Bishop Áed Ua Cáellaide is described as bishop of Airgialla/Louth and head of the canons, monks and nuns of Ireland.[56] Áed belonged to a well-established ecclesiastical family[57] and was one of St Malachy of Armagh's vanguard in implementing change in the Irish church, in line with changes occurring throughout western Christendom.

He was spiritual adviser to Diarmait mac Murchada, the Irish king who had sought the support of Henry II to restore his provincial kingdom of Leinster.[58] We can see Áed's influence, along with that of other leading bishops such as Lorcán Ua Tuathail, archbishop of Dublin, in the official establishment of new orders in Ireland, in foundation charters and in confirmations of land grants witnessed by bishops, abbots and kings, hence laying the ground for the widespread use in Ireland of standard administrative documents in ecclesiastical matters.[59] For example, a charter granting the lands of Baldoyle outside Dublin, the home farm of the Augustinian foundation of All Hallows, Dublin, was confirmed by Diarmait mac Murchada c.1162 to 'my spiritual father and confessor, Edanus, bishop of Louth, for the use of the canons ... and their successors etc.'.[60] Áed did not confine his support to Augustinian foundations alone: along with Gilla Meic Liac, archbishop of Armagh ('holding the Staff of Jesus in his hand') he witnessed a charter founding the Cistercian monastery of Newry c.1157.[61] But bishops such as Áed Ua Cáellaide who belonged to religious communities were not simply confirming charters and land grants. Like their counterparts in Britain and on the Continent they were also involved in altering the physical ecclesiastical landscape of Ireland. In a study of cathedral-building in thirteenth-century Ireland Roger Stalley has argued that native Irish bishops 'maintained a fairly limited view of the role of the status of a cathedral as a building, implying that diocesan reform, as confirmed in the synod of 1152, may not have been as radical as sometimes thought'. On the whole, in his estimation, Gothic cathedral-building projects came with the arrival of English bishops from the mid-thirteenth century onwards. Many Irish-born bishops were in charge of dioceses that did not have the wealth to support large-scale cathedrals.[62] Apart from factors such as lack of resources, it could be argued that many Irish dioceses did not need large cathedrals as they were not located in populous settlements and in addition the first task of the bishops was to lay out their diocesan seats, and if affiliated to an order, often be involved in building monastic complexes. Muirges Ua hÉnna is a case in point. If his witnessing of charters is any indication of any link to building projects, he was a witness to Domhnall Ua Briain's charter for the Cistercian Holycross Abbey dated to sometime between 1168 and 1185, a monastery in which he was buried in 1206.[63] He also witnessed Cathal Croibhdhearg's charter for the Cistercian abbey at Abbeyknockmoy (c.1201), and, more significantly in the context of cathedral-building, witnessed Domhnall Ua Briain's charter for Limerick Cathedral sometime between 1178 and 1180.[64] The bishop of Limerick at the time was a certain Brictius. In Áed Ua Cáellaide's case, this involved both cathedral and monastic projects: he is designated as 'bishop of the Airgialla', an extensive pre-Norman kingdom that stretched from the east midlands well towards the north-west. The traditional episcopal seat was at Clogher, Co. Tyrone but it was relocated, for reasons related to both church and royal politics, to Louth, the site of a small reliquary church dedicated to Mochta, a reputed disciple of St Patrick.[65] As part of this move it appears that Malachy introduced Arrouaisian canons to serve as the cathedral chapter of the diocese and dedicated their priory to the Blessed Virgin. This arrangement was further strengthened by the foundation of the abbey of SS Peter and Paul at nearby Knock, Co. Louth. Áed Ua Cáellaide was instrumental in building Knock as noted in the annals under 1148: 'The church of Cnoc-na-seangan was finished by the Bishop O'Caellaidhe and Donnchadh Ua Cearbhaill, and was consecrated by Ua Morgair, successor of Patrick; and a Neimheadh, i.e. ecclesiastical land, was assigned it in Lughmhadh' (AFM). The latter reference to a *nemed* being assigned to SS Peter and Paul's in Louth is noteworthy. It appears to mean that as a confirmation of the association between the houses at Knock and Louth that a portion of land for the church in Louth was granted to Knock. The term *nemed* is an early Irish legal term signifying a sacred space, a precinct or sanctuary.

Ailbe Ua Máel Muaid of Ferns in the south-east was another such energetic bishop who probably belonged to the midland dynasty that ruled the kingdom of Fir Cell.[66] His was a long and particularly complex career that was marked by his capacity to navigate through the byzantine web of the increasing power of the English Crown in Ireland in the late twelfth and early thirteenth centuries, an emerging Anglo-Norman episcopate, recalcitrant and divided Irish kings, and powerful Irish prelates. Ailbe is best known for his clash with Gerald of Wales during a provincial council held by John Cumin, archbishop of Dublin in March 1186: in a sermon, Ua Máel Muaid claimed that English clergy were a corrupting influence on the Irish, gaining a retort from Gerald that the Irish had no martyrs and that they were drunkards.[67] Another Irish bishop, Felix Ua Duib Sláine of Ossory, complained to the archbishop of Dublin about Gerald's remarks.[68] Yet, despite this, Ailbe was closely allied to John Cumin and to King John, and often during his career was involved in the implementation of the king's policy in Ireland, and especially in Leinster. This brought him into direct conflict with William Marshal (father and son) whose ever-increasing ambition was a worry to the English Crown, and also more locally to Ailbe, as the Marshals appropriated lands of his own episcopal see and also built a substantial castle overlooking the episcopal seat.[69] Ua Máel Muaid was appointed successor to Muirges Ua hÉnna as archbishop of Cashel but even though he had the king's support, he never succeeded in assuming that office.

Ailbe's monastic career was equally as complex. He was appointed c.1180 as abbot of the Cistercian house of Baltinglass, a daughter-house of Mellifont, founded *c*.1148 by Diarmait mac Murchada, the same king who granted land to Áed Ua Cáellaide's canons of All Hallows, Dublin. His own influence with King John no doubt led John to confirm the lands of Baltinglass Abbey in a charter dated to *c*.1185, just around the time he became bishop of Ferns.[70] As with Ua Cáellaide, Ailbe was part of a tight network of senior bishops who interacted closely in influencing the direction of the Irish Church. He was close to Felix Ua Duib Sláine, bishop of Ossory and Cistercian abbot of Jerpoint, and he and Ua Duib Sláine were involved in the promotion of Dunbrody Abbey, an English-endowed Cistercian house, and the Victorine house, St Thomas's Abbey, Dublin. He moved in a very different direction in regard to the great early monastery of Glendalough, by assisting the annexation of the Irish-dominated diocese of Glendalough by the English archbishop of Dublin. He did this despite the fact that he had probably been a protégé of Lorcán Ua Tuathail, abbot of Glendalough and archbishop of Dublin in his early career, and a life-long advocate of the canonisation of the very same famous churchman.

CONCLUSION

The lives of the first generation of Irish bishops in religious orders were far from secluded and required much skill in negotiating the high and low politics of the church and the laity. It meant coping with a new bureaucracy, as bishops and abbots, increased travel and journeys further afield than most of their predecessors would have ever undertaken. A few were suffragan bishops of English cathedrals, including Exeter, Winchester and Worcester. In taking the religious vows of an order, be it as monks or regular canons, they would have encountered new or revised liturgies and rules emanating from centres such as Arrouaise and Clairvaux. This might have entailed a higher level of literacy in Latin than many of their predecessors may have attained, although this may be an unfair judgement of many pre-eleventh-century Irish bishops. Large building projects needed direction as stone cathedrals and monastic complexes on a scale not previously seen in Ireland were completed during this period, often under the guidance of bishops. This was the tangible testimony to a changing church, a means to gain patronage and a powerful visible signal to the wider laity of this transformation. And yet, what was already there did not disappear, partially due to the origins of so many of these bishops from among the established ecclesiastical elite. It could be argued that for change to be implemented it had to be over a long period and involve compromises that took account of local practices and culture. This was a complicated business and was compounded by the arrival of a new elite and their followers intent on laying claim to and taking over an already well-settled landscape. It is no accident, therefore, that probably one of the most forceful generation of native bishops to emerge in the history of the Irish Church came to the fore at this time. Not all of them were also in religious orders, but a significant number were, a factor that should not be overlooked in our consideration of a tumultuous long century.

Notes

1. Franciscus Salesius Schmitt (ed.), *S. Anselmi Cantuariensis Archiepiscopi Opera Omnia*, V, (Seccovii, 1956), pp. 374–6 §§ 428–9 (letters to and from Anselm).

2. Shannon Williamson, 'Pseudo-Dionysius, Gilbert of Limerick and Innocent III: Order, Power and Constitutional Construction', in Robert C. Figueira (ed.), *Plenitude of Power. The Doctrines and Exercise of Authority in the Middle Ages. Essays in memory of Robert Louis Benson* (2006; repr. London, 2016), pp. 47–71.

3. John Fleming, *Gille of Limerick (c.1070–1147): Architect of a Medieval Church* (Dublin, 2001), pp. 151: 53–61, 161: 269–74.

4. Giles Constable, *The Reformation of the Twelfth Century* (Cambridge, 1996); Marie Therese Flanagan, *The Transformation of the Irish Church in the Twelfth Century* (Woodbridge, 2010).

5. This tension runs throughout Eadmer's Life of Anselm, see Eadmer, *The Life of St Anselm Archbishop of Canterbury by Eadmer*, ed. R. W. Southern (Oxford, 1962; repr. 1972).

6. F. S. Schmitt, *S. Anselmi Cantuariensis Archepiscopi Opera Omnia*, IV (Edinburgh, 1950), pp. 191–3 §§ 277–8.

7. Denis Bethell, 'English Monks and Irish Reform in the Eleventh and Twelfth Centuries', *Historical Studies*, 8 (1971), 111–35; Dagmar Ó Riain-Raedel, 'Irish Benedictine Monasteries on the Continent', in Martin Browne and Colmán Ó Clabaigh (eds), *The Irish Benedictines: A History* (Dublin, 2005), pp. 25–63; Edel Bhreathnach, 'Benedictine Influence in Ireland in the Late Eleventh and Early Twelfth Centuries: A Reflection', *Journal of Medieval Monastic Studies*, 1 (2012), 63–91.

8. Raghnall Ó Floinn, 'The Foundation Relics of Christ Church Cathedral and the Origins of the Diocese of Dublin', in Seán Duffy (ed.), *Medieval Dublin VII: Proceedings of the Friends of Medieval Dublin Symposium 2005* (Dublin, 2006), pp. 89–102.

9. Alf Tore Hommedal, 'St Sunniva, the Seljemenn and St Alban. The Benedictines and the Sanctuary at Selje, Norway', in Edel Bhreathnach, Małgorzata Krasnodębska-D'Aughton and Keith Smith (eds), *Monastic Europe: Landscape and Settlement* (Turnhout, forthcoming).

10. For the various rules emanating from these centres and others, see Jerome Bertram, *The Chrodegang Rules* (Farnham, 2005).

11. Pádraig Ó Riain, *A Martyrology of Four Cities: Metz, Cologne, Dublin, Lund* (London, 2009).

12. Aubrey Gwynn, *The Irish Church in the Eleventh and Twelfth Centuries*, ed. Gerard O'Brien (Dublin, 1992).

13. Flanagan, *Transformation of the Irish Church*; Marie Therese Flanagan, 'Reform in the Twelfth-Century Irish Church? a Revolution of Outlook?', *Kathleen Hughes Memorial Lectures*, 9 (Cambridge, 2012).

14. *Anselmi Opera Omnia*, IV and V.

15. Martin Holland, 'Dublin and the Reform of the Irish Church in the Eleventh and Twelfth Centuries', *Peritia*, 14 (2000), 111–60 (120).

16. *Anselmi Opera Omnia*, IV, letters 277–8.

17. R. Fleming, 'Christchurch's sisters and brothers', in Marc Anthony Meyer (ed.), *The Culture of Christendom: Essays in Medieval History in Commemoration of Denis L. T. Bethell* (London, 1993), pp. 115–53 (p. 146 (23)).

18. Eadmer, *Eadmeri Historia Novorum in Anglia*, ed. Martin Rule, RS, 81 (London, 1884), p. 73; Aubrey Gwynn, 'Bishop Samuel of Dublin', *Irish Ecclesiastical Record*, 60 (1942), 81–8.

19. Roderick O'Flaherty and James Hardiman, *A chorographical description of West of H-Iar Connaught written A.D. 1684* (Dublin, 1846), p. 370.

20. Nollaig Ó Muraíle (ed.), *The Great Book of Irish Genealogies. Leabhar Mór na nGenealach*, I (Dublin, 2003), § 204.10. Mac Fhirbhisigh notes the surname Ó hAingle among the Corca Loígde of West Cork (*Great Book*, II, §678.1) who are also listed in an earlier tract on the Corca Loígde, John O'Donovan (ed.), *The Genealogy of Corca Laidhe* in *Miscellany of the Celtic Society* (Dublin, 1849), *www.ucc.ie/celt* (accessed 18 October 2016).

21. For the details of Donngus and Samuel Ua hAingliu's careers and the sources see Ailbe Mac Samhráin, 'Donngus Ua hAingliu' and Aidan Breen, 'Samuel Ua hAingliu', in James McGuire and James Quinn (eds), *Dictionary of Irish Biography from the Earliest Times to the Year 2002* (Dublin, 2002), vol. 9, pp. 386–7; and Marie Therese Flanagan, 'Donngus' *ODNB*, vol. 55, pp. 842–3. For a detailed analysis of Dublin, see Holland, 'Dublin and the Reform of the Irish Church'.

22. Margaret C. Dobbs, 'The *Ban-Shenchus*', *Revue Celtique*, 48 (1931), 191.

23. Donal O'Connor, 'Malchus (*c.*1047–1135), monk of Winchester and first bishop of Waterford', *Decies*, 61 (2005), 122–50.

24. H. S. Sweetman (ed.), *Calendar of Documents relating to Ireland*, 5 vols (London, 1875–6), 1, p. 14 (93): 'grant to Thomas Fitz Maurice ... of five knights fees in the fee of Huamerith in Thomand on the river Shannon (September 6, 1199)'.

25. John O'Donovan (ed. and trans.), *Annala Rioghachta Eireann: Annals of the kingdom of Ireland by the Four Masters, from the earliest period to the year 1616*, 7 vols (Dublin, 1848–51; repr. Dublin, 1856; repr. Dublin, 1990); online *https://celt.ucc.ie* (accessed 10 January 2018).

26. Seán Mac Airt and Gearóid Mac Niocaill (ed. and trans.), *The Annals of Ulster (to A.D. 1131)* (Dublin, 1983); online *https://celt.ucc.ie* (accessed 10 January 2018); Whitley Stokes (ed. and trans.), 'The Annals of Tigernach', *Revue Celtique*, 16 (1895), 374–419; 17 (1896), 6–33, 116–263, 337–420; 18 (1897), 9–59, 150–303; repr. 2 vols, Felinfach, 1999 (online English translation by Gearóid Mac Niocaill: *https://celt.ucc.ie/* (accessed 10 January 2018)).

27. Muireann Ní Bhrolcháin, 'Maol Íosa Ó Brolcháin: an assessment', *Seanchas Ardmhacha*, 12 (1986), 43–67.

28. J. Leclercq andt H. -M. Rochais (eds), *Sancti Bernardi Opera III, Tractus et opuscula* (Rome, 1963), pp. 316–17; H. J. Lawlor, *St Bernard of Clairvaux's Life of St Malachy of Armagh* (London and New York, 1920), pp. 18–19.

29. Arthur E. J. Went, 'Fisheries of the Munster Blackwater', *Journal of the Royal Society of Antiquaries of Ireland*, 90 (1960), 97–131 (101, n. 13).

30. H. S. Sweetman (ed.), *Calendar of Documents relating to Ireland 1171–1251* (hereafter *CDI*) (London, 1875), I, 174 (1147).

31. Henry Richard Luard (ed.), *Annales Monastici*, 1, 67, RS 36 (London, 1864).

32. *CDI*, I, 311 (2098).

33. Patrick Power (ed.), *Life of St. Declan of Ardmore and Life of St. Mochuda of Lismore*, Irish Texts Society, 16 (London, 1914), pp. 136–7.

34. P. J. Dunning, 'Pope Innocent III and the Waterford-Lismore Controversy, 1198–1216', *Irish Theological Quarterly*, 28 (1961), 215–32; Richard Huscroft, 'Edward I's Government and the Irish Church: A Neglected Document from the Waterford-Lismore Controversy', *Irish Historical Studies*, 32 (2001), 423–32.

35. *Sancti Bernardi Opera*, III, pp. 316–17.

36. Flanagan, *Transformation of the Irish Church*, p. 231.

37. O'Donovan (ed. and trans.), *Annala Rioghachta Eireann*.

38. T. Ó Fiaich, *Gaelscrínte i gcéin* (Dublin, 1960), pp. 42, 62–5; Flanagan, *Transformation of the Irish Church*, p. 231.

39. Donnchad Ó Corráin, 'Dál Cais – church and dynasty', *Ériu*, 24 (1973), 52–63.

40. Flanagan, *Transformation of the Irish Church*, p. 114.

41. Ó Corráin, 'Dál Cais', 53

42. J. T. Gilbert (ed.), *Chartularies of St Mary's Abbey, Dublin*, 2 vols, RS (London, 1884), I, pp. 145–6. Ua hÉnna also confirmed grants to St Thomas's Abbey, Dublin, see *Register of the Abbey of St Thomas, Dublin*, ed. J. T. Gilbert (London, 1889), pp. 308, 317.

43. John O'Meara (ed.), *Giraldus Cambrensis, Topography of Ireland* (Dublin, 1951), pp. 99–100; K. W. Nicholls (ed.), 'A charter of John, lord of Ireland, in favour of Matthew Ua HÉnni, archbishop of Cashel', *Peritia*, 2 (1983), 267–76 (267–8).

44. Marie Therese Flanagan, 'Hiberno-papal relations in the late twelfth century', *Archivium Hibernicum*, 34 (1977), 55–70 (65–6).

45. Ó Corráin, 'Dál Cais', 60.

46. K. W. Nicholls (ed.), 'The Register of Clogher', *Clogher Historical Society*, 7 (1971/2), 361–431 (387).

47. Katharine Simms, 'Frontiers in the Irish Church – Regional and Cultural', in Terry Barry, Robin Frame and Katharine Simms (eds), *Colony and Frontier in Medieval Ireland. Essays presented to J. F. Lydon* (London, 1995), pp. 177–200.

48. Gearóid MacNiocaill, *Na Manaigh Liatha in Éirinn* (Dublin, 1959), p. 11.

49. Emilia Jamroziak, *The Cistercian Order in Medieval Europe, 1090–1500* (London, 2013).

50. Barry W. O'Dwyer (trans.), *Stephen of Lexington, Letters from Ireland 1228–1229* (Kalamazoo, 1992).

51. W. M. Hennessy (ed. and trans.), *The Annals of Loch Cé*, 2 vols (London, 1871; repr. Dublin, 1939).

52. Marie Therese Flanagan, 'John de Courcy, the first Ulster plantation and Irish church men', in B. Smith (ed.), *Britain and Ireland 900–1300: insular responses to medieval European change* (Cambridge, 1999), pp. 154–78 (pp. 161–3).

53. Flanagan, 'John de Courcy', p. 165.

54. P. J. Dunning, 'Letters of Pope Innocent III to Ireland. A Calendar Supplementary to that of *Calendar of Papal Registers I* (ed. W. H. Bliss)', *Archivium Hibernicum*, 13 (1947), 27–44: 42–3 (no. 25).

55. W. Reeves, *Ecclesiastical antiquities of Down, Connor, and Dromore, consisting of a Taxation of those Dioceses* (Dublin, 1847), p. 312 n. *m*, 313.

56. Marie Therese Flanagan, 'St. Mary's Abbey, Louth, and the Introduction of the Arrouaisian Observance into Ireland', *Clogher Record*, 10 (1980), 223–34; Marie Therese Flanagan, 'Irish Church Reform in the Twelfth Century and Áed Ua Cáellaide, Bishop of Louth: an Italian Dimension', in Michael Richter and Jean-Michel Picard (eds), *Ogma. Essays in Celtic Studies in honour of Próinséas Ní Chatháin* (Dublin, 2002), pp. 94–104.

57. Donncha Ó Corráin, 'The education of Diarmait mac Murchada', *Ériu*, 28 (1977), 71–81.

58. Flanagan, *Transformation of the Irish Church*, pp. 97, 116, 145–6.

59. M. T. Flanagan, *Irish Royal Charters: Texts and Contexts* (Oxford, 2005).

60. Flanagan, *Irish Royal Charters*, pp. 270–1, no. 3.

61. Flanagan, *Irish Royal Charters*, pp. 291–2, no. 5.

62. Roger Stalley, 'Cathedral-building in thirteenth-century Ireland', in Roger Stalley (ed.), *Irish Gothic Architecture: Construction, Decay and Reinvention* (Dublin, 2012), pp. 15–51 (pp. 21, 49).

63. Flanagan, *Irish Royal Charters*, pp. 308–9, no. 6.

64. Flanagan, *Irish Royal Charters*, pp. 316–7, no. 7 (Abbeyknockmoy charter).

65. Flanagan, 'St. Mary's Abbey, Louth'.

66. For a detailed study of Ailbe's career, see A. MacShamhráin, 'Ailbe Ua Máel Muaid, Uí Chennselaig and the *Vitae Sanctorum Hiberniae*', in Seán Duffy (ed.), *Princes, prelates and poets in medieval Ireland* (Dublin, 2013), pp. 309–38.

67. *Giraldus Cambrensis Opera, I*, pp. 65–72.

68. Flanagan, *Transformation of the Irish Church*, pp. 112–13.

69. W. L. Warren, 'Church and Stare in Angevin Ireland', *Chronicon*, 1 (1997), 1–17 (6), *www.ucc.ie/celt* (Warren notes) (accessed 14 October 2016).

70. K. W. Nicholls, 'The charter of John, Lord of Ireland, in favour of the Cistercian abbey of Baltinglass', *Peritia*, 4 (1985), 187–206.

6

Aʀt, aʀchitectuʀe, piety and patʀonage at Rievaulx Abbey, *c.*1300–1538

Michael Carter

INTRODUCTION

Rievaulx Abbey, Yorkshire, can be counted among the most significant monastic ruins in Europe.[1] It is thanks to Janet Burton that scholars now have a firmer understanding of the foundation of this great monastery in 1132, its early history, estates and economy.[2] The abbey has also benefitted from the attention of other scholars. Peter Fergusson and Stuart Harrison, who have done so much to enhance our understanding of this remarkable site, have described Rievaulx as the most important Cistercian abbey in England, both spiritually and architecturally.[3] The spiritual importance of Rievaulx is in large part due to two of its early abbots: William (ruled 1132–45), a native Yorkshireman and for a time Saint Bernard's own secretary, who in 1132 led the founding community from Clairvaux; and Aelred (ruled 1147–67), the third abbot and one of the most important churchmen of twelfth-century England. The rigour of the religious life at Rievaulx attracted the patronage of leading families, who endowed the monastery with extensive estates stretching across the northern counties.[4] The abbey was rapidly reduced to ruins after its suppression in 1538, but even in its ruinous state, the east end of the church, rebuilt on a magnificent scale from *c.*1220, can be counted among the glories of the Early English Gothic (see figure 8). However, according to traditional historiographical narratives, the presbytery at Rievaulx also marks the point when the abbey's community, and the Cistercian Order more generally, started to deviate from the ideals and austerity of its founders.[5] Thanks in large part to Janet Burton, many of the old orthodoxies of late medieval decline have recently been questioned, even overturned.[6] With this recent scholarship in mind, and focusing on art and architecture, this chapter will discuss evidence concerning religious life at Rievaulx between the fourteenth and sixteenth centuries, a period in which there were fundamental changes in the nature of Cistercian monasticism. The abbey unquestionably endured times of difficulty but as will be argued Rievaulx remained a place of piety and the spirit of William and Aelred endured at the monastery until the very moment of its suppression. Evidence for developments in the art and architecture of the abbey will be discussed within the wider context of changes in Cistercian spirituality, liturgy and devotion. It will also be shown that there was an enduring relationship between the monastery and its patrons who continued to esteem the prayers and spiritual services of the monks.

FIGURE 8: Rievaulx Abbey, presbytery, *c.*1220. Photograph: Michael Carter.

RIEVAULX ABBEY: A CASE STUDY
IN CISTERCIAN DECLINE?

The biography of Aelred written by Walter Daniel can leave little doubt of the vigour of religious life at Rievaulx during the time of its early abbots. The monastery attracted recruits from across Europe and in Aelred's time its community comprised 640 men. Rievaulx's name was familiar at the papal court in Rome and at the courts of the kings of England, France and Scotland.[7] However, a century later, Rievaulx and its sister houses across the north suffered a series of major reversals. In the 1270s and 1280s its flocks were devastated by epidemics of sheep scab, leaving the abbey badly in debt and even causing the temporary dispersal of the community.[8] The abbey's woes were compounded by warfare between England and Scotland in the early fourteenth century. On 14 October 1322 the Scots defeated the army of Edward II at the battle of Shaws or Scawton Moor, near Rievaulx. The victorious Scots sacked the abbey. A largely overlooked contemporary annotation in a manuscript from the monastery, a beautifully decorated thirteenth-century copy of Roger of Howden's *Historia Anglorum*, records this event, noting that the Scots despoiled the abbey and carried off 'books, chalices and the sacred ornaments' of the monastery.[9] The abbey complained to Cîteaux about the devastation caused to its estates by warfare, request-ing permission to convert directly managed granges into tenanted manors. Indeed, this period coincided with the decline of the Cistercian lay brother-hood, which ceased to be a significant part of the community by the end of the fourteenth century. In 1380, there were just fifteen choir-monks and three lay brothers at the abbey.[10]

However, this does not tell the full story. Evidence can also be cited showing the competent administration of Rievaulx and the quality of the religious life observed there. In 1517, Marmaduke Huby, the great reforming abbot of Fountains (ruled 1495–1526), asserted that it was in northern England that the religion and ceremonies of the Cistercian Order were especially well observed. Huby praised William Helmsley, abbot of Rievaulx between 1513 and 1528 as 'a well learned and religious man'.[11] A bachelor and doctor of divinity, Helmsley was energetic in his attempts to see the completion of Saint Bernard's, the Cistercian college at Oxford (now Saint John's).[12] Helmsley also sought appointment by the abbot of Cîteaux as a commissary for the reform of Cistercian houses in the north.[13]

Nevertheless, Rievaulx could not escape the reforms of Henry VIII and in 1538 was dissolved and rapidly reduced to ruins leaving only shattered remains. A detailed inventory was made of the furnishings of the abbey church and other buildings, invaluable evidence for the art and architecture of the monastery, to which this chapter will now turn.[14]

ESCAPING THE TWELFTH-CENTURY PRISM

Many of the abbey's buildings, including the nave of the church, chapter house and infirmary, date to Aelred's time and have the austerity expected of Cistercian architecture in the mid-twelfth century:[15] 'No pictures, no colour, nothing of great value', as Aelred himself wrote in his guide for novices.[16] At first sight, the Order's legislation forbade all forms of ostentation including most images, figurative and coloured window glass, elaborate bell-towers, and luxurious altar plate and rich vestments.[17] This legislation has provided a prism through which all Cistercian art and architecture is usually interpreted. However, its recent analysis has shown that it was not monolithic, evolved in a piecemeal fashion, that decrees were ambiguous, rarely unanimous, were never uniformly enforced and that there was always variation and variety in the Order's art and architecture.[18] Moreover, Cistercian monasticism was ever evolving with the world around it. By *c*.1300 all the Order's regulations on art and architecture had been replaced with a vaguely worded clause forbidding superfluity and novelty and capable of the widest possible interpretation.[19] A new constitution of the Order, usually known as the *Benedictina*, was issued in 1335 by Pope Benedict XII, Jacques Fournier, a Cistercian by profession, which recognised that Cistercian monasticism had evolved and changed from its twelfth-century origins and had nothing substantive to say about art and architecture.[20]

Evidence of such evolution can be seen in the buildings of Rievaulx. Between the fourteenth and early sixteenth centuries many were adapted and refurbished so as to make them more suitable to the needs of the late medieval community. The appearance of many of the buildings was modernised, including the church. The pitch of its roofs was lowered and they were covered with lead, and the nave was re-fenestrated. The lay brothers' stalls were cleared from the nave and the space given over to liturgical use; chapels were inserted into the eastern bays. At the end of the fifteenth century, an impressive new stone *pulpitum* screen was installed, the fragments of which have now been reassembled in the abbey's museum. The claustral buildings were also renovated. The former accommodation of the lay brothers in the west range was put to other uses and the enormous building was reduced in size, as was the monks' dormitory in the east range and the chapter house. The infirmary was converted into a president's lodging. All these works have parallels at other Cistercian abbeys.[21]

From the late thirteenth century onwards the full panoply of religious art could be encountered in a Cistercian context, Rievaulx included. Arguably the most important and beautiful surviving sculpture at the site is a depiction of Christ in Majesty, which dates to *c.*1260–70 (see figure 9), about the time when the Order's regulations on images were being relaxed. Christ in Majesty was of course a common image on portals, including the contemporary in-situ example on the Judgement Porch at Lincoln, and although the original

FIGURE 9: Rievaulx Abbey, fragmentary sculpture of Christ in Majesty, *c.*1260–70. Photograph: Historic England.

location of the sculpture from Rievaulx is unclear, a porch is a plausible context.[22] An idea of the other furnishings of the church can be gleaned from the Suppression-era inventory, including alabaster altarpieces, images of various saints, painted altar frontals and parclose screens, all of which were standard for any great monastic church.[23] Nevertheless, the inventory and survival material evidence are invaluable evidence of the religious life of the community at the abbey.

SPIRITUAL LIFE AND RELIGIOSITY AT THE LATE MEDIEVAL ABBEY: CONTINUITY AND CHANGE

Recent analysis of evidence including liturgical books has shown how well integrated Cistercians were in the religious traditions of the late medieval north, adopting the cults of local saints such as Cuthbert, Oswald, Wilfrid and William of York.[24] Rievaulx's own saints remained the focus of veneration until the very end of the Middle Ages. Cistercian sources from the early seventeenth century give William, the founding abbot, the status of *beatus* with a feast on 2 August, the day of his death. He was never formally canonised but there can be little doubt that a cult developed around him at Rievaulx. A largely overlooked late twelfth-century verse epitaph in a manuscript from Rufford, a daughter house of Rievaulx in Nottinghamshire, praises William as 'eminent in virtue and faith' and 'wholly Apostolic'.[25] There is also material evidence of William's cult at Rievaulx. In the mid-thirteenth century his relics were translated to a shrine inscribed *SCS Williamus Abbas* (see figure 10). Complete with an altar, the shrine was located at the entrance to the chapter house in the north opening. An inscription on the sill of the window in the south of the chapter house fixes the date of the translation to the year 1250, on 5 March, the anniversary of the foundation of the abbey. The shrine became a focus of burials, and several grave slabs can still be seen adjacent to it in the cloister walk.[26]

There is substantial evidence for the cult of Aelred in the late Middle Ages, both at Rievaulx and beyond. The magnificent architecture of the thirteenth-century presbytery can best be understood not as an expression of the abbey's pride but as a fitting setting for Aelred's translated relics. Shortly before the Suppression, the antiquary, John Leland, saw the tomb of Aelred in the church at Rievaulx, describing it as 'decorated with gold and silver'. This was probably the gilded shrine over the high altar mentioned in the Suppression-era inventory. In 1476, the Cistercian General Chapter granted formal permission for the celebration of Aelred's feast at Rievaulx, citing 'old and new miracles' in the church there. The feast was of high status and

FIGURE 10: Rievaulx Abbey, ex-situ stonework inscribed *SCS Williamus Abbas* from the shrine of Abbot William. Photograph: Historic England.

observed with twelve lections. In 1491, Jean de Cirey, the reforming abbot of Cîteaux, published a catalogue of Cistercian saints, which included the name of Aelred. The saint's *Vita* was among those gathered by the chronicler John of Tynemouth in 1330. The mid-fifteenth-century hagiographer John Capgrave also composed a life of Aelred, largely based on Walter Daniel's twelfth-century biography, for his *Nova Legenda Angliae*, an edition of which was published in 1516 by Wynkyn de Worde in London.[27]

A votive lead shoe from the abbey is possible evidence of pilgrimage to the shrines of Aelred and William, though it should be noted that no such pilgrimages are explicitly documented.[28] However, it is known that Aelred's shrine received oblations. As late as 1524 one John Rogerson bequeathed 'to Sancte Aldrede shryne a paire of beades'.[29] A relic of the saint at Rievaulx was valued by the laity, the abbey having a girdle of Aelred, lent to women to ease the pains and dangers of childbirth.[30]

In the medieval mind, motherhood brings us logically to the Virgin. All Cistercian abbeys were dedicated to the Virgin. It is clear from the Suppression-era inventory that her image proliferated at Rievaulx, with 'an image of our lady gyldyd' on the high altar, and other images adorning altars in the presbytery and nave aisles.[31] Although these images have long since perished, a limestone relief sculpture of the Annunciation to the Virgin survives. It is the only piece of figurative sculpture still in situ at the abbey and is located above the community's entrance to the late medieval abbots' house, which Abbot John Burton (ruled 1490–*c*.1510) created out of the former infirmary in *c*.1500 (see figure 11). Annunciation scenes were typically located in close proximity to doorways and other openings, a position related to Marian devotion, referring to the belief that the Gates of Heaven, closed by the sinfulness of Eve at the Fall, were reopened by the humility of the Virgin and the Incarnation at the Annunciation.[32] There is explicit evidence of devotion to the Annunciation at Rievaulx. When John Leland visited the abbey shortly

FIGURE 11: Rievaulx Abbey, limestone relief sculpture of the Annunciation to the Virgin, c.1500, above the entrance to the late medieval abbatial lodging. Photograph: Michael Carter.

before the Suppression he noted that its library included a copy of the now lost *Expositio super Missus est angelus Gabriel* by Walter Daniel.[33]

Images of other saints populated the church at Rievaulx. The inventory lists alabaster images of the Trinity and Saints Christopher, John the Baptist and John the Evangelist, Mary Magdalen and Margaret. Although all had a place in the liturgy of the Cistercians, their veneration was ubiquitous.[34] Rievaulx was a living institution, and religious life within the abbey shows evidence of developments in belief, devotion and liturgical practice of a type that occurred in the wider Church.[35] The Christ-centric affective piety found in the works of Richard Rolle (d.1349), who spent the final years of his life at the Cistercian nunnery of Hampole in Yorkshire, was deeply influenced by the writings of the early Yorkshire Cistercians, especially Aelred.[36] In the middle of the fifteenth century, Abbot William Spencer of Rievaulx (ruled 1436–49) donated to his abbey's library a copy of the *Speculum Christiani*, which is in both Latin and the vernacular.[37] Associated with clerics in the milieu of York Minster, this was an influential pastoral manual and drew heavily on several late medieval mystical authors, including Rolle.[38] The *Abbey of the Holy Ghost*, attributed to John Alcock (born in Beverley in c.1430; bishop of Ely between 1486 and 1500), was likewise an influential spiritual text in late medieval England and can also be counted among the surviving manuscripts from Rievaulx: it is the only surviving book from the abbey solely in the vernacular.[39] Its intended audience was lay people who wished to achieve the moral development associated with the regular life.[40]

The Christ-centric piety of the Cistercians meant that the Order was an early and enthusiastic promoter of the feast of Corpus Christi, which was formally sanctioned by the General Chapter in 1318.[41] The earliest surviving evidence for its observance by the English Cistercians is the office in a mid-fourteenth-century breviary from a Yorkshire Cistercian house. [42] Arguably the most important expression of devotion to the cult of Corpus Christi in northern England was the guild with that dedication founded in York in 1408.[43] Many Yorkshire Cistercians, including abbots William Spencer and William Helmsley of Rievaulx are known to have been members.[44]

There were also significant developments in the cult and iconography of the Virgin in the later Middle Ages, especially the emergence of devotion to Our Lady of Pity, or the Pietà. This representation of the Virgin often acted as the focus for burials, partly because the depiction of the grieving Virgin with her dead son upon her knees emphasised her intercessory role.[45] In 1515 Sir Ralph Scrope stated in his will that he wished to be buried before the image of Our Lady of Pity at Rievaulx,[46] clear evidence of the dialogue between the Order's spirituality, use of images and wider religiosity.

RIEVAULX AND ITS BENEFACTORS:
AN ENDURING RELATIONSHIP

Finally, evidence concerning the burial of the laity provides further insights into the religious life of Rievaulx in the late Middle Ages, as well as the abbey's enduring relationship with its benefactors. The Order initially had detailed legislation specifying who could be buried at its abbeys and where their graves could be located. This gradually became more permissive and after the middle of the thirteenth century, burial of the laity within the walls of Cistercian monasteries became a widespread practice. Burials were initially restricted to liminal areas, such as the galilee porch.[47] There are eight monuments in the porch of Rievaulx, one of which is inscribed with the name Isabel de Roos, who died in 1264, a descendant of the founder, Walter Espec.[48] However, at around this time the de Roos family chose another of Espec's foundations, the Augustinian priory at Kirkham, to be their mausoleum, partly because this house had a more permissive attitude towards lay burials. It was not until the end of the fourteenth century that the de Roos family again turned to Rievaulx as their place of burial as, by this time, patrons were being permitted burial within the liturgical heart of the monastery at Rievaulx. In 1384, Thomas de Roos was buried before the high altar at Rievaulx. In 1394 Sir John de Roos ordered that his body be laid to rest in the choir, to the south of the high altar; in the same year his wife, Mary, requested burial next to him.[49] The spiritual advantages of the location of the de Roos burials are obvious, being next to the high altar, visible to the community in their stalls, and close to the shrine of Aelred. The fact that the de Roos lords of Helmsley favoured Rievaulx with their burials is eloquent testimony of the quality of religious life at Rievaulx, belief in the efficacy of the prayers of its monks and also the enduring prestige of the monastery.

Rievaulx also continued to enjoy the support of other important secular benefactors. In 1511, John Clervaux, whose family were long-standing tenants of the abbey, asked to be buried before the image of the Virgin at the choir door of the monastery, thus benefitting from the intercessory opportunities afforded by the liturgy and the location of images.[50] Benefactors also established chantries within the church. In 1301, Master Simon de Clervaux, rector of Lythe, near Whitby, established perpetual chantries at three altars at Rievaulx.[51] Bequests from local clergy and laity enriched the abbey financially and materially. A typical example was that made in 1481 by William Overton of Helmsley, who bequeathed the abbey 23s. 4d on condition that the community attended his requiem at Helmsley and he also left the monastery two silver salts with covers, whereas in 1483

Christopher Conyers, rector of Rudby, left the abbot his amber rosary and the convent 20s. in cash.[52]

CONCLUSION

This chapter has presented evidence regarding the religious life of Rievaulx and patronage at the abbey that directly challenges traditional notions of the abbey's spiritual decline in the late Middle Ages. Yes, the art and architecture of the abbey evolved and images of saints proliferated. However, this does not show that the community had abandoned its Cistercian identity. William and Aelred remained a powerful presence and the monks responded to, and were even at the forefront of, developments in late medieval piety and were able to attract the sustained patronage of leading families. The prayers of Cistercian monks were still considered a sure road to heaven. If all this evidence is interpreted within the context of the late Middle Ages, and not through the prism of the twelfth century, the Rievaulx that emerges was still very much, in the words of Walter Daniel, 'a home of piety and peace, the abode of perfect love for God and neighbour'.[53]

Notes

1. It is a pleasure to contribute to Janet Burton's Festschrift and to be able to offer these thoughts on the art and architecture of Rievaulx Abbey in the later Middle Ages. My research on Rievaulx and the other northern Cistercian houses has benefitted immeasurably from Janet's advice and support. Versions of this chapter were presented to the British Archaeological Association and the Leeds International Medieval Congress in 2016. Since then it has benefited from the comments of Jeremy Ashbee, David Bell, Glyn Coppack, Stuart Harrison and Emilia Jamroziak.

2. For discussion of the foundation of Rievaulx and Cistercian settlement of Yorkshire, see Burton, *Monastic Order*, pp. 98–124 and her articles, 'The estates and economy of Rievaulx Abbey in Yorkshire', *Cîteaux: Commentarii Cistercienses*, 49 (1998), 29–94 and 'Rievaulx Abbey: the early years', in Terryl Kinder (ed.), *Perspectives for an Architecture of Solitude: Essays on Cistercians, Art and Architecture in Honour of Peter Fergusson* (Turnhout, 2004), pp. 47–53.

3. Peter Fergusson and Stuart Harrison, *Rievaulx Abbey: Community, Architecture and Memory* (New Haven and London, 1999), p. vii.

4. For the abbey's relations with its patrons and accumulation of estates, see Emilia Jamroziak, *Rievaulx Abbey and its Social Context, 1132–1300: Memory, Locality, and Networks* (Turnhout, 2005).

5. For a critical discussion of such historiographical interpretations of the Cistercians in the late Middle Ages, see the introduction in Martin Heale (ed.), *Monasticism in*

Late Medieval England, c.1300–1535 (Manchester, 2009), pp. 3–4. For an overview of the historiography of the art and architecture of the Cistercians, see Peter Fergusson, 'Cistercian Architecture', in Conrad Rudolph (ed.), *A Companion to Medieval Art* (Oxford, 2010), pp. 577–99.

6. The literature is already substantial, and important works include Janet Burton and Karen Stöber (eds), *Monasteries and Society in the British Isles* (Woodbridge, 2008), Heale (ed.), *Monasticism in Late Medieval England*, and the collections of essays in James Clark (ed.), *The Religious Orders in Pre-Reformation England* (Woodbridge, 2002) and Julian Luxford, *The Art and Architecture of English Benedictine Monasteries, 1300–1540: a Patronage History* (Woodbridge, 2005). For an important study reframing the debate on the Cistercians in the late Middle Ages, see Terryl N. Kinder, *Cistercian Europe: the architecture of contemplation* (Grand Rapids and Cambridge, 2002), Janet Burton and Julie Kerr, *The Cistercians in the Middle Ages* (Woodbridge, 2011) and Emilia Jamroziak, *The Cistercian Order in Medieval Europe, 1090–1500* (London, 2013), esp. pp. 238–84.

7. Walter Daniel, *Life of Aelred of Rievaulx*, ed. and trans. Maurice Powicke, Cistercian Fathers Series, 57 (1994).

8. For a summary of the abbey's difficulties in this period, see William Page, 'House of Cistercian Monks: Rievaulx', in William Page (ed.), *A History of the County of York*, III (London, 1974), pp. 149–53.

9. London, Inner Temple, MS 511.2, fol. 58r, '*Et anno domini MᶜCCCʹxxij Scoti dilapidauerunt et destruxerunt atque asportauerunt libros, calices et sacra ornamenta monasterii de Ryevall in festo sancto Kalixti pape et martiris*'.

10. For the conversion of the abbey's granges and those of other northern Cistercian houses into manors, see Janet Burton, 'The Estates and Economy of Rievaulx Abbey in Yorkshire', *Cîteaux: Commentarii Cistercienses*, 49 (1998), pp. 89–90, and R. A. Donkin, *The Cistercians: Studies in the Geography of Medieval England and Wales* (Toronto, 1978), p. 127. For the most recent discussion of the reasons behind the decline of the Cistercian lay brotherhood, see James France, *Separate but Equal: Cistercian Lay Brothers, 1120–1350* (Kalamazoo, 2012), pp. 300–22. For the number of monks at Rievaulx at the end of the fourteenth century, see David Knowles and R. Neville Hadcock, *Medieval Religious Houses. England and Wales* (London, 1953), p. 114.

11. C. H. Talbot (ed.), *Letters from the English Abbots to the Chapter at Cîteaux 1442–1521*, Camden Society, Fourth Series (1967), p. 252.

12. For Helmsley's career at Oxford, see Alfred B. Emden, *A Biographical Register of the University of Oxford to A.D. 1500*, II (Oxford, 1958), p. 905. His efforts to ensure the completion of Saint Bernard's College were praised by Huby in 1517; see, Talbot (ed.), *Letters from the English Abbots to the Chapter at Cîteaux*, p. 243.

13. Talbot (ed.), *Letters from the English Abbots to the Chapter at Cîteaux*, pp. 239–41.

14. Glyn Coppack, 'Appendix D: Suppression documents', in Fergusson and Harrison, *Rievaulx Abbey*, pp. 227–31.

15. For discussion of these buildings and the influence of Aelred as patron, see Fergusson and Harrison, *Rievaulx Abbey*, pp. 59–82, 95–9, 123–30. For Cistercian architecture in twelfth-century England, see Peter Fergusson, *The Architecture of Solitude: Cistercian Abbeys in Twelfth-Century England* (Princeton, 1984).

16. Aelred of Rievaulx, *Mirror of Charity*, trans. Elizabeth Connor (Kalamazoo, 1990), p. 212.

17. For the legislation on art and architecture, see Christopher Norton, 'Table of Cistercian Legislation on Art and Architecture', in Christopher Norton and David Park (eds), *Cistercian Art and Architecture in the British Isles* (Cambridge 1986), pp. 315–93. The articles in this volume discuss the application, or otherwise, of this *legislatio*.

18. Chrysogonus Waddell, *Twelfth-Century Statutes from the Cistercian General Chapter, Latin Text with English Notes and Commentary*, Cîteaux: Commentarii Cistercienses, Studia et Documenta, XII (2002). For comment on the significance of Waddell's reinterpretation of Cistercian statues on art and architecture, see Fergusson, 'Cistercian Architecture', p. 590.

19. *superfluae novitates et notabiles curiositates*; Norton, 'Table of Cistercian Legislation', pp. 384, 388.

20. With the exception of a provision forbidding the construction of private cells for all but the most senior monks, the bull made no reference to matters artistic or architectural. For discussion of the *Benedictina*'s significance to the interpretation of Cistercian monasticism in the late Middle Ages, see Peter McDonald, 'The Papacy and Monastic Observance in the Later Middle Ages: the *Benedictina* in England', *Journal of Religious History*, 14 (1986), 117–32.

21. Glyn Coppack, 'The Planning of Cistercian Monasteries in the Later Middle Ages: the Evidence from Fountains, Rievaulx, Sawley and Rushen', in J. Clark (ed.), *The Religious Orders in Pre-Reformation England* (Woodbridge, 2002), pp. 197–210; Fergusson and Harrison, *Rievaulx Abbey*, esp. pp. 99–101, 132–5.

22. For discussion of the Christ in Majesty at Rievaulx and its relationship with the image at Lincoln, see Jonathan Alexander and Paul Binski (eds), *Age of Chivalry: Art in Plantagenet England*, catalogue of an exhibition at the Royal Academy, London, 1987 (London, 1987), pp. 344–5.

23. Coppack, 'Suppression documents', in Fergusson and Harrison, *Rievaulx Abbey*, pp. 227–31.

24. For these volumes, see the articles by Michael Carter, 'A Printed Missal from an English Cistercian Abbey', *Cistercian Studies Quarterly*, 49 (2014), 243–59 and 'Unanswered Prayers: a Printed Cistercian Missal at York Minster Library', *Antiquaries Journal*, 95 (2015), 267–77. The third missal was recently discovered in the collections of Leeds City Library and publication by Philip Wilde is expected shortly. The appropriation of the religious traditions of northern England by the Cistercians is discussed by Michael Carter, '"*So it was abowte iiiiᵗ yeres agoo*": Retrospection in the Art and Architecture of the

Cistercian in Northern England in the Late Middle Ages', *Journal of Medieval Monastic Studies*, 4 (2015), 107–32.

25. William's epitaph is in BL, Cotton MS Titus D XXIV, fol. 81v: *Epitaphium domini Willelmi Abbatis Rieuallensis / Dormit in hoc tumulo quondam celeberrimus ille / Ordinis interpres, religionis odor; / Sol patriae, pater ecclesiae, lux fusa per orbem; / Cuius fundator et patriacha domus; / Insignis virtute, fide, spectabilis ortu, Abbas Willelmus totus apostolicus.* ('Epitaph of Lord William, Abbot of Rievaulx. In this tomb sleeps the late very celebrated expounder of the order, the fragrance of religion; the sun of his native land, the father of the church, the light poured forth through the world; the founder and father of his house; eminent in virtue, in faith, in the dawning [or rise] of what is admirable, Abbot William, the wholly apostolic man.') The epitaph has received little scholarly comment, but see Megan Cassidy-Welch, *Monastic Spaces and their Meanings: Thirteenth-Century English Cistercian Monasteries* (Turnhout, 2001), p. 70 and J. H. Mozley, 'The Collection of Mediaeval Latin Verse in MS Cotton Titus D. XXIV', *Medium Ævum*, 11 (1942), 1–45.

26. Evidence of William's cult is discussed in Charles Peers, 'Rievaulx Abbey: the Shrine in the Chapter House', *Archaeological Journal*, 86 (1929), 20–8 and Fergusson and Harrison, *Rievaulx Abbey*, pp. 99, 166–7.

27. Medieval evidence for the cult of Aelred at Rievaulx, including Leland's description of the saint's tomb, is discussed in Fergusson and Harrison, *Rievaulx Abbey*, pp. 167–9. The catalogue of Cistercian saints published by de Cirey is conveniently reproduced in Phillipe Guignard (ed.), *Les monuments primitifs de al règle Cistercienne* (Dijon, 1878), pp. 650–2. The evidence the catalogue provides of Cistercian identity and devotion in the late Middle Ages is discussed by Jamroziak, *The Cistercian Order in Medieval Europe*, p. 257. The decree of the General Chapter approving Aelred's cult is printed in *Statuta Capitulorum Generalium Ordinis Cisterciensis ad anno 1116–1786*, V, ed. Joseph Marie Canivez (Louvain, 1941), pp. 348–9. See also, John Caprave, *Nova Legenda Angliae* (London, 1516), ff. XIr–XIIIr.

28. G. C. Dunning, 'Heraldic and Decorated Metalwork and Other Finds from Rievaulx Abbey, Yorkshire', *Antiquaries Journal*, 45 (1965), 55–63; Fergusson and Harrison, *Rievaulx Abbey*, p. 167.

29. James Raine and John William Clay (eds), *Testamenta Eboracensia: a Selection of Wills from the Registry at York*, V, Surtees Society, 79 (1884), p. 194. An altar dedicated to Aelred at Fountains was also receiving oblations; see Joseph Fowler (ed.), *Memorials of the Abbey of St Mary of Fountains*, III, Surtees Society, 130 (1918), pp. xiv, 40, 79.

30. J. S. Brewer, J. Gairdner and R. H. Brodie (eds), *Letters and Papers of the Reign of Henry VIII*, 23 vols in 38 (London, 1862–1932), X, p. 364.

31. Coppack, 'Suppression documents', in Fergusson and Harrison, *Rievaulx Abbey*, pp. 227–8.

32. For discussion of the iconography and location of the sculpture, see Michael Carter, 'Late Medieval Relief Sculptures of the Annunciation to the Virgin from

the Cistercian Abbeys of Rievaulx and Fountains', *Cîteaux: Commentarii Cistercienses*, 60 (2009), 139–60.

33. For the work by Walter Daniel mentioned by Leland, see *http://mlgb3.bodleian.ox.ac.uk/authortitle/medieval_catalogues/Z21/* (accessed 29 March 2018).

34. Coppack, 'Suppression documents', in Fergusson and Harrison, *Rievaulx Abbey*, pp. 227–9. For discussion of the importance of the place of these saints and use of their images in late medieval England, see Richard Marks, *Image and Devotion in Late Medieval England* (Stroud, 2004), esp. pp. 86–120; and Eamon Duffy, *The Stripping of the Altars: Traditional Religion in England 1400–1580*, 2nd edn (New Haven and London, 2004), esp. pp. 155–205.

35. For an overview of how the Order responded to the evolution of late medieval religiosity, see Jamroziak, *The Cistercian Order in Medieval Europe*, pp. 255–9.

36. For Rolle's Cistercian influences, see Nicholas Watson, *Richard Rolle and the Invention of Authority* (Cambridge, 1991), p. 55. For Aelred's influence on Rolle, see Robert Boenig, 'Contemplations of the Dread and Love of God, Richard Rolle, and Aelred of Rievaulx', *Mystics Quarterly*, 16 (1990), 27–33.

37. Oxford, Corpus Christi, MS 151, fols 146–205v.

38. For comment on this work, see Vincent Gillespie, 'The Evolution of the *Speculum Christiani*', in A. J. Minnis (ed.), *Latin and Vernacular: Studies in Late-Medieval Texts and Manuscripts* (Cambridge, 1989), pp. 39–62. The northern English religious and devotional context of this work is discussed by Jonathan Hughes, *Pastors and Visionaries: Religion and Secular Life in Late Medieval Yorkshire* (Woodbridge, 1988), pp. 194–6.

39. BL, MS Cotton Vespasian D XIII, fols 181–201.

40. R. N. Swanson, *Catholic England: Faith, Religion and Observance before the Reformation* (Manchester, 1993), pp. 17–18.

41. The cult of the host was rooted in the Christ-centric affective spirituality of the Cistercians, and Matthew, cantor at Rievaulx (d.1220), was the author of Eucharistic hymns; see Jamroziak, *The Cistercian Order in Medieval Europe*, p. 257. For Cistercian support of the foundress of the cult of Corpus Christi, see Barbara R. Walters, 'The Feast and its Founder', in Barbara R Walter, Vincent J. Corrigan and Peter T. Ricketts (eds), *The Feast of Corpus Christi* (Pennsylvania, 2006), pp. 5–57.

42. BL, MS Burney 335, fol. 329r. For comment on this manuscript, including its evidence for the office and likely provenance, see D. F. L. Chadd, 'Liturgy and Liturgical Music: the Limits of Uniformity', in Norton and Park (eds), *Cistercian Art and Architecture in the British Isles*, pp. 312–13 and Richard W. Pfaff, *The Liturgy in Medieval England: a History* (Cambridge, 2009), p. 259. Fountains is given as the most likely house of origin for this manuscript by both authors, but there is nothing in the calendar, litany or office to confirm such a precise localisation.

43. For the history of the guild, see David J. F. Crouch, *Piety, Fraternity and Power: Religious Gilds in Late Medieval Yorkshire, 1389–1547* (Woodbridge, 2000), pp. 160–96.

44. R. H. Skaife (ed.), *The Register of the Guild of Corpus Christi in the City of York*, Surtees Society, 57 (1871), pp. 71, 185.

45. For a discussion of devotion to Our Lady of Pity in late medieval England and the use of this type of image, see Marks, *Image and Devotion*, pp. 123–43.

46. Raine (ed.), *Testamenta Eboracensia*, V, p. 63.

47. For Cistercian legislation on lay burials, see Jackie Hall, Sheila Sneddon and Nadine Sohr, 'Table of Legislation Concerning the Burial of Laity and Other Patrons in Cistercian Abbeys', in Jackie Hall and Christine Kratzke (eds), *Sepulturae Cistercienses: Burial, Memorial and Patronage in Medieval Cistercian Monasteries, Cîteaux: Commentarii Cistercienses*, 56 (2005), 373–416. The legislation is discussed by Jackie Hall, 'The Legislative Background to the Burial of Laity and Other Patrons in Cistercian Abbeys', in Hall and Kratzke (eds), *Sepulturae Cistercienses*, 363–70.

48. Fergusson and Harrison, *Rievaulx Abbey*, p. 4.

49. Burials by the de Roos family at Kirkham and Rievaulx are discussed by Jamroziak, *Rievaulx Abbey*, pp. 49–50; see also Janet Burton, *Kirkham Priory from Foundation to Dissolution*, Borthwick Papers, 86 (York, 1995).

50. Raine (ed.), *Testamenta Eboracensia*, V, pp. 20–1.

51. J. C. Atkinson (ed.), *Cartularium Abbathiae de Rievalle Ordinis Cisterciensis Fundatae Anno MCXXXII*, Surtees Society, 83 (1887), pp. xcvii–viii.

52. James Raine (ed.), *Testamenta Eboracensia*, III, Surtees Society, 45 (1864), pp. 262, 289.

53. Daniel, *Life of Aelred of Rievaulx*, pp. 117–18.

7

The last days of Bridlington Priory

Claire Cross

Of the twelve Yorkshire houses of Augustinian canons the priories of Guisborough in the North Riding and Bridlington in the East Riding were by a considerable margin the richest, largest and most important, and until the early sixteenth century their histories ran on largely parallel lines. Their fate in the 1530s, however, could scarcely have been more different. Not suppressed until 1539 Guisborough fared relatively well, its prior receiving a generous settlement and its canons obtaining at least adequate pensions. For Bridlington, in contrast, the dissolution proved an unmitigated disaster, with the priory confiscated in the aftermath of the Pilgrimage of Grace, its canons thrust penniless into the secular world and its prior paying for his treasonable activities with his life. The responsibility for this catastrophe lies almost entirely with Bridlington's last prior, William Wood, and with the company he kept during some of the most crucial years of the Henrician Reformation.

Founded some six years before Guisborough in 1113 by Walter de Gant with the active support of Henry I and Archbishop Thomas II of York and endowed with no fewer than sixteen appropriated churches in addition to several chapelries, the greater part lying within a four-mile radius of the priory, Bridlington rose rapidly to become one of the wealthiest priories in the whole of Yorkshire. After about 1200 when patrons began transferring their support first to the Cistercians and later to the friars, like most of the other Augustinian houses in the county it no longer attracted any more major benefactions, but unlike its sister houses it experienced a second spring and a considerable improvement in its economic fortunes on its transformation into a cult centre at the end of the fourteenth century.[1]

The priory owed its new prominence to John Thwing, a member of a minor gentry family from the Wolds village of the same name some nine miles from Bridlington. Born around 1319 and professed some twenty years later, he served in a succession of monastic offices before his election as prior in 1360. Revered for his piety, austerity and charity, he was said to have worked miracles even in his lifetime, and after his death in 1379 more miracles occurred at his tomb. Encouraged by Richard II, the archbishop of York, Alexander Neville, began proceedings for his canonisation within a decade, and in 1401 Boniface IX pronounced him a saint, the last Englishman to be so honoured before the Reformation. The community responded by translating his body to a shrine behind the high altar in the priory church, and in 1409 Boniface's successor, Alexander V, conferred a yet further mark of papal approval upon the house by according the prior the right to wear the mitre, ring and other pontifical insignia. The future Henry IV made a pilgrimage to the priory on his return from the crusade in 1391, and Henry V, who had a special devotion to St John of Bridlington, visited the shrine on at least two occasions. With such royal patronage the priory rapidly developed into one of the most important pilgrimage sites in late medieval England.[2]

From its earliest days, when prior Robert had produced glosses on books of both the Old and New Testament, Bridlington had developed a reputation for learning, and over the centuries it accumulated an impressive library, which in addition to numerous biblical commentaries contained works by Jerome, Augustine, Bede and Anselm when inspected by Leland in 1534. If, however, the commonplace book of Thomas Ashby, ordained priest from the priory in 1503, can be taken as a guide, the canons seem to have remained conservative in their intellectual tastes, and to have shown far more interest in stories of their local saint, papal indulgences, the symbolism of the prior's mitre, guardian angels and the miraculous properties of the text *In principio erat verbum* than in the new Christian humanism beginning to permeate England from the Continent.[3]

Be this as it may, at least in its last decades the priory was fulfilling its obligation of sending some of its more promising young monks to the university. Peter Hardy graduated as a bachelor of divinity at Cambridge in 1505–6, Robert Charde (or Charder) as a bachelor of arts in 1510 and master of arts in 1514, and William Wood as a bachelor of canon law in 1513. On their return to their house university-educated monks frequently made rapid progress through the monastic hierarchy, and Hardy, the most senior of the three, had become subprior sometime before 1519. By 1530 both he and Charde seem to have died, so it is not surprising that, when the aged William Brownefleet (or Broomfleet) decided to resign, the community elected the third member of the trio, William Wood, as their new prior on 20 June 1531.[4]

Ordained subdeacon on 5 April 1511 and deacon just under two years later on 19 February 1513, Wood seems to have been in his early forties when he succeeded Brownefleet. By all accounts he inherited a house in good array. Throughout the later Middle Ages the priory had a sufficiently large endowment to maintain around twenty canons and there may have been slightly above this number in the convent just before the dissolution. Even more significantly the community seems to have been a predominately youthful one. On the assumption that the priory presented its novices for ordination to the priesthood on reaching the statutory age of twenty-five, in 1536 the convent contained only two canons aged over fifty, John Colman being by some way the most senior at around fifty-nine, three, including the prior, between forty and fifty, nine between twenty-five and forty, and no fewer than seven who were still deacons or subdeacons and so presumably under the age of twenty-five. The archiepiscopal registers, which routinely record the location of those admitted to the first of the minor orders, suggest that in common with the majority of Yorkshire houses the priory recruited its members from a geographically confined area. Of the eleven canons who had been ordained acolytes before entering the community two, Thomas Paitson and John Skeresbeke, originated from Bridlington itself, Sebastian Freston from nearby Bessingby, a priory appropriation, Robet Todde from Newbald and William Toye from Beverley. Outside the East Riding three came from the North Riding, three from the east of the West Riding and none at all from outside Yorkshire.[5]

Living in some state in the recently refurbished Prior's Lodging with its great hall, separate dining chamber, sleeping chamber, various other fair chambers, private chapel, servants' quarters and kitchen, for a brief period after his election Wood was able to perform without outside interference the duties in local society expected of the head of a major religious house. In 1532, for example, he acted alongside the abbot of Meaux, Sir John Constable and others as one of the government's commissioners for weirs and fishgarths in the East Riding, and around the same time conducted a spirited defence in the courts of the priory's property rights in the manor of Speton. More and more, however, events occurring at Westminster intervened to curtail his freedom of action.[6]

The first intimation of future trials came in October 1535 in a letter from Cromwell offering Wood the choice of either recognising the Crown as the priory's founder or of appearing before the council by the end of the month. Pleading infirmity, the prior dispatched one of his brethren with the priory's charters to show that the house had been founded not by Henry I but by Walter de Gant. It proved a hollow victory for later that autumn, having completed their visitation of monasteries in the south of England, Dr Richard Layton and Sir Thomas Legh turned their attention to the northern province, and descended upon Bridlington. Compared with some neighbouring houses which they portrayed as dens of immorality, the priory escaped relatively lightly. The visitors cast no aspersions on the prior, and accused only one canon, John Gibson, of having had a sexual relationship with a woman, and two others, John Ward and Robert Smith, of having committed self-abuse. When complying with a subsequent order to forward his charters to London,

Wood enclosed a 'poor fee' for Cromwell, upgraded to an annuity of ten marks in the following May.[7]

From this stage onwards Wood was greatly affected by the opinions of his closest associates. He seems to have enjoyed good relations with the local gentry, dining on occasion with Matthew Boynton of Boynton, though by far his most intimate ties were with the priory's steward, Sir Robert Constable of Flamborough, a mere two or three miles from Bridlington. A one-time soldier, who as a young man in 1511 had joined a military expedition against the Moors and two years later fought at the battle of Flodden, after succeeding his father in 1518 Constable had taken an active part in administration of the East Riding. Conservative in religion and an outspoken opponent of heresy he had ready access to Wood, often choosing to stay in the priory in the newly built chamber which bore his name.[8]

The man who exerted the most influence upon Wood in these crucial months, however, was John Pickering, a Dominican friar. A northerner and perhaps a native of Bridlington, Pickering had been ordained priest from the York friary in 1516, and then studied in Cambridge for nine years for the degree of bachelor of divinity before becoming warden of the York convent in about 1524. Throughout his time at the university he had turned his face against the 'new learning', and he spoke out in support of Henry VIII's marriage to Catherine of Aragon and of the papal supremacy later in the decade when consultations were being held on the king's 'great matter'. In 1532 he bitterly opposed the northern convocation's recognition of the king's headship of the English church, and perhaps in protest resigned as warden around this time. Befriended by Dr Marmaduke Waldby, a Yorkshire cleric with connections to the imperial court, he then seems to have gone abroad to study for a doctorate at a continental university. By the early autumn of 1536 he was back in the north of England, and temporarily residing not as might have been expected in one of the Yorkshire Dominican convents but in Bridlington Priory.[9]

Resentment at the recent intrusion of the state into the priory's affairs may well have lain behind Wood's harbouring of a known opponent of government policy. Be this as it may, the two men were certainly living under the same roof at the beginning of October when news reached the priory of the Lincolnshire rebellion. Wood subsequently claimed to have been appalled when told that the commons of the East Riding were also planning to rise. This, though, may have been special pleading, since soon afterwards he responded to the appeal for assistance from the captains of the rebels by sending no fewer than eleven men on horseback and two of his younger canons, John Lambert and William Broomfleet, the namesake and probable relative of the previous prior. After gaining an assurance that the host would not harm the priory's goods, he then went on to contribute twenty nobles to Robert Aske, paid a further £4 to the commons of Holderness to prevent them from confiscating his cattle, and gave four horsemen to a local yeoman, John Hallam, who had come to the priory seeking aid in the siege of Scarborough Castle. While Wood later maintained that he had done all this under constraint, he did not deny having had conversations with Pickering in which the friar had asserted 'that the insurrection was well done for the wealth of the church'.[10]

On his visit to the priory Hallam had brought with him 'certain rhymes made against my Lord Privy Seal, my Lord Chancellor, the Chancellor of the Augmentations and divers bishops of the new learning, which rhymes had been sung abroad by minstrels'. At his suggestion Pickering then incorporated them in a long, Latinate poem exhorting the 'faithful people of the boreal region' 'to make reformation Of great mischief and horrible offense'. Through the machinations of Cromwell, Sir Thomas Audley, Sir Richard Rich, the archbishop of Canterbury, Thomas Cranmer, the bishop of Worcester, Hugh Latimer and Nicholas Shaxton, the bishop of Salisbury 'Christ's church very like is spoiled to be And all abbeys suppressed'. The realm could only be saved 'And the bishops reformed in a new array' if Cromwell suffered the same punishment as Hamon, King Ashasuerus's wicked minister in the Old Testament story of Esther. The fight pertained not solely to England but to the whole of Christendom, and if the present government failed to reverse its policies, the northerners might hope to receive aid 'out of a strange land'.[11]

As soon as he had finished his poem Pickering showed it to Wood and some of the rest of the community. The prior praised it effusively, and gave it to one of the canons to transcribe. A servant of Sir Robert Constable obtained a copy, and within a month, as Wood later admitted, 'the rhyme was in every man's mouth about Bridlington and Pomfret'. At the same time as Robert Aske was leading the Pilgrims south towards Doncaster, the archbishop of York, Edward Lee, was assembling a small group of theologians and canon lawyers in Pontefract to discuss such contentious matters as the royal supremacy, the payment of first fruits and tenths, the benefit of clergy, the fate of the monasteries, the worship of saints and images and the retention of holy days. At the end of November he summoned Pickering to join in the deliberations and Wood provided him with a horse and three crowns for the journey. In the ensuing clerical debates at Pontefract Priory Pickering re-stated his conviction that 'the king might not be the supreme head'. He shared in the general dismay when the archbishop changed sides and maintained in his public sermon on 3 December that it was not lawful for the commons to make battle against their prince, and together with the archbishop's chancellor, Cuthbert Marshall, forced Lee to retain the clause in the assembly's articles which recognised the pope's headship over the English church.[12]

Unlike Aske, Pickering had no trust in the king's honouring the promises made by the duke of Norfolk of a royal pardon and of a parliament to be held in York which led the Pilgrims to disband a few days later, and on his return to the East Riding he may well have shared his reservations with Wood. There can be no shadow of a doubt of Pickering's complicity in the second rising. He carried letters between Sir Francis Bigod and John Hallam and attended the council meeting in Bigod's house in Settrington on 14 January 1537 which planned the joint attack on Scarborough and Hull. He then seems to have accompanied George Lumley, the son and heir of John, fifth baron Lumley, to Scarborough, and apparently remained there after Hallam's failure to take Hull, Lumley's surrender and the revolt's collapse at the end of the month. In a letter to Norfolk on 27 February Henry VIII singled out Pickering as a particular object of his wrath and ordered his immediate capture. He was not in fact taken until two months later. Dispatched to London, tried and found guilty of high treason, he was hanged at Tyburn on 25 May.[13]

Wood's active participation in the second revolt is far less clear. Cromwell, who from the start contended that 'the prior of Bridlington and Dr Pickering were busy in both insurrections', had Wood brought to London in April 1537. Two government lawyers, Richard Layton and William Petre, then subjected him to a series of interrogations. They questioned him in particular on the 'divers subsidies given by him to the ... insurrection, and much traitorous conferences had between him and Dr Pickering', and alleged 'that he knew of Sir Francis Bigod's [commotion] and that George Lumley sent unto him to have men for that commotion', before going on to accuse him of putting 'all his household servants and tenants in harness when George Lumley sent to him', and insinuating 'that Friar Pickering was a principal inciter thereunto'. Wood tried desperately to counter the charges. He claimed that he had alerted Matthew Boynton as soon as he had heard that Bigod had raised the commons in Buckrose, that the two men had made plans to stay the rebels, and that when Lumley had sent to him for men the next day, Bridlington was so quietened that he had virtually no success and eventually 'stole privily away'. Wood could not, however, disavow his friendship with Pickering and this is what damned him in the end. He was executed for treason alongside the abbot of Jervaulx and the quondam abbot of Fountains on 25 May; George Lumley was put to death at Tyburn on 2 June, and Sir Robert Constable hanged in Hull on 6 July.[14]

From the moment of Wood's conviction Bridlington Priory ceased to exist as a corporate entity and automatically reverted to the Crown, since the government had taken the decision to treat the lands and goods of the heads of religious houses condemned for treason exactly as they treated the possessions of secular traitors. The task of dissolving the priory, estimated to be worth a little over £547 a year in 1535, devolved upon Norfolk, then engaged in the pacification of the north in the aftermath of the Pilgrimage of Grace. He reported to Cromwell on 18 May that he had an inventory made of all the priory's goods, and had removed the most valuable to his residence at Sheriff Hutton. Cromwell, who preferred his own officers to undertake the formal survey, instructed the duke in the meanwhile to dismantle the shrine of St John of Bridlington 'that people be not seduced into offering their money', to dispatch all the plate and jewels to London, with the exception of any that he might be willing to buy himself, and to dispose of all the priory's corn, cattle and growing crops for the king's profit. He also required him to pay the priory's debts, later estimated to be around £200, sanctioned the spending of up to £20 on the repair of Bridlington harbour, previously the responsibility of the priory, and promised him further directions concerning the recovery of the lead from the major monastic buildings once he had the full survey.[15]

At this juncture Norfolk focused his attention mainly on the priory church, the nave of which served as the parish church for 1,500 townspeople. He dispatched to London in two sealed boxes all the gold work, which Thomas Magnus, the archdeacon of the East Riding, had torn from the shrine, together with the most precious ornaments, which included a Root of Jesse 'to be set upon an altar', but kept the silver gear amounting in all to about 3,470 ounces, which he suggested to the king could either be retained at Sheriff Hutton until his projected visitation of the north, or sold locally for his best advantage. The supervision of the minutiae of the dissolution then passed from Norfolk to Richard Pollard, who had attended the duke at the suppression of priory and had very recently applied for the post of receiver of its forfeited estates. On 14 June he informed Cromwell that he had succeeded in extracting more gold and silver from the church but that the poor people had stolen much of its 'stuff' before he arrived. He enclosed with his letter a detailed survey of the entire monastic site. The wainscotted chancel of the priory church with its newly carved choir stalls had particularly caught his eye, together with 'the reredos at the high altar representing Christ at the assumption of Our Lady and the 12 apostles with divers other great images'. The lead, however, was his main concern. Having already received an offer of 500 marks for the lead from the great barn, he later estimated that the lead from all the priory's buildings might fetch in the region of £1,000. At the end of July Cromwell authorised him to have it stripped out and melted into sows, though it took until the following spring for the work to be completed.[16]

Compared with the time expended on realising the maximum profit from the priory's possessions Cromwell's officers paid only scant attention to the fate of the Bridlington religious. Perhaps with the intention of improving their future prospects the priory itself had presented an abnormally large number of novices for ordination at the church of the York Austin friars on 24 February 1537, when Robert Burdus, Matthew Charder, Sebastian Freston and Robert Watson had been made subdeacons and John Pullane, Peter Williamson and Robert Smyth deacons. Within weeks of the ceremony Wood had been arrested and taken down to London, and the community had been left leaderless until the arrival of the royal commissioners on 17 May. Clearly under instructions to act as expeditiously as possible they offered the canons the choice of either seeking a dispensation to take a benefice in the secular church or of transferring to another house of their order as set out in the Act for the Dissolution of the Lesser Monasteries of 1536. Fourteen applied for dispensations, though in the event only thirteen took them up, while five opted to persevere in the religious life, Robert Burdus going to Bolton Priory, John Pullane and John Ward to Nostell Priory, Robert Watson to Guisborough Priory and Peter Williamson to Kirkham Priory.[17]

The very short interval which elapsed between the failure of the second rising and the dissolution of the priory meant that Bridlington, unlike the other major Yorkshire Augustinian houses, had little opportunity to make use of its appropriations to provide for its members, and only two canons, William Toye, who became curate of Bessingby chapel, worth a mere £5 6s. 8d a year, and John Coltman, who became vicar of Foxholes where the priory had enjoyed part of the tithes, secured benefices which had previously belonged to the priory. All the rest of the community in receipt of dispensations seem to have had to make their own way in the world. Two if not three went on to earn a livelihood as chantry priests, with the elderly Robert Todde serving as chantry in Beverley minster, the much younger William Walker a chantry in Sykehouse chapel in Fishlake, and just possibly William Mason a chantry in Ilkley parish church. Robert Anlaby may have obtained a curacy in Bubwith, Laurence Chapman a curacy in Nafferton and John Lambert may have ended his career as vicar of Pannal. No evidence has survived on the fate of the other five.[18]

Although they could not possibly have foreseen this at the time, the five canons who decided to persevere in the religious life made by far the best economic choice, since all the inmates of the major monasteries voluntarily surrendered to the Crown from 1537 onwards were granted pensions. Consequently Robert Watson received a pension of £5 6s. 8d from Guisborough Priory, John Ward and his younger colleague John Pullane pensions of £5 6s. 8d and £5 respectively from Nostell Priory, Peter Williamson a pension of £5 6s. 8d from Kirkham Priory, and the very junior Robert Burdus a pension of £4 from Bolton Priory. Thus cushioned John Ward went on to minister as a chantry priest in Helmsley parish church, Robert Burdus as a curate in Wymondley in Hertfordshire and Robert Watson possibly as a curate in Birdsall in the

East Riding. A John Pullane, who can perhaps be identified with the former Bridlington canon, having previously been a curate in the parish, became the rector of Kirkheaton in 1554. As there is no record of the payment of his pension Peter Williamson probably died soon after the suppression of Kirkham Priory.[19]

Alive and still drawing his pension in 1573, Robert Watson may have been the last of the former religious to die. Forced to find a living wherever they could, hardly any of the canons, apart from William Toye, seem to have stayed in the area long enough to see the roof of their house stripped of its lead, its walls torn down and the stone carted away. With the clergy powerless to act, some local gentry families intervened to save a very few of the priory's furnishings, and around this time the North Riding churches of Leake and Over Silton acquired some of the bench-ends from the choir stalls, and Flamborough parish church the Tudor screen which almost certainly had once formed part of the great screen dividing the canons' chancel from the nave, but in Bridlington itself by the end of the century only the truncated church and the gatehouse remained to bear witness to one of the most important Augustinian houses in the north of England.[20]

Notes

1. J. Burton, 'The Regular Canons and Diocesan Reform in Northern England', in J. Burton and K. Stöber (eds), *The Regular Canons in the Medieval British Isles* (Turnhout, 2011), pp. 42–6; W. Page (ed.), *VCH Yorkshire*, 3 (London, 1913), pp. 199–205; D. Neave, *Port, Resort and Market Town: A History of Bridlington* (Howden, 2000), pp. 7–19; T. N. Burrows, 'The Geography of Monastic Property in Medieval England: A Case Study of Nostell and Bridlington Priories (Yorkshire)', *Yorkshire Archaeological Journal*, 57 (1985), 79–86.

2. J. S. Purvis, 'St John of Bridlington', *Journal of the Bridlington Augustinian Society*, 2 (1924), 1–50; R. Lutton, 'Bridlington Priory in Late Medieval England and the Cult of John Thweng', in P. Weston and D. Weston (eds), *Celebrating the Heritage: Bridlington Priory in its Historical Context 1113–2013* (Bridlington, 2015), pp. 19–32; C. Sanok, 'John of Bridlington, Mitred Prior and Model of the Mixed Life', in P. H. Cullum and K. J. Lewis (eds), *Religious Men and Masculine Identity in the Middle Ages* (Woodbridge, 2013), pp. 143–59; Page (ed.), *VCH Yorkshire*, 3, pp. 199–205.

3. A. Mathers-Lawrence, 'The Augustinian Canons in Northumbria: Region, Tradition, and Textuality in a Colonizing Order', in Burton and Stöber (eds), *The Regular Canons in the Medieval British Isles*, p. 67; M. Prickett, *An Historical and Architectural Description of the Priory Church of Bridlington* (Cambridge, 1831), pp. 21–2; T. Webber and A. G. Watson (eds), *The Libraries of the Augustinian Canons*, Corpus of Medieval Library Catalogues, 6 (1998), pp. 8–24; A. G. Dickens, 'The Writers of Tudor Yorkshire', *Transactions of the Royal Historical Society*, Fifth Series, 13 (1963), 51–2.

4. J. and J. A. Venn, *Alumni Cantabrigienses*, Part 1, vol. 2 (Cambridge, 1922), p. 304;

J. S. Purvis, 'The Ripon Carvers and the Lost Choir-Stalls of Bridlington Priory', *Yorkshire Archaeological Journal*, 29 (1929), 198–9; C. Cross and N. Vickers (eds), *Monks, Friars and Nuns in Sixteenth Century Yorkshire*, Yorkshire Archaeological Society, Record Series, 150 (1995), pp. 252, 253, 255.

5. C. Cross (compiled), *York Clergy Ordinations 1500–1509*, Borthwick List and Index 30 (York, 2001), pp. 63, 255; C. Cross (compiled), *York Clergy Ordinations 1510–1519*, Borthwick List and Index 31 (York, 2002), pp. 123, 210; C. Cross (compiled), *York Clergy Ordinations 1520–1559*, Borthwick List and Index 32 (York, 2002), pp. 4, 32, 35, 42, 43, 73, 77, 116, 146, 154, 179, 176, 199, 204, 206, 209, 217; Borthwick Institute for Archives, York Prob. Reg. 9, fol. 216r (Alice Paiteson).

6. Prickett, *Priory Church of Bridlington*, pp. 109–10; *Letters and Papers of the Reign of Henry VIII*, ed. J. S. Brewer, J. Gairdner and R. H. Brodie, 23 vols in 38 (London, 1862–1932), V, no. 725; H. B. McCall (ed.), *Yorkshire Star Chamber Proceedings, II*, Yorkshire Archaeological Society Record Series, 45 (1911), p. 147.

7. *LP Hen. VIII*, IX, nos 670, 1173; *LP Hen. VIII*, X, nos 364 (p. 139), 501, 998; TNA SP1/102, fol. 90r; all these and subsequent references to the priory in the Henrician state papers were first assembled in a pioneering essay by Canon Purvis in 1923: J. S. Purvis, 'The Dissolution of Bridlington Priory', *Journal of the Bridlington Augustinian Society*, 1 (1923), 5–23.

8. *LP Hen. VIII*, XII, pt 1, no. 1019; *LP Hen. VIII*, XII, pt 2, no. 161; Prickett, *Priory Church of Bridlington*, p. 111; C. M. Newman, 'Constable, Sir Robert (1478?–1537), *ODNB*, 13, pp. 22–3.

9. S. E. James, '"Against them all for to fight"; Friar John Pickering and the Pilgrimage of Grace', *Bulletin of the John Rylands University Library*, 85, 1 (2003), 38–46; *LP Hen. VIII*, XII, pt 1, no. 1080.

10. James, '"Against them all for to fight"', 46–7; *LP Hen. VIII*, XII, pt 1, no. 1019.

11. *LP Hen. VIII*, XII, pt 1, no. 1021; James, '"Against them all for to fight"', 48–52, 61, 62, 63, 64.

12. *LP Hen. VIII*, XII, pt 1, nos 1019, 1021; James, '"Against them all for to fight"', 52–6.

13. *LP Hen. VIII*, XII, pt 1, nos 479, 1021; James, '"Against them all for to fight"', 57–60.

14. *LP Hen. VIII*, XII, pt 1, nos 1020 (ii), 1088, 1087 (p. 499), 1019, 1285.

15. John Burton, *Monasticon Eboracense* (York, 1758), p. 203; *LP Hen. VIII*, XII, pt 1, nos 1237, 1257, 1307 (2).

16. *LP Hen. VIII*, XII, pt 1, nos 1307 (2); *LP Hen VIII*, XII, pt 2, nos 34, 82, 92, 234, 432, 1083; Prickett, *Priory Church of Bridlington*, pp. 108–12.

17. *York Clergy Ordinations 1520–1559*, pp. 35, 43, 73, 154, 179, 206, 209, 217, 237; D. S. Chambers, *Faculty Office Registers, 1534–1549* (Oxford, 1966), p. 119.

18. Cross and Vickers (eds), *Monks, Friars and Nuns*, pp. 255, 256, 257, 258, 259, 260.

19. Cross and Vickers (eds), *Monks, Friars and Nuns*, pp. 244, 245–6, 271, 283, 299, 307, 332, 338–9, 341.

20. Purvis, 'The Ripon Carvers', 160, 163, 172; Neave, *Port, Resort and Market Town*, pp. 16, 38–9.

8

Galwegians and Gauls: Aelred of Rievaulx's dramatisation of xenophobia in *Relatio de Standardo**

Marsha L. Dutton

Scholars of Cistercian thought and history portray Aelred, abbot of Rievaulx from 1147 to 1167, as consistent in advocacy for peace and order. The principal historical source for that portrait is the *Vita Aelredi* by Walter Daniel, who quotes Aelred's saying of Rievaulx, 'this house is a holy place because it generates for its God sons who are peacemakers'.[1] Elizabeth Freeman has recently reinforced this view, noting Aelred's opposition to twelfth-century English animosity towards the Celtic people of Scotland:

> At around this time influential 12th-century historians such as William of Malmesbury, Richard of Hexham, and Henry of Huntingdon … were producing literary images of English culture founded on the argument that all Celts … were savage barbaric 'others' … But Aelred painted quite a different picture; for him, the Celtic world was a source of holy exemplars, not of barbarism.[2]

Scottish historians, however, point to a different Aelred. While acknowledging his warm portrayal of Saint Ninian, founder of the Scottish see of Whithorn, in Galloway, they also point to his invective in *Relatio de Standardo* (henceforth Relatio) towards the Galwegians (Latin *Galwenses*), especially those who in the 1138 Battle of the Standard led the Scottish attack against the Anglo-Norman army.[3] William B. Aird, for example, says, 'The exaggerated language employed by Ailred of Rievaulx and his contemporaries to describe the Scots, represents the cultural antipathy that the "civilised" Anglo-Norman elite felt for their Celtic neighbours.'[4]

* Having for many years depended on the astute, meticulous and trustworthy scholarship of Janet Burton, I am honoured to share in celebrating her life and work with this book.

Such views reveal a gap between Aelred's irenic reputation and his xeno-phobic portrait of the Galwegian troops in Relatio. While some scholars have tried to explain his motives, none resolves the problem. Freeman and Mariann Garrity both interpret the work as relevant to monastic values: Freeman states that the work's 'manuscript history spoke very precisely to Cistercian concerns' with the ability of memory, assisted by history, to lead one to God, and Garrity describes Relatio as 'a metaphor for the timeless struggle between good and evil', 'an exquisite metaphor for the monastic life'.[5] Neither considers the extensive Galwegian passages. Aird argues that Aelred wrote to advance the pol-icy of twelfth-century ecclesiastical reform, and Aelred Glidden suggests that the work represents Aelred's desire 'to defend the character of King David of Scotland' from charges showing David as 'a bloody-handed butcher responsible for sacrilege and atrocities'.[6] Similarly Daphne Brooke, writing of 'the con-spicuously central position occupied by Ailred in the vilification of Galloway', adds, 'Ailred performed the feat of preserving David's good name, and he did this partly by scapegoating the Gallovidians.'[7]

Such suggestions fail to reconcile Aelred's horrifying depiction of the Galwegians with the peace-loving author of spiritual treatises. The simple truth may be that the two voices cannot be reconciled – that ignoring the problem is the best way to deal with a shockingly brutal narrative. It is possible, however, to reach towards some understanding of what lies behind Aelred's portrait, recognising it as not merely an attempt to defend David (if that), but above all an effort to resolve the emotional conflict caused by his divided loyalties.

GALLOWAY AND THE GALWEGIANS

Galloway, the home of the Galwegians, is in the Southern Uplands of Scotland, jutting into the Irish seaways with a coastline stretching along the North Channel, Irish Sea and Solway Firth. Ian A. Morrison comments of its location that 'Historically … it seems more profitable to regard Galloway as less of an out-of-the-way corner of Scotland than as an intrinsic part of the Irish Sea province, in terms of economic, political and demographic links.'[8] Not surprisingly, in the ninth and tenth centuries it seems to have drawn immigrants from Ireland, including Scandinavians from Dublin, probably asso-ciated with the Gaelic-speaking people known as Gall-Gaidhel, or 'foreign Gaels'. Edward Cowan explains the name: 'The Irish annals are littered with examples of the word *gall*, stranger, foreigner, non-Gael … the islands of the west became Innse Gall, "the islands of the foreigners".'[9] Brooke says that the ninth-century Gallgaidhil [*sic*] 'were apparently mercenaries – freelance fighters at the disposal of any warlord whose activities promised sufficient plunder …

It was almost to be expected that Gallovidian mercenaries would be operating in the conditions of social breakdown of the mid-ninth century.[10] Richard Oram similarly considers the twelfth-century Galwegians mercenaries for the Scottish kings:

> Throughout the Middle Ages Galloway was seen as a reservoir of military man-power, providing contingents to Scottish and English armies and establishing its rulers as power-brokers in the political manoeuvrings of their day … It could be argued, therefore, that the Galwegians serving in the eleventh- and twelfth-century Scottish armies were present on occasion as hired troops, not as the product of a military levy.[11]

The Galwegians were widely known for their fierce aggression in battle, wearing no armour and few garments but intimidating their enemies by fierce shouts and what Matthew Strickland calls 'the terrifying effect of their wild charges'.[12] Guibert of Nogent, writing of the first Crusade in *Gesta Dei per Francos* (1107–8), describes the Scots – presumably the Galwegians – as 'fierce in their own country, unwarlike elsewhere, bare-legged, with their shaggy cloaks, a scrip hanging from their haunches, coming from their marshy homeland, and presenting the help of their faith and devotion to us'.[13]

THE BATTLE OF THE STANDARD, AND AELRED'S ACCOUNT

On 22 August 1138, during the war over the English throne, King David of Scotland, ostensibly fighting on behalf of the Empress Matilda, his niece, attacked Anglo-Norman troops fighting for Stephen, king of England. The resulting battle took place near Northallerton, about thirty miles from York, with the Scots arrayed against the Anglo-Norman army. The Anglo-Norman troops, summoned by Archbishop Thurstan of York 'to defend the church of Christ against the barbarians' (PL 195: 703), arranged themselves around the standard that gave the battle its name, a ship's mast bearing a pyx with a host and flying the banners of three saints – Saints Peter of York, Wilfrid of Ripon and John of Beverley. As Freeman has said, the army was 'enveloped in a saintly glow'.[14]

The Scottish army, comprised of numerous regional and tribal groups, went in with a clear advantage, outnumbering the Anglo-Norman army about three to one. Having two months earlier resoundingly defeated Stephen's forces at Clitheroe (Lancs), they expected to prevail again here. But in about two hours they were scattered, with the lightly armed Galwegians in the vanguard dispersed by the assault of the Anglo-Norman archers and David pushed back into Scotland, with his son Henry lost behind the English lines.[15]

Aelred probably wrote his *Relatio de Standardo* in the eleven months after the November 1153 signing of the Treaty of Westminster declaring Henry of Anjou heir to the throne but before the death of King Stephen in October 1154.[16] He brought to his account personal familiarity with and obligation to the leaders of both armies. Not only had he spent ten youthful years at the court of Scotland, growing up with Prince Henry and serving David as steward, but he also had long, close relationships with Thurstan of York and Walter Espec. As archbishop of York since 1119, Thurstan had been the ecclesiastical overlord of Aelred's father, residing across the marketplace from the church of St Andrew when he visited Hexham; he may have played a role in arranging a bright future for the priest's capable son.[17] Aelred had presumably also known Walter Espec, the leader of the Anglo-Norman troops, for some time, perhaps from Walter's visits to David's court; Walter Daniel reports that Aelred spent two nights at Walter's manor in Helmsley before his first visit to Rievaulx.[18] Walter's role as Rievaulx's founding patron gave the two men many subsequent years of friendship.

Aelred's is the longest of the three principal twelfth-century English narratives of the battle, with the ones by Henry of Huntingdon and Richard of Hexham; it is an independent treatise rather than, like theirs, a segment in an extended chronicle.[19] The other immediately obvious difference is that while Henry and Richard begin with the battle's background, including the Scots' depredations in the north of England and emphasising the unprovoked nature of their attacks on what Richard repeatedly calls 'the territory of Saint Cuthbert', Aelred leaves such contextual information to be recounted in speeches within the work.[20] He begins with two succinct sentences: 'When King Stephen had occupied the southern districts, the king of the Scots assembled an immense army ... Advancing with great pride and ferocity, he intended either to subdue all the northern part of England or to depopulate it by fire and sword' (PL 195: 701–3). He borrows this beginning from within Henry's account, but whereas Henry specified 'the southern regions of England', Aelred omits *of England*, thereby seeming to imply that rather than being distracted at the other end of the country, Stephen had invaded Scotland, so prompting David's incursion.[21]

Like Aelred's other works, *Relatio* focuses less on events than on dialogue and personal portraiture. By dramatising both sides of the conflict, Aelred introduces his audience to the participants in the battle and allows them to listen in on the speakers' words. Like the other chroniclers, he writes from within the Anglo-Norman camp, emphasising its leaders' holiness of purpose and the righteousness of their cause. But he elides many of the details of the battle, focusing instead on the armies' leaders and the debate among the Scottish warriors.[22] For example, he precedes the first such speech, by the Anglo-Norman Walter Espec, with a cameo view of the man himself, exploring his character and person, introducing him as being 'of penetrating intelligence, prudent in counsel, forbearing in peacetime and farsighted in war' and then describing his appearance and voice before telling of the founding of four monasteries (PL 195: 703). This introduction helps to give his work a dramatic, even cinematic, impact.

AELRED ON THE GALWEGIANS

The most striking aspect of this work's personalising approach is its extended focus on the Galwegians as villains. While Aelred shows King David as almost persuaded by a friend to turn back, he portrays the Galwegians as self-serving, lacking not only virtue but also a rational awareness of their situation. In fact, he makes it clear that by directing their combativeness against their fellow Scottish troops rather than against the opposing army, they cause the defeat of David's army.

The Galwegians enter the narrative not by act but by reputation, with Aelred reserving most of his own description of their actions for the end of the work. Until then, he allows them to be presented in speeches by two Anglo-Normans, Walter Espec and Robert de Brus, speeches separated by a brief dramatic episode in which the Galwegians speak to David, two Scots react, and David makes a fatal error of judgement. The three-part portrait that emerges from this sequence establishes the Galwegians as a composite character in the work's dialogue.

Walter begins by praising King Stephen and warning his troops of the battle's dangers for England, then provides a lengthy graphic exemplum about Galwegian atrocities. The bitter debate among the Scots follows, and finally Robert offers a second lengthy description of Galwegian atrocities, ending with a warning of their threat to the Anglo-Normans and urging David to rid himself and his army of them. The structure of these three passages taken together is chiastic, beginning and ending with statements of the Galwegian threat to England and centred in lengthy descriptions of their atrocities. Much later, Aelred in his own voice describes the Galwegians' frantic retreat and their final act of perfidy.

Before speaking of the Galwegians, Walter Espec urges the Anglo-Normans to battle. He does not claim that they are responding to Scottish aggression, as one might expect, but declares the legitimacy of their king, echoing Stephen's words at the beginning of his coronation charter:

But we are not undertaking an unjust war on behalf of our king, who has not invaded a kingdom not rightfully his,[23] as enemies falsely claim, but who has accepted it as an offering, he whom the people sought, the clergy chose, the pope anointed, and apostolic authority confirmed in his kingdom.[24]

He then alerts his troops to the danger to their country, their wives, their children and their churches 'if the Scots conquer', characterising the Scots as subhuman committers of atrocities:

> I am silent about the slaughter, the rapine, the fires that the enemy employed in something like a human way … They spared no age, no rank, no sex. The high-born, boys as well as girls, were led into captivity. Honourable matrimony was defiled by unspeakable lust. (PL 195: 706)

Although Walter here focuses on the Scots, who are after all the enemy, he at once moves almost imperceptibly into horrific specificity about the Galwegians:

> Little children, thrown into the air and caught on the lance's point, furnished an entertaining spectacle to the Galwegians. A pregnant woman was cut through, and a wicked hand dashed the tender foetus snatched from her womb against the rocks. (PL 195: 706)

As he goes on, he expands his charges to cannibalism, along with a Galwegian mock-Eucharist embedded within the gleeful slaughter of children:

> Wearied by the slaughter of innocents, they cut the meat they were wolfing down with the unwashed knives with which they had sliced out the entrails of the sufferers. Mixing human blood with water, they satisfied their thirst with the cruel cup, calling themselves happy in that fortune had preserved them for the time when they could drink the blood of the Gauls. By chance they found many children in a single house. A Galwegian was standing there; seizing one after another by the foot, he smashed their heads on the doorpost. When he had collected them in a pile, he laughed and said to his friend, 'See how many Gauls I have killed all by myself today!' I shudder to say how they entered the temple of God, how they defiled his sanctuary, how they trampled the sacraments of Christian salvation under their feet. (PL 195: 706)

Here Walter calls particular attention to the Galwegians' paganism and dismissal of their victims as Gauls, 'foreigners'.

Now Walter points out to his troops what their enemies' inhuman acts require of them: 'You are fighting not against men but against beasts! There is no humanity in them, no reverence … the seas have not overwhelmed them for any reason other than to save them for your victories, so that they may die at your hands' (PL 195: 706). He concludes by recalling the king, anticipating the rewards awaiting the victorious army:

> Think of your absent king, how great will be your glory when you report the triumph of a king without the king's presence. Yours will be the court, yours the kingdom; everything will be done by your counsel through whom today a kingdom is sought for the king, peace for the kingdom, and glory for the peace. (PL 195: 706)

Thus the speech ends as it began, reminding all who listen of the Anglo-Normans' glorious purpose.

In the interlude that follows in the Scottish camp, the Galwegians insist on leading the Scots into battle. Aelred sets the scene as David lays out his battle plan, with the armed knights and archers leading the attack. But the Galwegians interrupt, demanding that they be allowed 'to make the first charge against the enemy and to encourage the rest of the army by their prowess'. When David's barons point out the dangers of this tactic, the Galwegians boast of their unstoppable valour, even against armed men:

> 'Why are you afraid, O King?' they said. 'Why do you tremble so much at those iron tunics that you see in the distance? We have iron sides, breasts of brass, and minds devoid of fear; our feet have never known flight, and our backs have never felt a wound … At Clitheroe we brought back a victory over men clothed in mail; today, using strength of mind as our shield, we will overthrow these men too with our lances.' (PL 195: 707)

In reaction to the Galwegians, one of David's supporters, Malise of Strathearn, proclaims his own desire for precedence in battle, casually insulting the Galwegians by calling them Gauls: 'Why is it, O King', he said, 'that you give in to the will of these Gauls [*Gallorum*]? None of those with arms will go into battle today ahead of me, unarmed as I am!'[25] He too claims a place at the front of the battle, declaring his intent also to go forward unarmed. But when Alan de Percy, 'exceedingly able in military affairs', angrily objects, David gives way, letting the Galwegians have their way. Remarkably, then, even though David's barons have argued for placing the armed knights and archers in the lead, 'so that as far as possible knights should contend with knights and archers oppose archers' (PL 185: 707), the Galwegians prevail, with David apparently unable to control his men.[26]

After this conflict comes the second major Anglo-Norman speech, beginning with another venomous diatribe against the Galwegians. When the English Robert de Brus, torn between loyalty to King Stephen and affection for his old friend David, attempts to persuade David to withdraw, he disassociates the Scots and the Galwegians. As Walter had done, he again recalls the vital Anglo-Norman support formerly rendered to the Scots. In contrast, Robert declares, the Galwegians are traditional enemies of the Scots: 'This reliance on the Galwegians is new to you. Today you are attacking with arms those through whom you have up till now ruled, beloved by the Scots and terrible to the Galwegians' (PL 195: 709). He goes on to point out the dangers of including the Galwegians in the Scottish army, echoing Walter Espec's charges to encourage David's repulsion:

> Beware especially of implicating yourself in the sins of wicked men, at whose hands come the slaughter of children, the grief of pregnant women, violence to priests, and contempt for the Godhead itself. Against them not Abel's blood alone but the blood of innumerable innocents cries out from the earth. (PL 195: 709–10)

After a brief pause Robert increases the personal nature of his appeal, with insistent first-person plural pronouns specifying the consequences for the Anglo-Normans – David's own friends and kinsmen – if David's army conquers:

> If you conquer, we will surely die. We will die, I tell you. Our little children will die, our priests will have their throats cut on the altars, our wives will be defiled by shameful lust. We have chosen either to conquer or to die gloriously, although we have no doubt as to the victory. (PL 195: 710)

At no point does Aelred show the Galwegians actually committing atrocities or desiring to do so: he simply relies on the joint power of Walter's and Robert's stories and his audience's predisposition to hate Galwegians. And once he has led that audience to admire Walter and Robert and, with Walter's soldiers, to believe their stories, they too are prepared to fear and despise the Galwegians, and to hope for their defeat.

Once the battle is over, with the Anglo-Normans having decisively destroyed their opponents, Aelred returns for a last time to the Galwegians, now tacitly recalling their earlier boast of invulnerability as their battle charge turns to craven retreat. Whereas Walter and Robert portrayed them as inhuman in their fury, Aelred reduces them to wounded animals:

> The wedge of the Galwegians, shouting harshly three times according to their custom, rushed on the southerners with such force that they drove the first lancers back from their position. But repulsed in their turn by the strength of the soldiers, they then received the courage and power of their foe … You might see a Galwegian stuck all around by arrows like the spines of a hedgehog, but shaking his sword nonetheless, now rushing forward to slaughter the enemy as if in a blind madness, now beating the empty air with futile blows. At last, completely terrified, they melted away in flight. (PL 195: 710–11)

A little later he provides a final view: 'Then the Galwegians, who could not hold out against the shower of arrows and the swords of the soldiers any longer, began to flee, first killing their two leaders, Wigric and Donald' (PL 195: 711). So they leave the scene, revealing in one last act both their pusillanimity and their wickedness.

Aelred did not exhaust his venom towards the Galwegians in Relatio. A year or so later, with Stephen dead and Henry on the throne, he returned to the subject in *De Sanctis Haugustaldensis*, probably initially a sermon given to the Augustinian priors of Hexham on 15 March 1155.[27] This work contains two scenes with the Galwegians again serving kings of Scotland (Malcolm III and then David), and Aelred again portrays them as ruthless adversaries of the English. In both cases, though, they take no action; in their first appearance they are dispersed by the fog through which Saint Cuthbert (d.687) saves the people of Hexham, and in the other case they are mentioned only once, in a scene-setting subordinate clause. Because the focus of this work is the translation of the relics of five bishops of Hexham, the Galwegians function only incidentally, though once again representing the threat of demonic violence against the good people of England.

AELRED'S CONTEXT

Aelred's Relatio raises several questions, the most obvious of which is the date: why does he only write of the battle fifteen or sixteen years afterward? Why does he express such animosity towards the Galwegians? Why does he betray his long affection for David by depicting him as weak-willed, unable to do what is reasonable and right? Why does he go out of his way to insist on Stephen's legitimacy, knowing that Stephen had violated his oath to support Matilda as Henry's heir? Is Relatio merely a political hack job, an attempt to curry favour? Finally, why is Aelred here so unlike his reputation as a lover of peace and charity?

The answer may lie in Aelred's history. His time in the Scottish court must have instilled in him some residue of the hostility created by three centuries of tension between the rulers of Scotland and the people of Galloway, and the Scottish raids on the north of England after the death of Henry I must have resulted in his sharing some of the anti-Scottish sentiment widespread in Northumbria and Yorkshire. Despite his deep affection for David and his family, he too must have struggled with fear and animosity toward the Scottish invaders. So in 1153–4 he revisited that time, now partially displacing these earlier emotions onto a small group of aliens, enemies of both Anglo-Normans and Scots, endeavouring to resolve the conflict between his friendship for King David, Prince Henry and other Scots and his loyalty to his current friends and patrons among the Anglo-Normans. He may even have been reacting against the Galwegian egotism that subverted David's goals and revealed his weakness. As both the Anglo-Normans and the Scots had ample reason to hate these people, long perceived as barbaric, savage and alien, they were an easy target. Perhaps the vituperative passages reveal Aelred's effort to displace his fear for and anger towards his friends onto a group of warriors for hire, fighting only for themselves, ready at a moment's notice to betray foes and friends alike.

All of this is only supposition, of course, with too many instances of *may have* and *must have* to be entirely satisfactory. But the hostility Aelred expresses towards the Galwegians certainly reflects the political and military situation of 1138, as well as his own experience of the danger his homeland faced from people he admired and loved and whom he might still have been serving. But in 1153–4, with the battle long past, the outcome well known and the combatants whom he knew best dead, he obviously needed to revisit that time, and the question was how to do it.

The virulence towards the Galwegians in Relatio that Aelred places on the lips of Walter Espec and Robert de Brus is of course his own – there is no getting around that – but it seems likely to be virulence employed to negotiate and resolve his memories.[28]

Notes

1. Walter Daniel, *The Life of Aelred of Rievaulx*, ed. and trans. Maurice Powicke, Cistercian Fathers Series (hereafter CF), 57 (Kalamazoo, 1994), p. 118.
2. Elizabeth Freeman, 'Aelred as a Historian among Historians', in Marsha L. Dutton (ed.), *Aelred of Rievaulx: A Companion (1110–1167)*, Brill's Companions to the Christian Tradition, 76 (Leiden and Boston, 2017), pp. 113–46 (pp. 136–46).

3. Relatio 1; PL 195: 701–2; 'The Battle of the Standard', in Aelred of Rievaulx, *The Historical Works*, trans. Jane Patricia Freeland and ed. Marsha L. Dutton, CF, 56 (Kalamazoo, 2005), pp. 245–69.

4. William B. Aird, '"Sweet Civility and Barbarous Rudeness": A View from the Frontier, Abbot Ailred of Rievaulx and the Scots', in Steven G. Ellis and Lud'a Klusáková (eds), *Imagining Frontiers, Contesting Identities* (Pisa, 2007), pp. 59–75 (p. 67).

5. Elizabeth Freeman, 'Aelred of Rievaulx's *De Bello Standardii*: Cistercian Historiography and the Creation of Community Memories', *Cîteaux, Commentarii Cistercienses*, 49, 1–2 (1998), 5–28 (10, 13); Mariann Garrity, '"Hidden Honey": The Many Meanings of Aelred of Rievaulx's *De bello standardii*', *Cistercian Studies Quarterly*, 44, 1 (2009), 57–64 (57).

6. Aird, 'Sweet Civility', pp. 60, 67; Aelred Glidden, 'Aelred the Historian: The Account of the Battle of the Standard', in John R. Sommerfeldt (ed.), *Erudition at God's Service, Studies in Medieval Cistercian History, XI*, Cistercian Studies Series, 98 (1987), pp. 175–84 (pp. 175, 182).

7. Daphne Brooke, *Wild Men and Holy Places* (Edinburgh, 1994), p. 99.

8. Ian A. Morrison, 'Galloway: Locality and Landscape Evolution', in Richard D. Oram and Geoffrey P. Stell (eds), *Galloway: Land and Lordship* (Edinburgh, 1991), pp. 1–16 (p. 3). For a careful analysis of the origin of the Galwegians, see Richard D. Oram, *The Lordship of Galloway* (Edinburgh, 2000), pp. 1–9.

9. Edward J. Cowan, 'Myth and Identity in Early Medieval Scotland', *The Scottish Historical Review*, 63 (1984), 111–35 (113).

10. Brooke, *Wild Men*, p. 61.

11. R. D. Oram, 'Fergus, Galloway and the Scots', in Oram and Stell (eds), *Galloway: Land and Lordship*, pp. 117–30 (p. 24).

12. Matthew Strickland, 'Securing the North: Invasion and the Strategy of Defence in Twelfth-Century Anglo-Scottish Warfare', in Matthew Strickland (ed.), *Anglo-Norman Warfare: Studies in Late Anglo-Saxon and Anglo-Norman Military Organization and Warfare* (Woodbridge, 1992), pp. 208–29 (p. 222).

13. PL 156: 686, trans. from A. A. Duncan, 'The Dress of the Scots', *The Scottish Historical Review*, 29 (1950), 201–12; cited by Matthew Strickland, 'Securing the North', p. 223, n. 100. The speech by Walter Espec in Relatio similarly refers to the Scots while describing the Galwegians: 'Who therefore would not laugh rather than fear when the worthless Scot with his nearly bare buttocks runs to fight …?' (PL 195: 705).

14. Elizabeth Freeman, *Narratives of a New Order: Cistercian Historical Writing in England, 1150–1220*, Medieval Church Studies, 2 (Turnhout, 2002), p. 46.

15. For a thorough analysis of the battle, see Jean Truax, *Aelred the Peacemaker: The Public Life of a Cistercian Abbot*, CS, 251 (Collegeville, MN, 2017), ch. 6.

16. For the date of the work, see Marsha L. Dutton, 'Aelred of Rievaulx: Abbot, Teacher, and Author', in Dutton (ed.), *A Companion to Aelred of Rievaulx*, pp. 17–47.

17. See Marsha Dutton, 'The Conversion and Vocation of Aelred of Rievaulx: A Historical Hypothesis', in Daniel Williams (ed.), *England in the Twelfth Century* (London, 1990), pp. 31–49 (p. 39).

18. Walter Daniel, *The Life of Aelred*, p. 99.

19. Henry, archdeacon of Huntingdon, *Historia Anglorum: The History of the English People*, ed. and trans. Diana Greenway (Oxford, 1996); Richard of Hexham, 'De Gestis Regis Stephani et de Bello Standardii', in Richard Howlett (ed.), *Chronicles of the Reigns of Stephen, Henry II and Richard I*, vol. III (London, 1886), pp. 139–99.

20. Richard of Hexham, 'De Gestis', e.g., pp. 158, 161.

21. Henry: *Occupatio igitur rege circa partes australes Angliæ Dauid Scotorum rex innumerabilem exercitum promouit in Angliam* (Henry, *Historia Anglorum*, p. 712); Aelred: *Dominicæ Incarnationis 1138 rege Stephano circa partes australes occupato innumerabilem coegit exercitum* (PL 195: 701–2). Aelred may be intentionally conflating this event with an earlier one in Henry's account: *Rex igitur Stephanus insurgens combussi et destruxit australes partes regni regis Dauid* (Henry, *Historia Anglorum*, p. 711).

22. See John R. E. Bliese's articles: 'Aelred of Rievaulx's Rhetoric and Morale at the Battle of the Standard, 1138', *Albion*, 20, 4 (1988), 543–56; 'The Battle Rhetoric of Aelred of Rievaulx', *Haskins Society Journal*, 1 (1989), 99–107.

23. *qui regnum non … invasit indebitum* (PL 195: 105).

24. The charter begins, *Ego Stephanus Dei gratia, assensu cleri et populi in regem Anglorum electus, et a Willelmo Cantuariensi archiepiscopo et sancte Romane ecclesie legato consecratus, et ab Innocentio sancte romane sedis pontifice confirmatus* ('Charte du Roi Étienne [1136]', in Charles Bémont and Alphonse Picard (eds), *Chartes des Libertés Anglaises [1100–1305]* (Paris, 1892), pp. 8–9).

25. I am grateful to Ronald Greenwald of the University of Liverpool for pointing out to me that the CP translation reads *Galwegians* here (CF 56: 258), although all three manuscripts read *Gallorum*. Mr. Greenwald's letter prompted my study of this topic.

26. Jim Bradbury has noted that the Anglo-Normans used tactics that were not native to the English but had become increasingly common among continental armies ('Battles in England and Normandy, 1066–1154', in Strickland (ed.), *Anglo-Norman Warfare*, pp. 182–93 (p. 193)). It thus seems likely that the Galwegian rejection of the advice of David's military advisors meant that the Scots' strategy was not only foolish but outmoded.

27. Aelred could have written of the Galwegians a third time in his *Vita S. Niniani*, a work probably requested by the church of Whithorn, but in this work he never refers to Galloway or Galwegians and indicates no connection between the people of Ninian's church and the mercenary warriors in the other two works (PL 195: 737–90).

28. Since I wrote this chapter, Domenico Pezzini's critical edition of Relatio has appeared in *Corpus Christianorum, Continuatio Mediaevalis* III, pp. 57–73.

9

The cloister of the soul: Robert Grosseteste and the monastic houses of his diocese

Philippa Hoskin

According to the monastic chronicler Matthew Paris, the actions of Robert Grosseteste (bishop of Lincoln 1235–53) towards the monastic houses of his diocese were those of a tyrant. At the bishop's death, even though Paris reported miracles at Grosseteste's tomb, which suggested the former bishop's sanctity, and noted that the bishop's virtues were greater than his vices, he also felt it right to remind his readers that Grosseteste had, 'made terrible threats against religious persons'.[1] In the years before Grosseteste's death, however, Paris had been less conciliatory. His Great Chronicle had recorded the bishop's 'acts of tyranny'. Grosseteste had unfairly deposed the abbot of Bardney, thus provoking the monks of Canterbury to excommunicate him in return. During his visitation of Ramsey Abbey he destroyed any item that was fastened down, and went through the monks' dormitory, seizing personal possessions, breaking open chests and smashing the precious items stored within them. His treatment of nuns during his visitations shocked Matthew: the bishop had their breasts squeezed to ensure that they were not pregnant.[2] Grosseteste's relationship with the monastic houses of his diocese is a part of the interplay of monastic and episcopal authority. In a volume dedicated to Janet Burton, this is particularly fitting: my experience of working with Janet has been in the English Episcopal Acta project, working on the documents of bishops and the relationship between bishops and monks marries the two parts of Janet's extensive work.

As a Benedictine monk himself, and a member of a house that prized its position outside direct episcopal jurisdiction, Paris could be expected to have viewed Grosseteste's interference in the work of the religious with suspicion. The bishop, however, could not with justice be described as acting tyrannically towards monastic houses. The tyrant was a man who ruled for himself not for others,[3] and Grosseteste saw his interventions in religious houses as very much for the benefit of the monks, nuns and canons there. Whilst Grosseteste was assiduous in his visitation, and he certainly did depose heads of religious houses, his sermons and dicta (notes on lectures and sermons), his letters and administrative records demonstrate that he held the religious in high esteem. Stephenson noted as early as 1899 that Grosseteste's reputation amongst contemporary chroniclers for hating monks and favouring the new orders of friars was undeserved. Rather, whilst he criticised the monastic orders for their 'lax interpretation and observance of their monastic rule', he had a clear vision of the ideal monastic life, and when the religious lived in accordance with their vows he was in fact inclined to champion and protect them.[4]

These explanations of Grosseteste's approach to the religious, however, risk treating them in isolation from the bishop's diocesan work as a whole. They both suggest that Grosseteste held monks and canons to higher standards than he did others in the see, and failed to integrate them fully within his pastoral model. When considered as part of Grosseteste's pastoral strategy, it is clear that the religious were not singled out: the bishop was equally critical of the friars – reprimanding them sharply on occasion[5] – and of the secular clergy. During his parochial visitations he carried out enquiries as searching as those he held in monastic houses and he removed vicars and rectors whose behaviour, or suitability for their posts, was in question. Grosseteste's attitude towards the religious of the see of Lincoln can also be placed in the broader context of his pastoral concerns. There were two dimensions to this concern. First, although these monks, nuns and canons had a far smaller role in the direct provision of pastoral care within the see than did the friars or parish priests, the part they did play could bring them into conflict with the bishop. Secondly, Grosseteste was concerned with the internal pastoral care within these religious houses and with his own role in overseeing that pastoral care. The individual souls of monks, nuns and canons needed the same careful oversight as those of secular clergy and the laity. The spiritual efforts of monks and nuns, seeking a closer union with God, were also a core component of Grosseteste's strategy to bring about the reunion of God with his creation, the overall goal of his pastoral care.

What exactly did Grosseteste aspire to for the religious? Grosseteste's academic and theological work examined the nature and function of the religious, in the context of the Benedictine rule's emphasis on the need for the monk to be separate from the world.[6] As Ginther and Stephenson noted, he emphasised the separation of the religious from the world. The religious should be guided towards a life of prayer. They should take as their model the contemplative Mary not the active Martha.[7] Their meditation might lead them to a direct experience of God, the contact Grosseteste wrote of in his commentary of the 1230s upon the *Mystical Theology* of Pseudo-Dionysius.[8] This life of meditation and prayer was what separated the religious from the secular clergy and would, said Grosseteste, provide them with the light of the sun – the direct experience of God – rather than the secondary light of the moon which could be gained through academic speculation.[9] In his *Sermo ad Religiosis* he describes the religious as needing to be free of worldly desire, not just through the renunciation of property but also by giving up any wish to possess it, and focusing instead on spiritual, rather than temporal, realities. It was the desire for ownership of goods, which demonstrated a continuing connection with the temporal world, that Grosseteste scorned as he smashed the belongings of the monks of Ramsey. Their fastening down of property demonstrated their clinging to the world, rather than a willingness to release themselves from it.[10] The pathway to the perfection of a contemplative life was through obedience: to the head of their house and to their Rule. The religious who practised this would find stability, not through withdrawing from all the practicalities of daily life, but in their attitude to worldly existence. Grosseteste noted that monks asked themselves how, if they separated themselves from the world, they would be able to carry out their daily tasks and ensure that they were fed. A contemplative life, however, he said, involved a permanent mental, rather than physical, dwelling within the cloister. Even when they walked through the world, their minds could remain in contemplation.[11] This was the solitude which Grosseteste says is at the heart of one possible meaning of the word *monachus*. By pursuing this path the religious would reach the life of dedication to prayer, focused on God, which Grosseteste urged in his letter to the monks of Bury St Edmunds in *c.*1238 should be their aspiration.[12] This focus on the spiritual world was not, for Grosseteste, necessary only for the religious. In his *Hexaemeron* he related it to the distinction between *affectus* and *aspectus* (will and reason) arguing that for anyone to obtain genuine spiritual understanding required turning their mind away from their own will and from the material world.[13] For the monk, however, separation from the world was his vocation and his reason for existence. The monk who lived this life would truly reunite his soul in perfection with God and weaken the devil's power.[14]

Yet the religious could not entirely free themselves from material concerns, and Grosseteste still required them to play a practical role in the delivery of his master plan of pastoral care. Grosseteste's pastoral theory had at its heart the idea that it was possible to restore the unity of God and his creation. The salvation of men and women in whom the divine and temporal met could overcome the separation between God and man that had occurred at the fall, perfectly reuniting creator and created.[15] The Church's hierarchy of authority had to play a central part in achieving this end. For Grosseteste, the purpose of this hierarchical arrangement was the effective delivery of pastoral care.[16] His reading of the treatises of Pseudo-Dionysius on the celestial and ecclesiastical hierarchies had helped him to formulate his ideas about the role of all secular ecclesiastics, from the pope down to the parish priest, their purpose being to express God's goodness and mercy to humanity.[17] Whilst the pope and the bishop must consider the spiritual health of their clergy, the parish clergyman had an equal responsibility to his parishioners. Grosseteste describes an unworthy clergyman as spiritually dead, a murderer of souls, an antichrist.[18] Yet the greatest responsibility for the saving of souls belonged to the bishop, and for Grosseteste this meant that he, personally, had the duty of ensuring the quality of pastoral care in the diocese of Lincoln, being ultimately responsible for the salvation of everyone – parishioner, priest or monk – in his very extensive diocese. If he neglected his obligations and allowed, for example, the appointment of an unsuitable parish clergyman, the consequence would be his personal damnation. In writing to William Raleigh, then treasurer of Exeter Cathedral, about his rejection of the ill-educated W. de Grana for a pastoral cure, he declared that if he gave a parish to such a man he would expose himself to hellfire.[19] Nor could he ever depute these responsibilities, for, as he wrote to the dean and chapter of Lincoln, whilst spiritual authority could be shared, it could never be devolved.[20]

Within this network of pastoral care and episcopal obligation the religious houses of the diocese had their place. They played a part, even if not a large one, in day-to-day pastoral care within the Lincoln diocese. It was not only the secular clergy who had a duty towards the salvation of others: everyone had a part to play. Grosseteste was clear that the laity had a role and all those who had patronage of churches had pastoral responsibilities. These lay patrons had the right to present a new clergyman to the bishop in the case of a vacancy in a parish church, and therefore shared the responsibility for the provision of well-educated, experienced and dedicated parish priests who would fulfil their obligations to their parishes and parishioners.[21] Some religious too had a part in practical pastoral care. Those living in communities of canons were often ordained to higher orders and could – and did – act as parish clergy themselves. In such instances they provided the lived example of the parish priest, which could be copied by ordinary men and women, and upon which western pastoral care of the twelfth and thirteenth centuries was built.[22] The monks of the thirteenth century, however, even when they were priests, could not, according to their Rules, preach and teach the laity in the parishes. Nor, even when outside the cloister, do they seem to have been expected to provide a lived example of piety for lay men and women. Although Grosseteste returned to Fleury Abbey unsuitable monks sent by them to their daughter house of Minting, men who were known for their love of property and who had been convicted within the diocese of adultery or violence, he seems to have objected to the poor exempla they offered to other monks rather than to the lessons they may have been teaching the laity.[23]

Houses of monks and nuns, however, were often patrons of benefices, and like lay patrons had a role to play in providing suitable parish clergy, although Grosseteste recognised this with a clear sense of unease. In the diocese of Lincoln their role in selecting parochial clergy was significant: 60 per cent of churches within the see in the mid-thirteenth century were under religious patronage.[24] In this sense, although meant to be separate from the world, these monks and nuns were often very present in it, embedded in the networks of secular obligation in which the granting of benefices played an important part. In their role as patrons they were responsible for providing suitable rectors for their parishes and they seem, usually, to have presented unexceptional clergy, but they also sometimes presented individuals, including clerks related to the house's own secular patrons, who were not ordained to higher orders and thus would not be able to perform their duty as parish priests but would instead need to have a substitute clergyman.[25] Monastic houses developed even closer relationships to parishes when they came into possession of not only the patronage but the rectory itself, and the valuable rectorial tithes, by the process known as appropriation.[26] Since an institution could not actually serve the benefice as rector, another clergyman – a vicar – was put in place. To Grosseteste these vicars were a potential pastoral problem. Although he recognised the need to work within these legally accepted systems of parochial management, including appropriation, he knew that vicars never received the best of the tithes, which went to the rectors, and their poor remuneration tempted them to hold churches in plurality, leaving, as he said, their flock to the mercy of spiritual wolves.[27] As with the presentees of lay patrons, Grosseteste was prepared to reject the doubtfully literate or to make their institutions conditional on future examination.[28]

Religious houses also had responsibility for their own, internal pastoral care; however, a responsibility that they shared with Grosseteste as their bishop. Grosseteste viewed the heads of all kinds of communities as having a duty towards the spiritual welfare of those subject to them: the king for his kingdom; the nobleman for his household; the parish priest for his parishioners.[29] The religious community was no different. The head of the house was its spiritual leader: as the Rule of St Benedict said, they held the place of Christ within the community.[30] In one of his dicta Grosseteste described such a leader as the heart of the tree, the trunk through which spiritual nutrients were drawn. If a monk set aside the authority of his prior or abbot and to attempt to interpret the Rule for himself, he in effect separated himself from the community, and became a withered branch, to be cut off and thrown into the fire.[31] In another dictum the abbot was described as embodying the house: the wills of all its members should be subsumed within his, and the community would then be united in him. Just as the body could not function unless the humours worked together to keep it united, or as a hive could not work if all the bees did not subsume their wills to that of their king,[32] the monastic house must practise that unity which, Grosseteste believed, all nature should aim towards. In this way they would, together, 'serve in chains of peace'.[33] The character and abilities of the head of the house were, therefore, vitally important: they must lead the community by example, just as the parish priest should guide their parishioners. Unlike the parishioners of a parish, however, or even the members of a noble household, the monks, nuns and canons had, through their right of election, a responsibility for the choice of their spiritual leader and this meant that they required particular guidance. To Fleury Abbey, seeking a new prior for their daughter house at Minting, Grosseteste wrote describing what such a man should be: one who sees the truth through the light of God and who has the ability to lead his followers along the road to salvation.[34] Similarly, he urged the canons of Missenden to be careful in their selection of a new head of their house, fearing that they might put less care into their choice than they would that of a new pig-keeper, and reminding them that they were choosing a man who would be responsible for the guidance of their souls.[35]

In keeping with his own sense of episcopal responsibility for pastoral care, it is unsurprising that Grosseteste was careful in overseeing the choice of such heads. He brought monastic houses as far as he could under episcopal authority, following both the instructions of the Fourth Lateran Council – which sought to increase episcopal control over monastic houses – and his own sense of personal obligation.[36] He was clear about what was necessary in the head of a religious house and although his letters above demonstrate that he recognised the communities' rights of election, he exercised fully the episcopal duty of care before confirming these elections and would remove those elected who could not fulfil their duties. Although a number of those he removed had their elections set aside only for technicalities and were almost immediately reinstated, others were removed permanently or refused instalment altogether.[37] It was this sense of his obligation and authority that led Grosseteste to tell Philip of Kyme, secular patron of Kyme Priory, that a layman had no right to choose a new head of a religious house, or to be consulted in that choice, whatever his relationship to that community. The appointment of a suitable abbot was, after all, more important than an individual's claims to authority.[38] Ultimately he believed it to be the bishop's responsibility to ensure good pastoral guidance for the religious as well as for the laity.

Grosseteste's sense of personal obligation towards those in religious houses also stretched beyond the provision of heads of houses, to a concern for each individual member of a religious house. In his dealings with his secular clergy, his belief that he was unable to delegate authority led him to become directly involved in his parishes, through his parochial visitations, which involved the taking of detailed statements under oath from the laity as well as the clergy of his parishes.[39] Similarly, in the religious communities of the diocese he intervened at the level of the individual monk, undertaking the recently established practice of monastic visitation, a degree of attention that led Matthew Paris to express his resentment. In this process he removed heads of monastic houses, but also individual monks: he returned to Fleury Abbey those unsuitable monks sent by them to Minting.[40] He also involved himself in other individual circumstances, becoming personally involved with the case of a former canon of Dorchester, sent away from his own house to Leicester to perform penance, who in his old age wished to return to his former home.[41]

For a thirteenth-century bishop to maintain oversight of the religious houses of his diocese was not unusual, but Grosseteste's care differed in its quality and in the theory of pastoral care which informed it. In his zealous visitations, as in the sermons he preached to monastic houses, Grosseteste's urged upon the religious the separation from the world required of them in their own Rule, through spiritual solitude and contemplation. Also important, however, was the role the religious played in Grosseteste's theory and practice of pastoral care. For those who were not canons, their practical role within the network of pastoral care at parish level that Grosseteste created was limited to their involvement – albeit important – as patrons of particular churches. They were, moreover, within their own communities the recipients of pastoral care, and since they were souls to be saved living within Grosseteste's diocese, in Grosseteste's view, they were his personal responsibility. Just as he concerned himself with individual laymen and women in the parishes, as well as with their parish priests, so his concern for the religious stretched to the individual members of those houses. Grosseteste was not hostile to the religious: in their contemplative lives, striving for unity with God, they were an important part in bringing about the perfect reunion of God and man. It was Grosseteste's understanding of their important work that was behind his acute interest in their affairs.

Notes

1.   Matthew Paris, *Matthaei Parisiensis monachi Sancti Albani Chronica Majora*, ed. H. R. Luard, RS, 7 vols (London, 1872–83), V, p. 419.

2.   *Chronica Majora*, IV, pp. 245–8; V, p. 226.

3. For Grosseteste's examination of this in his commentary on the Nicomachean Ethics by Aristotle, see W. Stinissen (ed.), *Aristoteles Over de Vrienschap: Boeken VIII en IX van de Nicomachische Ethiek met de commentaren van Apasius en Michael in de Latijnse vertaling van Grosseteste* (Brussels, 1963), pp. 38–9.

4. F. Stevenson, *Robert Grosseteste Bishop of Lincoln* (London, 1899), p. 163.

5. For stories in which Grosseteste was driven to refuse to speak to the friars and suspected them of offering a bribe, see James McEvoy, *Robert Grosseteste* (Oxford, 1995), pp. 58–60; James McEvoy, *The Philosophy of Robert Grosseteste* (Oxford, 1982), pp. 43–6; Thomas of Eccleston, *De Adventu Fratrum Minorum in Angliam*, ed. A. G. Little (Manchester, 1951), pp. 91–4, 98–9.

6. *Regula* 4.20; quoted by Grosseteste in a letter to the archbishop of Canterbury (Robert Grosseteste, *Letters of Robert Grosseteste bishop of Lincoln*, ed. F. A. C. Mantello and J. Goering (Toronto, 2010), no. 72*, p. 235; H. R. Luard (ed.), *Roberti Grosseteste Episcopi Quondam Lincolniensis Epistolae*, RS (London, 1861), p. 212).

7. James McEvoy, 'Nostra Conversacio in Celis est (Phil 3:20). Sermo ad religiosos of Robert Grosseteste', in Maura O'Carroll (ed.), *Robert Grosseteste and the Beginnings of a British Theological Tradition* (Rome, 2003), pp. 128–32, 135–7; James McEvoy, 'Maria Optimam Partem (Luc 10:42). A sermon on Martha and Mary attributed to Robert Grosseteste', in O'Carroll (ed.), *Robert Grosseteste and the Beginnings of a British Theological Tradition*, pp. 145–7; Dictum 50, Bodl., MS Bodley 798, fol. 34r.

8. J. McEvoy (ed.), *Mystical Theology: the Glosses by Thomas Gallus and the commentary of Robert Grosseteste on De Mystica Theologia* (Paris, 2003), p. 99.

9. J. R. Ginther, 'Monastic ideals and episcopal visitations: the Sermo ad Religiosos of Robert Grosseteste', in Carolyn Muessig (ed.), *Medieval Monastic Preaching* (Lieden, 1998), p. 239, and see also the edition of the sermon, pp. 249–50.

10. *Chronica Majora*, IV, p. 435.

11. Dictum 135, Bodl., MS Bodley 798, fol. 109r–v.

12. *Letters of Robert Grosseteste*, no. 57, p. 200 (*Epistolae Grosseteste*, p. 173).

13. This phrase recurs repeatedly in Grosseteste's work, see D. A. Callus, 'Robert Grosseteste as Scholar', in D. A. Callus (ed.), *Robert Grosseteste, Scholar and Bishop* (Oxford, 1955), pp. 16, 21; Robert Grosseteste, *Hexaemeron*, ed. Richard C. Dale and Servus Gieben (Auctores Britannici Medii Aevi, British Academy, 1982), part II, ch. IX, 2; *Robert Grosseteste: On the Six Days of Creation: A Translation of the Hexaëmeron*, trans. C. F. J. Martin (Oxford, 1996), Part II, ch. IX, 2; Richard C. Dales, 'The Influence of Robert Grosseteste's Hexaemeron on the Sentences Commentaries of Richard Fishacre O. P. and Richard Rufus of Cornwall O. F. M.', *Viator*, 2 (1971), 293–6; Lawrence E. Lynch, 'The Doctrine of Divine Ideas and Illumination in Robert Grosseteste, bishop of Lincoln', *Mediaeval Studies*, 3 (1941), 168–70.

14. *Letters of Robert Grosseteste*, no. 57, pp. 203–4 (*Epistolae Grosseteste*, pp. 174–6).

15. James R. Ginther, 'Robert Grosseteste's Theology of Pastoral Care', in J. Caskey, A. S. Cohen and L. Safran (eds), *A Companion to Pastoral Care in the Late Middle Ages (1200–1500)* (Leiden, 2010), pp. 95–122.

16. Ginther, 'Monastic ideals and episcopal visitations', p. 239. Writing on Grosseteste's view of hierarchies is extensive and several authors have noted how for him this hierarchy's central importance was to ensure the exercise of pastoral care: an emphasis not found in Pseudo-Dionysius's work. See McEvoy, *The Philosophy of Robert Grosseteste*, p. 121; C. Taylor-Hogan, 'Pseudo-Dionysius and the Ecclesiology of Robert Grosseteste: a Fruitful Symbiosis', in J. McEvoy (ed.), *Robert Grosseteste: New Perspectives on His Thought and Scholarship*, Instrumenta Patristica, 37 (Turnhout, 1995), pp. 189–212, particularly pp. 190–8; Candice Taylor Quinn, 'Robert Grosseteste and the Corpus Dionysiacum: Accessing Spiritual Realities through the Word', in E. A. Mackie and J. Goering (eds), *Editing Robert Grosseteste* (Toronto, 2003), pp. 79–95; Ginther, 'Robert Grosseteste's Theology of Pastoral Care', pp. 107–8; Servus Gieben, 'Robert Grosseteste at the Papal Curia, Lyons, 1250: Edition of the Documents', *Collectanea Franciscana*, 41 (1971), 387. Calendared in W. A. Pantin, 'Grosseteste's Relations with the Papacy and the Crown', in D. Callus (ed.), *Robert Grosseteste: Scholar and Bishop* (Oxford, 1955), p. 213.

17. Candice Taylor Hogan, 'Robert Grosseteste, Pseudo-Dionysius and Hierarchy: a medieval trinity. Including an edition of Grosseteste's translation of and commentary on "De Ecclesiastica Hierarchia"', 2 vols (unpublished PhD thesis, Cornell University, 1991), I, 163–4.

18. For Grosseteste's consideration in 1250, see Gieben, 'Robert Grosseteste at the Papal Curia', 378. Here, although the pope's own position is clearly part of the consideration, it is notable that an archbishop too can be a 'super-tyrant' if he neglects his obligations. The links between the two types of authority were also noted by Pantin, 'Grosseteste's Relations with the Papacy and the Crown', pp. 178–215, particularly p. 212. For the role of the parish priest see quotation from a currently unidentified letter transcribed and translated in Grosseteste, *Letters of Robert Grosseteste*, pp. 12–13 (introduction). Grosseteste also speaks of his horror of the unqualified priest and the harm he can do in his Dicta. See for example Dictum 51, considering the man who undertakes rule of souls without proper understanding, he declares, '*Cum tamen si hic erratur non possessio sola, non vita qualiscumque, sed vita eterna periclitatur. Non sit in vobis tam audax presumpcio.*' Bodl., MS Bodley 798, fol. 38r.

19. *Letters of Robert Grosseteste*, no. 17, p. 96 (*Epistolae Grosseteste*, p. 65).

20. *Letters of Robert Grosseteste*, no. 127, pp. 376–7, 380, 381–2, 396 (*Epistolae Grosseteste*, pp. 360–1, 364–5, 369–370).

21. Philippa Hoskin, 'Robert Grosseteste and the simple benefice: a novel solution to the complexities of lay presentation', *Journal of Medieval History*, 40 (2014), 24–43.

22. Caroline Walker Bynum, *Jesus as Mother* (Cambridge, 1984), pp. 16–19. For Grosseteste's own expression of this see Dicta 50, 51, 90 and 101, Bodl., MS Bodley 798, fols 30r, 37v, 67r–v, 82v–3r.

23. *Letters of Robert Grosseteste*, nos 53, 108, pp. 193–5, 336–8 (*Epistolae Grosseteste*, pp. 166–8, 318–21).

24. David M. Smith, 'The Administration of Hugh of Wells, Bishop of Lincoln 1209–1235', 2 vols (unpublished PhD thesis, University of Nottingham, 1970), II, 40.

25. Philippa M. Hoskin (ed.), *Robert Grosseteste as Bishop of Lincoln: the episcopal rolls 1235–1253*, Kathleen Major Series of Medieval Records, 1 (Woodbridge, 2015), no. 1792 (for Tewkesbury Abbey's institution of one of the Clare family, its patrons, as rector of Great Marlow even though the candidate does not seem to have been ordained to higher orders); nos 145, 213 (for nominees judged illiterate and subject to later examination).

26. See, for example, J. H. Denton and Philippa M. Hoskin (eds), *English Episcopal Acta 43: Coventry and Lichfield 1215–1256* (Oxford, 2015), nos 20 (where the church of Alspath is appropriated to Coventry Priory following the loss of their books); 23 and 27 (the appropriation of the chapel of Osmanton and Scarcliffe church to Darley Abbey to help maintain their hospitality); 41 and 42 (the appropriation of King's Newnham and St Mary, Kenilworth churches to Kenilworth Priory for the same purpose).

27. Gieben, 'Grosseteste at the Papal Curia', 375.

28. Hoskin (ed.), *Robert Grosseteste as Bishop of Lincoln: the episcopal rolls 1235–1253*, nos 132, 145, 187, 1045, 1290, 1415, 1422, 1433, 1438, 1457, 1609, 1623, 1965.

29. *Letters of Robert Grosseteste*, no. 124, p. 367 (*Epistolae Grosseteste*, pp. 348–9) for Grosseteste's letter to the king about his duties. See also his letter to Margaret de Quincy, countess of Winchester, emphasising her responsibility for the sins of her bailiff (*Letters of Robert Grosseteste*, no. 5, p. 70 (*Epistolae Grosseteste*, p. 38: '*ne ministorum vitium congrua severitate non repressum, vobis reputetur in peccatum*')) and his advice to the countess of Lincoln about setting an example to her household (Robert Grosseteste, 'Les Reules Seynt Roberd', in Dorothea Oschinsky (ed.), *Walter of Henley, and Other Treatises in Estate Management and Accounting* (Oxford, 1971), pp. 121–45).

30. *Regula* 63:13, quoted by Grosseteste in a letter to the archbishop of Canterbury (*Letters of Grosseteste*, no. 72*, p. 233; *Epistolae Grosseteste*, p. 212).

31. Dictum 115, Bodl., MS Bodley 798, fol. 95r–v.

32. Until the mid-sixteenth century hives were thought to be led by kings rather than queens and were often held up as ideal, ordered communities, suitable to be imitated by kingdoms and also often by monastic communities; see Fiona J. Griffiths, *The Garden of Delights: reform and renaissance for women in the twelfth century* (Philadelphia, 2007), p. 72; Renato G. Mazzolini, 'Adam Gottlob Schirach's Experiments on Bees', in J. D. North and J. J. Roche (eds), *The Light of Nature: essays in the history and philosophy of science presented to A. C Crombie* (Dordrecht, 1985), pp. 167–8.

33. Dictum 135, Bodl., MS Bodley 798, fol. 110r. On Grosseteste and the unity of nature, see Ginther, 'Robert Grosseteste's Theology of Pastoral Care', pp. 107–8.

34. *Letters of Robert Grosseteste*, no. 54, pp. 195–6 (*Epistolae Grosseteste*, pp. 169–71).

35. *Letters of Robert Grosseteste*, no. 85, pp. 287–9 (*Epistolae Grosseteste*, pp. 268–70).

36. N. P. Tanner, *Decrees of the Ecumenical Councils. From Nicaea I to Vatican II* (London and Washington DC, 1990), Fourth Lateran Council, canons 12–13.

37. Hoskin (ed.), *Robert Grosseteste as Bishop of Lincoln: the episcopal rolls 1235–1253*, nos 115, 145, 147, 183, 213, 368, 382, 397, 684, 1328, 1344, 1642, 2008.

38. Grosseteste claimed in the same letter to have rejected candidates presented by the king as heads of religious houses as well, *Letters of Robert Grosseteste*, no. 30, pp. 142–4 (*Epistolae Grosseteste*, pp. 116–17).

39. On Grosseteste's parochial visitations, see F. M. Powick and C. R. Cheney (eds), *Councils and Synods with other documents relating to the English Church II AD 1205–1313* (Oxford, 1964), pp. 261–5, 470; *Chronica Majora*, V, pp. 226–7, 256–7; H. R. Luard (ed.), *Annales Monastici*, 5 vols, RS (London, 1864–9), IV, pp. 579–80.

40. *Letters of Robert Grosseteste*, nos 53 and 108, pp. 193–5, 336–8 (*Epistolae Grosseteste*, pp. 166–8, 318–21).

41. *Letters of Robert Grosseteste*, no. 55, pp. 196–7 (*Epistolae Grosseteste*, pp. 169–71).

10

The abbey of St Benet of Holme
and the English Rising of 1381

Andrew Prescott

Some of the most dramatic and violent events of the great revolt in England in 1381 took place in what Trenholme called the monastic boroughs, such as St Albans, Bury, Dunstable and Abingdon, where there was longstanding resentment among townsfolk at the control exerted by local religious houses.[1] In St Albans, the inhabitants of the town went to London to seek support against the abbey from Wat Tyler and forced the abbot to grant them a new charter. In the brutal suppression of the revolt, many leading townsfolk of St Albans were hanged. At Bury St Edmunds, the ancient enmity between the town's population and the abbey meant that the Suffolk rebels led by the chaplain John Wraw were welcomed into the town. The prior of Bury and the monk who administered the abbey's estates were beheaded, and documents and jewels of the abbey were seized. The inhabitants of Bury were afterwards excluded from the amnesty for the rebels, and a fine was imposed on them which took five years to pay. In Bedfordshire, the prior of Dunstable was forced during the revolt to concede a charter to the town.[2] While there do not appear to have been large-scale disturbances in Abingdon, orders were nevertheless issued for the arrest of seven inhabitants of Abingdon for insurgency.[3]

The motives of the townsfolk of St Albans, Bury and Dunstable for joining the rising are often portrayed as somehow different to those of the bulk of the rebels. They are seen as allies of the rebels who took advantage of the breakdown of law and order to pursue their own local interests.[4] Yet it is difficult to differentiate sharply between the grievances of the townsfolk and the rural insurgents. The townsfolk of St Albans bitterly resented their designation as bondsmen by the monks, and their demands for common pastures and fisheries and the right to grind their own corn were similar to those voiced by rural insurgents. Likewise, the action of the mayor and inhabitants of Cambridge in destroying enclosures erected by Barnwell Priory on land claimed as commons by the town is difficult to distinguish from attempts by rural insurgents to claim land and fisheries as commons.

In exploring the relationship between urban and rural participation in the revolt, an examination of the attacks on religious houses and orders provides a useful case study. While urban disturbances such as those in St Albans and Bury have received considerable attention, there has been far less interest in attacks on monasteries in more rural areas. One of the largest attacks on a monastery during the rising of 1381 was on the small Benedictine foundation of St Benet of Holme in Norfolk, which stood in an isolated setting over-looking marshland on the River Bure and whose estates were concentrated in the east of the county.[5] An analysis of the disturbances connected with the abbey of St Benet of Holme illustrates the complexity of the structure of the rising. While the attacks on the abbey were largely directed against its role as a landowner, the activities of rebel leaders involved in these incidents suggest a close connection with urban insurgents in towns such as Norwich and an awareness of wider political and social grievances. The potency of the rising arose from the way in which it fused various traditions of protest across a range of social groups in both country and town.

Monastic and religious orders were among the most prominent victims of the rising. One of the first major attacks in Kent occurred on 3 June when a group of rebels from Erith burst into Lessness Abbey, an Augustinian house, and forced the abbot to swear to support the rising.[6] As the rising developed in Kent, the tenants of the prioress and convent of Dartford withdrew their services[7] and the tenants of the abbess of Malling forced her to release them from their obligations.[8] The prior of the Augustinian house at Combwell was compelled to give one of the rebels a horse.[9] Across the county border in Surrey, tenants of the prior of Christ Church Canterbury at Merstham occupied a wood that they claimed as commons.[10] When the rebels arrived in London, they not only destroyed the preceptory of the Hospitallers at Clerkenwell Priory and burst into Westminster Abbey to seize and kill the unpopular gaoler Richard Imworth,[11] but also destroyed forges belonging to the Hospitallers in Fleet Street,[12] while a group of Londoners forced the Cistercian abbot of St Mary Graces to make them grants of land.[13] In Middlesex, the tenants of Harmondsworth Priory threatened to kill the prior and burn the priory, and burnt the foundation charter, court books and other records of the priory.[14] The records of the prior of Bury's manor at Sawbridgeworth were also burnt.[15]

In Essex, a group of men from Brightlingsea and St Osyth burst into the abbey there on 16 June, burnt the court rolls and other records of the abbey, imprisoned the abbot for three days and assaulted the abbey's parker and collector of rents so badly that they could not work again for four years.[16] Rebels also burst into the abbeys of Barking, Stratford Longthorne and Waltham Holy Cross and burnt records. The preceptory of the Hospitallers at Cressing

Temple was destroyed and at Ingatestone records of the Hospitallers' property there were burnt.[17] Among other records destroyed were those belonging to the prior of Bury at Harlow,[18] the abbot of Westminster at Moulsham,[19] the prior of Christchurch Canterbury in Bocking, Prittlewell and Southchurch, St Mary's Priory at Wivenhoe[20] and the prior of St Bartholomew Smithfield at Clavering.[21] In Cambridgeshire, rebel leaders made proclamations from the pulpit of Ely Abbey,[22] and property of the Ely monks at Wratting and Wentworth was attacked.[23] There was particular hostility towards the Hospitallers in Cambridgeshire, with attacks on their property at Shingay, Chippenham and Duxford.[24] In Suffolk, as well as the rising in Bury, the records of the Augustinian house of Butley were destroyed.[25] Further afield, there were attacks on the Hospital of St John in Bridgwater in Somerset, Breadsall Priory in Derbyshire was attacked, and tenants of the abbot of Chester and the prior of Worcester withheld their services.[26]

In many of these cases, these attacks were not primarily due to antipathy towards monasteries but were instead part of a general protest against large landowners. This is vividly illustrated in Harmondsworth, where the threats against the prior and the destruction of the priory's records were the culmination of a dispute between the priory and its tenants which stretched back to the thirteenth century.[27] The 1370s had seen a resistance campaign by the tenants against the prior which included refusal to take part in haymaking and harvesting, trespassing in the prior's woods and poaching in his ponds. Similarly, the attack on Breadsall Priory in Derbyshire was a consequence of a long-running dispute between the Stahum family and John of Gaunt over the ownership of the manor of Morley.[28] Considering whether the attacks on Hospitaller properties such as Cressing Temple were due to the unpopularity of the Master of the Hospitallers, Robert Hales as treasurer or antagonism towards the order itself, Helen Nicholson came to the conclusion that 'As a religious order, the Hospital came under attack for the same reason as other religious orders in England: because it was a landowner and many of its tenants held by unfavourable terms.'[29] This judgement seems to hold true for most of the attacks on monasteries in 1381.

The most widespread attacks against religious houses and clergy took place in Norfolk which was probably the county most badly affected by violence in 1381. On 18 June, rebels threatened Margery de Inges, the prioress of Carrow Priory near Norwich, and forced her to hand over the priory's records which were burnt.[30] On 19 June, another group entered the abbey of West Dereham and took valuables worth £100 belonging to John de Methwold, a steward of John of Gaunt, stored there.[31] The prior of Coxford was assaulted by a group of six armed men,[32] and money was violently extorted from the prior of Bromholm,[33] as well as from the Master of the Hospital of St John at Carbrooke.[34] Records were burnt belonging to the abbot and convent of Bury at Southery and Aylsham,[35] the prior of Binham at Thorpe Market,[36] the prior of Long Bennington at Field Dalling,[37] the prior of Bromholm at Bacton[38] and the prior of Hickling.[39] The largest of these attacks in Norfolk was at the abbey of St Benet of Holme where between 18 and 20 June the abbot and monks were forced to surrender records which were burnt in what André Réville described as 'an unrelenting war on parchment'.[40] The records of the abbey's estates at Antingham, Great Hautbois, Horning, Neatishead with Irstead, Potter Heigham, Thurne, Ashby, Thurgarton and North Walsham were destroyed.[41] When the bishop of Norwich began to take military action against the rebels, the abbot and monks were again threatened and the disturbances there were sufficiently serious that when the earl of Suffolk's commission began its judicial action against the rebels, special sessions were held at the nearby town of Horning.

The ecclesiastic targets selected by the rebels were not exclusively monastic. The secular clergy also suffered. William de Ellerton, the parson of Thursford, was denounced as a traitor in a bill presented to the Norfolk rebel leader Geoffrey Lister, apparently because he was suspected of offering shelter to John Holkham, a local Justice of the Peace who was hated by the rebels.[42] Houses belonging to the bishop of Norwich at Hevingham in Norfolk and to the archdeacon of Norwich at Cawston were attacked.[43] A group of insurgents led by a local carpenter entered the church of Tottington while the vicar was there and forced him to pay 40 s. by threatening him with beheading.[44] The vicars of Egmere and Hainford were also threatened with beheading unless they paid a fine,[45] and the vicar of Mattishall was assaulted.[46] Goods were also seized from the rectory of Wickmere.[47]

As with the monasteries, the attacks on secular clergy do not seem to have been directed against them as representatives of the church, but were due to their position as landholders and their connections with a corrupt county elite. For example, the attack on the parson of Thursford was prompted by his friendship with an unpopular local justice. Likewise, the attack on the parson of Skeyton was apparently directed against his role as a landlord. A group of men from the village broke into the parson's property, took goods and chattels worth £40 and burnt his charters, writings, rentals and other muniments.[48]

Samuel Cohn and Douglas Aiton have emphasised the prominence of minor clergy and clerks among the insurgents, and suggest that the participation of clergy was a distinctive feature of popular protest in Britain compared with Europe.[49] These clerical participants included the Suffolk rebel leader, John Wraw, said to have been formerly parson of Ringsfield in Suffolk,[50] and Geoffrey Parfray, vicar of All Saints Sudbury.[51] In Norfolk, William de Quynburgh, chaplain of Scottow, imprisoned Brother John de Repas until he made a fine for his release and also killed Hugh Avelin of Hautbois because he had criticised the theft of goods by the rebels.[52] The extent to which clerical participants in the revolt were motivated by religious concerns requires further investigation, but cases like that of David Calveley and Nicholas Frompton, papal provisors who used the revolt to try and advance their claims, suggest that issues of personal advancement loomed large for some of these clergy.[53]

For a long time, historians regarded the rising in Norfolk as random pillage. Barrie Dobson declared that the revolt in Norfolk consisted of '"village ruffianism" … rather than any attempt to express common political and social grievances'.[54] However, as subsequent studies by Andy Reid and Herbert Eiden have emphasised, this is not an accurate view.[55] The disturbances in Norfolk were extremely widespread, but the Norfolk rebels were well coordinated and selective in their choice of targets.

The rising spread into Norfolk from 14 June 1381 through contact with rebels in Suffolk and Cambridgeshire on the southern and western borders of the county.[56] Three major bands have been identified as active in the south and west, rapidly criss-crossing the area. The movements of these rebel bands are reminiscent of the chevauchées used by the English in France, and may reflect military experience. The political and social grievances of these bands are apparent from their choice of targets, which included John of Gaunt's manors at Methwold and Hilgay, property of John Methwold, one of Gaunt's stewards, and Edmund Gurnay, a Justice of the Peace and chief steward of Gaunt in Norfolk who fled for his life in a boat. Insurgents in south and west Norfolk came together on 17 June for a major attack on the property of John Reed, an unpopular poll tax collector and money lender, at Rougham. These bands in south and east Norfolk also formed links with townsfolk in King's Lynn who had joined the rising, who helped spread the rising in the north and the county.

Meanwhile, from 14 June onwards, agitators had been making proclamations in such places in north and east Norfolk as Scottow and Swanton Abbot in the name of Geoffrey Lister, a dyer from Felmingham, urging the people to rise up.[57] On 18 June, Lister was at the head of a large assembly on Mousehold Heath containing not only insurgents from many places in east and north Norfolk but also some members of the bands that had been active in south and west Norfolk. Again, this suggests complex and sophisticated coordination which might recall the experience of the chevauchée. Among those who joined Lister at Mousehold was Sir Roger Bacon, a member of the local gentry who was aggrieved about a property transaction and had recently been recruited to raise a retinue for the unsuccessful attempts to send an armed force to relieve the earl of Buckingham in Brittany.[58] This rebel army captured and killed the soldier Sir Robert Salle, whose family were from Norwich.[59]

Walsingham claimed that the citizens of Norwich paid Lister's men a large sum of money to prevent them ransacking the city.[60] While the trouble in Norwich was apparently not on the scale of that in towns like Bury or Cambridge, Reginald Eccles, a JP, was nevertheless seized and beheaded and his property attacked,[61] and houses of Robert Salle were destroyed.[62] There was a large-scale attack on the house of a prominent citizen of Norwich, Henry Lomynour, a former bailiff of Norwich who in 1378 had negotiated with parliament over the issue of a new charter for the town which gave much more power to elite citizens.[63] Money was also seized from Walter Bixton, another former bailiff who had accompanied Lomynour in the 1378 negotiations over the new charter.[64]

On the following day, 18 June, Lister and Bacon entered Yarmouth, to the south of Norwich, where they seized a charter that was resented locally because of the control it gave Yarmouth over the herring fisheries. They tore the charter in two, sending one half to John Wraw and his associates in Suffolk. Bacon ordered that customs should be collected in the disputed port of Kirkley Road. The local prison was opened and four prisoners, three of them Flemings, were beheaded. The houses of Hugh Fastolf and William Ellis, whose oppressions had been the subject of complaint in the Good Parliament,[65] were attacked and customs and other records kept there were destroyed.[66]

In the days after the killing of Salle and Eccles at Norwich, north and east Norfolk were engulfed by widespread disturbances. The events in Norwich were the signal for an immense uprising, propagated by those who had been in the 'great society' on Mousehold Heath. The attacks on the abbey and manors of St Benet of Holme were the focal point of these protests. There appears to have been a systematic and coordinated attack on the abbey's infrastructure, with the burning of records apparently intended to bring the administration of the abbey's lands to a halt.

Most of our information about the attacks on the abbey comes from the proceedings of a commission under the earl of Suffolk against the rebels in Suffolk and Norfolk issued on 24 June 1381.[67] This commission was ordered to make public proclamations against the rebels and to chastise and punish the realm according to the law of the realm and the careful consideration of the commissioners. This gave the commissioners the power to override due legal process if they thought it necessary. The commissioners began their work in Suffolk where they held sessions between 27 June and 3 July. Their first session in Norfolk was held at Norwich on 6 July. They then gave priority to the disturbances in the area around St Benet of Holme, holding a session at Horning on 9 July and another at nearby Hickling on 15 July.[68] The way in which these proceedings verged on vengeance is reflected in the composition of the jury at Horning which was headed by John Fastolf, who took the opportunity to make accusations against one of his own servants concerning the attack on his house at Caister.[69]

The commissioners used their power to proceed in an extra legal fashion to make arrest and executions on the basis of allegations by single individuals. At their session at Horning, John Mundeford, the steward of the abbey of St Benet of Holme, appeared and claimed that John Thomson and John Ellis of Horning on 18 June 1381 had gone to the abbey with others in a warlike fashion and threatened the abbot and monks with death and the burning of their property unless they gave them the abbey's court rolls and other muniments. The abbot handed over the documents, and Thomson and Ellis had then burnt the court rolls and muniments at Horning. The sheriff had arrested the two men, who were brought before Thomas Morreux, one of the commissioners. They acknowledged that they had burnt these court rolls, and were beheaded.[70]

Other indictments taken by the commissioners indicate that Thomson and Ellis did not act alone. The indictments suggest that there may have been successive attacks on the abbey on 18, 19 and 20 June, but jurors seem often to have been hit and miss in the accuracy of their dating and it may be that all these indictments refer to a single incident. What is clear is that there was a sustained attempt to burn the records of the abbey and that these burnings often took place in public rituals. An indictment from Happing Hundred states that a group of rebels from Potter Heigham, Scottow, Ludham, Dilham and elsewhere, including a number of men such as John, son of Alice Chamber of Potter Heigham, Adam Martin and Henry Reyse of Dilham who had been at Norwich and participated in such events as the killing of Salle and Eccles, entered the abbey of St Benet of Holme on 20 June 'with various people from divers hundreds' and forced the abbot, William de Methwold, to give up all custumals, rentals, court rolls and muniments, which they burnt at Horning.[71] One of these men, Alan Dix of Potter Heigham, was accused of forcing the abbot to hand over records on 19 June, and was said to have been a chief burner of books and muniments pertaining to the manors of Sutton, Hickling and Ingham. Unlike Thomson and Ellis, Dix was granted a jury trial, but was found guilty and beheaded.[72]

The public and ritual character of the burning of these records is apparent from an indictment against Robert Capoun who was accused of going to the market at Hickling to persuade the local inhabitants to join him in the burning of the charters, court rolls, accounts and other evidences of the manor of Ingham.[73] The date given for this incident by the indictment (28 June) is surprisingly late, but the public nature of the action is very clear. Given the complex manorial structures in Norfolk, it is frequently difficult to tie reports of the burning of documents in the indictments to particular landowners, but Herbert Eiden has calculated that records of the abbey's property were destroyed for Antingham, Great Hautbois, Horning, Neatishead with Irstead, Potter Heigham, Thurne, Ashby, Thurgarton and North Walsham.[74] He suggests that records of the abbey at Ludham were also destroyed.[75] This shows how the destruction of the records of the abbey was not restricted to those seized from the abbey itself but also involved documents held locally in its manors.

The abbot initiated some private actions of trespass arising from the abbey's losses in the revolt. Many such private actions of trespass did not reach trial, but can be identified in notes of the mesne process designed to compel the defendants to appear in court from references to the burning of records.[76] The abbot brought four such actions, all in the plea side of the court of King's Bench. He brought a plea of trespass against John atte Wood of Catfield and Adam atte Wood stating that they broke a close of the abbot at Horning and took charters, writings, court rolls, rentals and other muniments, which they burnt. Proceedings were started to outlaw John and Adam, but they do not seem ever to have appeared to answer the abbot.[77] The abbot also brought a trespass case against John Bettes, probably from North Walsham and not to be confused with John Bettes or Creek of Wymondham who was allegedly a prominent rebel leader elsewhere in Norfolk.[78] The abbot claimed that John Bettes and Martin Rust had broken into property of the abbot at Horning, North Walsham and Antingham and taken court rolls, rentals and other muniments. Again, the abbot was unsuccessful in getting Bettes to appear to answer his case.[79]

These first two trespass cases brought by the abbot of St Benet of Holme are very typical of private litigation relating to the revolt, both in their distinctive reference to the burning of records and their failure to secure the appearance of the defendants. This raises the question of what private litigants such as the abbot of St Benet hoped to achieve by their prosecutions. While a successful trespass action might have brought some monetary compensation for losses incurred during the revolt, it offered no assistance in reconstituting lost documents. It is striking that the abbot brought far fewer trespass actions after the revolt than other victims of the rising such as Henry Lomynour in Norwich who prosecuted over 600 people over the destruction of his property in Norwich.[80] This may reflect the fact that the abbey of St Benet of

Holme had not suffered the kind of capital loss experienced by Lomynour in Norwich. It may also be that the relatively poor house of St Benet had to be more cautious about running up large legal bills.

The other two trespass cases brought by the abbot of St Benet of Holme perhaps offer some hints as to what the abbot hoped to gain from these prosecutions. The abbot brought a case against William Swinebrook, the parson of Bylaugh, and Thomas Grave of Ludham alleging that they broke closes of the abbot at Horning and Ludham.[81] At Ludham, they took six horses, eight oxen and three cows worth 10 s., while at Horning they took goods and chattels worth 20 s. and burnt charters, rolls and other memoranda. William and Thomas never appeared to answer the case against them, but their removal of livestock said to have been owned by the abbey has the appearance of an incident relating to a dispute over the use of land for common grazing or the retention by the abbot of livestock for tenurial offences. The abbot would have been anxious not to lose ground in such matters and this may have been the reason why he brought this prosecution.

Tenurial disputes also perhaps explain the prosecution brought by the abbot through his attorney William Balsham against Clement Paston and Roger Leech alleging that on 20 June 1381 at North Walsham they seized goods belonging to the abbot including timber and wool as well as court rolls, feodaries and rentals, which they took and carried away. They also assaulted the abbot's servants there, namely Robert Thurkeld, John Walsingham and Richard Cok, injuring them so that the abbot lost their service for a month.[82]

The defendant in this action was presumably the Clement Paston identified in a fifteenth-century memorandum as a ploughman who was the great-grandfather of Sir John Paston.[83] Clement Paston's appearance as one of those attacking the property of the abbot of St Benet during the rising provides a striking illustration of the way in which many of the insurgents were from the aspirational members of the village elite. Clement afterwards made an advantageous marriage and was able to send his son William to an expensive school. At his death in 1419 he left bequests to Bromholm Priory and other churches in the area. Nevertheless, the suggestion that Clement was a bond tenant dogged the Paston family for generations. The fact that Clement was already quite well off in 1381 is shown by the fact that he was represented in the trespass case brought against him by the abbot of St Benet by the attorney Henry Lessingham.

Clement claimed that he was not guilty of the allegations brought against him. Attempts to persuade a jury to appear in the King's Bench to pronounce of the case dragged on until at least 1387 and it was never resolved. However, the fact that Clement and Roger were accused of taking timber and wool belonging to the abbot suggests that their actions in 1381 may possibly have been connected with an attempt to pasture sheep on common land and treat woods as common. By about 1413, Clement was pasturing his animals on the prior of Bromholm's commons at North Walsham and fishing the prior's fishponds.[84] It looks as if his actions in 1381 may have been an attempt to exercise similar rights on the abbey of St Benet's lands. A determination to resist such claims might explain the abbot's willingness to bring an ultimately fruitless prosecution over the incident.

The trespass prosecutions brought by the abbot of St Benet following the rising again suggest that the disturbances there were chiefly protests against the abbey's role as landowner. However, the most frightening time of the rising for the small abbey on the banks of the River Bure was yet to come. By 20 June, the bishop of Norwich with a small armed force had taken military action against rebels in Cambridgeshire and had reached the Suffolk border.[85] Lister had ordered three of his supporters to go to London with two knights he was holding hostage in order to negotiate with the king. Meeting Lister's deputation, the bishop killed the rebels and freed the knights. He then pressed on into Norfolk.

According to an indictment from Tunstead hundred,[86] during the night of 21 June, about 400 men, led by William Kimberley, a carter of the abbey of St Benet, and the son and brother of John Chamber of Potter Heigham who had been involved in the burning of documents at Horning, surrounded the abbey. They wished to use the stronghold of the abbey to hold out against the bishop when he arrived. The monks had been at matins when the rebel army appeared but they abandoned their prayers and armed themselves, staying up for the rest of the night to protect the abbey. Herbert Eiden suggests that this attack reflected resentment at the abbey's connections with Despenser,[87] but there is no evidence of any particularly strong connection of the abbey with the bishop. It is likely rather that this incident reflected the fact that the abbey was a key strategic point in the area and would be a valuable asset in any resistance by the rebels against the bishop.

The way in which the abbey got caught up in attempts to rally resistance against the bishop of Norwich emphasises how the attacks at St Benet of Holme cannot be considered in isolation. The economic, social and cultural networks of the abbey were disrupted in many directions. The neighbouring priory of Hickling also suffered the loss of its records for land in Hickling, Sea Palling and Horsey.[88] Other associates of the abbey suffered losses, such as John Fastolf whose house at Caister was attacked by a mob led by Robert Stronghobbe, one of Fastolf's own servants, who stripped the lead from the house.[89] The abbey had property in Norwich, and cannot have regarded events there with equanimity.

While the attacks on the abbey of St Benet of Holme seem on the surface to have been primarily directed against its role as landowner, how do the events at the abbey fit into the structure of the rising as a whole in Norfolk? Should we see it as completely disconnected from urban grievances in towns like Norwich or King's Lynn? It is tempting to see the war on parchment in places like Horning and North Walsham as the aftermath of the dramatic events in Norwich. However, closer examination suggests complex cross-currents and connections between the two, and illustrate how in interpreting the 1381 revolt we should be wary of creating a false polarity between country and town.

As has been noted, the assembly on Mousehold Heath was preceded by a period of intensive activity in which the rising was proclaimed at various venues in north and east Norfolk. A jury from South Erpingham hundred declared that on 14 June at Scottow, Swanton Wood and elsewhere John Watts of Scottow, John Gentilhomme, Richard Filmond and others had made proclamations from town to town in the name of Geoffrey Lister.[90] The jurors from Happing hundred at the sessions in Horning also identify these men as having made proclamations and congregations from town to town to encourage congregations, risings and rumour.[91] Another name frequently mentioned in connection with these agitators was John Chamber of Potter Heigham. Watts, Gentilhomme, Filmond and Chamber all took part in the seizure of the records of the abbey of St Benet, and John Chamber was said to have sought to rally resistance against the bishop of Norwich.[92]

One Norwich jury provides an intriguing and circumstantial account of the death of Reginald Eccles which suggests that it was a carefully stage-managed execution and that the abbey of St Benet played a role in these events.[93] It states that Adam Pulter of Potter Heigham, Thomas Aslake, a cordwainer of Norwich, and John Norwich, a cook, seized Eccles while he was at the abbey's manor in Potter Heigham. They took him back to Norwich, then led him to a pillory which had been set up for the occasion before the great gathering at Mousehold. Thomas Aslake stabbed Reginald through the heart with a dagger and Henry Reyse of Dilham then beheaded him. Other juries accused other leaders of also joining in. One said that John Chamber of Potter Heigham had also stabbed Eccles[94] and Walter Clerk, a servant of the prior of Wymondham was said to have urged the rebels to kill Eccles,[95] but nevertheless there is a strong suggestion that the execution of Eccles was a staged event in which rebels from both Norwich and the surrounding countryside participated.

Towns like Norwich and Yarmouth have often been depicted as the victim of a largely rural insurgency. Phillippa Maddern argued that the rising in Norwich did not display the social conflict evident in towns like London,

York or Beverley. She pointed out that victims like Eccles and Salle were not members of the urban government and suggested that few Norwich citizens joined the disturbances.[96] Ben McRee, while describing how the elite citizens of Norwich sent Henry Lomynour and Walter Bixton to London in 1378 to secure special powers to make ordinances for the city, notes that these powers were never invoked and suggests that there was no general movement against the city elites in 1381, with Norwich suffering a 'minimum of disruption'.[97] McRee attributes this to the way in which the city government accommodated different demands.

However, there are some indications that Norwich did indeed suffer from some internal social conflicts during the rising. Christopher Baswell has described how a friar at Norwich sometime not long after the rising made annotations referring to the disturbances at Norwich in a copy of the *Aeneid*.[98] The friar commented on one part of the *Aeneid* 'Note how the peasants and the low-born commons rise up against the magnates.' A couple of lines later, he observes 'Here he shows what such a throng does when it rises up. John Latimer in Norwich and Horyn in London.' The mention of Horyn refers to the allegations made against John Horn and other aldermen in London that they had allowed the insurgents from Kent and Essex into the city, and the annotator clearly felt that, just as in London, the disturbances in Norwich had been exacerbated by social conflicts within the city. John Latimer was a wealthy citizen of Norwich who had served as bailiff and Member of Parliament for the city. However, he was accused of being involved in the agitation for the elections for city officials to be organised on a craft rather than a ward basis. Latimer was among the Norwich citizens ordered to be arrested for rebellious assemblies in 1371. The implication of the annotation in the *Aeneid* is clear, namely that Latimer and his supporters in Norwich sought to pursue their own ends during the rising of 1381.

The suggestion that in some way Norwich escaped lightly during 1381 does not take account of the large scale of the attack on the property of Henry Lomynour in Norwich which is only evident from trespass actions brought by Lomynour discovered by me some years ago.[99] These actions name altogether over 600 people involved in the attack on Lomynour's property and are comparable in scale with the trespass actions brought over such incidents in London as the attack on the Savoy and the destruction of houses belonging to John Butterwick, the under-sheriff of Middlesex. Given that the population of Norwich at that time was about 8,000 people, a mob of over 600 people would have been terrifying.[100]

Lomynour's trespass actions reveal that, while the bulk of those who attacked his property came from the surrounding countryside, there was also a significant Norwich contingent. Of course, we cannot be sure how Lomynour got his information about the identity of those who attacked his property, but these trespass actions indicate that there was an assumption that people from Norwich joined the attack. Moreover, it is striking that the two citizens of Norwich who were singled out for attack in 1381, Walter Bixton and Henry Lomynour, were the same men who had been sent secretly to negotiate a new charter in 1378.

The most striking feature of Lomynour's trespass actions is the way in which inhabitants of Norwich are acting besides insurgents from villages in the area around the abbey of St Benet of Holme. Just as the killing of Reginald Eccles was said to have been carried out by men from Potter Heigham, Dilham and Norwich, so the attack on Lomynour's property was carried out by an alliance of men from Norwich with people from places like Frettenham, Aylesham, Antingham and Dilham. William, the parson of Bylaugh who sought to grab land and rights belonging to the abbot of St Benet of Holme, was also said to have been present at the attack on Lomynour's property in Norwich.[101] The question is how far the faction from Norwich was responsible for selecting Lomynour as a target. Lomynour had not simply been prominent in the government of Norwich. He had also been a commissioner to investigate evasion of the poll tax and had assisted Sir John White, a retainer of John of Gaunt, in acquiring land in Scottow and Lammas immediately before the rising.[102]

Just as the insurgents who attacked Lomynour were a mixture of townsfolk and rural inhabitants, so the motives for attacking him also seem to have blended local civic discontent with wider political and social grievances. Samuel Cohn and Douglas Aiton have recently drawn attention to the scale and persistence of popular protest in English towns during the later Middle Ages.[103] They argue that historians have underestimated the significance of urban protest in England, although it never attained the size and frequency of urban revolts in continental Europe. Cohn and Aiton criticise the suggestion that it was the rural peasantry who were potentially the most anti-feudal class in medieval England and that the aspirations of urban rebels were more localised and circumscribed.

Cohn and Aiton's analysis raises in a new and more urgent form the question of the relationship between the urban and rural aspects of the rising in 1381. Because of the neglect of the traditions of protest in towns, disturbances there have been seen as subsidiary to the main rising. Underpinning much discussion of the 1381 rising has been an assumption that in some way, the disturbances in rural areas might represent a 'purer' form of revolt directed to the overthrow of feudalism. The attacks on the abbey of St Benet of Holme might be seen as at one level epitomising this rural aspect of the revolt. However, the way in which the disturbances there were closely integrated with the organisation of large-scale protests in towns like Norwich and Yarmouth, and the links formed between rural rebels from places like Scottow or Potter Heigham with insurgents from Norwich, indicates that the traditions of urban and rural protest were interwoven together in 1381 in a complex and powerful fashion.

Indeed, it appears that the potency and danger of the rising in 1381 came not simply from the devastating attacks on the feudal infrastructure by such actions as the burning of the records of the abbey of St Benet of Holme. It came rather from the way in which traditions of urban and rural insurgency were fused together as is shown by the way in which the tenants of St Benet's abbey collaborated with insurgents from Norwich in 1381. One of the chief features of recent historiography of the rising has been the way in which there has been an increased awareness that the insurgents comprised not only workers on the land but also craftsmen, clerks, artisans and inhabitants of towns. In analysing the structure of the rising, the priority should be not to look for the purest expression of a peasant insurgency, but rather to consider how these various urban, rural and other elements came together to form such a powerful and threatening uprising.

The means by which the abbey of St Benet of Holme rebuilt its estate infrastructure after the destruction of documents during the 1381 rising is illustrated by the records of its manors at Ashby and Thorne.[104] The court roll for 10 August 1381 declares that all the rolls and custumals touching the lordship had been burnt by the bondmen and those holding bond land. The land was seized into the lord's hands. In order to get their lands back, the tenants had to perform homage and pay a fine for re-registration of the land. The homage of Ashby and Thorne was also fined 20 s. at the same court for failing to make hay either at the monastery or the manor, and a further 20 s. for ignoring a summons to hoe corn. Some tenants at Ashby and Thorne continued to withhold services during 1382. The comparison between Ashby and Thorne and the nearby manor of Martham which belonged to the cathedral priory may help explain some of the antagonism towards the abbey of St Benet during the rising. Customary services in Ashby and Thorne were much more onerous and the abbey was more active in attempting to stop villeins leaving its manors. While the abbot of St Benet readmitted his tenants at the old rents and services after the 1381 rising, the prior of Norwich took the opportunity to negotiate new less onerous terms for his tenants.

The dangers for the abbey of St Benet of Holme did not end when the earl of Suffolk and his commission against the rebels held its sessions at nearby

Horning in July 1381.[105] Thomas Walsingham describes how in September 1382 a group of conspirators proposed to renew the revolt. Their plan was to capture the bishop of Norwich and other magnates of the county and kill them. They would then go to St Faith's Fair, held just north of Norwich, and force all the people there to follow them, or be killed. They also planned 'to occupy the abbey of St Benet of Hulme secretly; for this abbey struck these perfidious men as a powerful stronghold if they were to encounter any dangers in the future'.[106] One of the conspirators, however, revealed details of the plot. The conspirators were seized and beheaded at Norwich. Escheators' records show that they were from the villages of Blofield, Beighton, Thrigby and Wymondham, and were apparently among the poorer inhabitants of the village.

While some plotted a renewal of the rising, others however found different exit routes from the rising. One of those accused of burning the records of the prior of Hickling at Hickling, Sea Palling and Horsey was Richard Crisping of Catfield. The prior brought a trespass case against Richard, but in 1383 Richard was allowed to go *sine die* because he was serving in the company of Henry de Bello Monte in the expedition of the bishop of Norwich to Flanders.[107] It is interesting to speculate how Bishop Despenser, celebrated for his vigorous action against the insurgents in 1381, would have reacted if he realised that his army contained erstwhile rebels from Norfolk.

Notes

1. For a thorough and well-referenced narrative of the rising, see now Juliet Barker, *England, Arise: The People, the King and the Great Revolt of 1381* (London, 2015). For a recent discussion of the unrest in monastic boroughs, see Samuel Cohn and Douglas Aiton, *Popular Protest in Late Medieval English Towns* (Cambridge, 2012), pp. 203–24.

2. Andrew Prescott, '"Great and Horrible Rumour": Shaping the English Revolt of 1381', in Justine Firnhaber-Baker with Dirk Schoenaers (eds), *The Routledge History Handbook of Medieval Revolt* (London, 2017), p. 89.

3. Prescott, 'Great and Horrible Rumour', p. 87.

4. See, for example, Rodney Hilton, *Bond Men Made Free: Medieval Peasant Movements and the English Rising of 1381* (London, 1973), pp. 198–207.

5. There is a brief account of the abbey and its involvement in the events of 1381 by W. F. Edwards, 'The Peasants' Rising of 1381 and the Abbey of St Benet's-at-Holme', in Barbara Cornford (ed.), *Studies Towards a History of the Rising of 1381 in Norfolk* (Norwich, 1984), pp. 34–8.

6. TNA, KB 27/486 rex m. 2, printed in André Réville, *Le soulèvement des travailleurs d'Angleterre en 1381* (Paris, 1898), pp. 183–4, where the membrane number is given wrongly.

7. *Cal. Close Rolls 1381–5*, p. 74.

8. Edgar Powell and G. M. Trevelyan, *The Peasants' Rising and the Lollards* (London, 1899), p. 10.

9. Powell and Trevelyan, *Peasants' Rising*, p. 3.

10. TNA, JUST 3/216/5 m. 184; JUST 5/163 m. 14d; KB 27/483 m. 26.

11. Barker, *England, Arise*, p. 222; Helen Nicholson, 'The Hospitallers and the "Peasants' Revolt" of 1381 Revisited', in Victor Mallia-Milanes (ed.), *The Military Orders. Volume 3. History and Heritage* (Aldershot, 2007), pp. 225–33.

12. TNA, SC8/20/986-987; *Cal. Close Rolls 1381–5*, pp. 390, 593–4.

13. Powell and Trevelyan, *Peasants' Rising*, p. 17.

14. Barker, *England, Arise*, pp. 71–2; TNA, SC 8/116/5755. A writ dated 22 January 1382 ordering Roger Cook of Harmondsworth, Robert Freke of Harmondsworth, Richard ate Soler of Harlington, William Helway of Harlington, John Sander of Stanwell, Thomas Bynorth of Stanwell, Andrew Freke of Stanwell, William Ravening of Drayton, Hugh William of Drayton and Peter Penyfader of Colnbrook, carpenter, to answer the suit of the prior of Harmondsworth for breaking the houses of the priory there and burning charters, writings and other muniments is TNA, KB 136/5/5/2/2 (unnumbered membranes).

15. TNA, CP 40/491 m. 358d.

16. TNA, KB 27/484 m. 20d.

17. TNA, CP 40/487 m. 33d.

18. TNA, CP 40/490 m. 167.

19. TNA, CP 40/490 m. 517.

20. Herbert Eiden, 'Joint Action against "Bad" Lordship: The Peasants' Revolt in Essex and Norfolk', *History*, 83 (1998), 5–30 (15).

21. TNA, KB 136/5/5/3/2 (unnumbered membranes): writ dated 20 April 1382 ordering Richard Sohom, John Letherel, Thomas Buk, William Buk, William Friday, Richard Davy, John Allen and Thomas Carter, all of Langley, to answer the suit of the prior of St Bartholomew that they broke the close of the prior of Clavering and burnt his muniments there.

22. TNA, JUST 1/103 m. 10.

23. TNA, JUST 1/103 mm. 6, 11.

24. TNA, JUST 1/103 mm. 3, 4.

25. TNA, KB 136/5/5/4/2 (unnumbered membranes): writ dated 8 June 1382 ordering John Radon, William del Medew, William Baxter, Roger Perys, Richard Icok, John Koo, John Lowan, Adam Taylor, William Hale and Robert the servant of Thomas Smith of Alderton to answer the suit of the prior of Butley that they burnt a chest together with the charters, writings and other muniments contained therein at Butley.

26. Prescott, 'Great and Horrible Rumour', pp. 83–4, 88–9; Powell and Trevelyan, *Peasants' Rising*, pp. 13–16.

27. Diane K. Bolton, H. P. F. King, Gillian Wyld and D. C. Yaxley, 'Harmondsworth: Economic and social history', in T. F. T. Baker, J. S. Cockburn and R. B. Pugh (eds), *VCH Middlesex*, 4 (London, 1971), pp. 10–15, *British History Online, www.british-history. ac.uk/vch/middx/vol4/pp10-15* (accessed 17 May 2017).

28. David Crook, 'Derbyshire and the English Rising of 1381', *Bulletin of the Institute of Historical Research*, 60 (1987), 9–23.

29. Nicholson, 'The Hospitallers and the "Peasants' Revolt" of 1381', p. 229.

30. TNA, KB 9/166/1 m. 119; TNA, CP 40/487 m. 362d.

31. TNA, KB 9/166/1 m. 46.

32. TNA, KB 9/166/1 m. 46.

33. TNA, KB 9/166/1 m. 71.

34. TNA, KB 9/166/1 m. 64.

35. TNA, KB 9/166/1 mm. 71, 95.

36. TNA, KB 9/166/1 m. 63.

37. TNA, KB 27/486 m. 57; TNA, KB 27/488 m. 27d.

38. Eiden, 'Joint Action against "Bad" Lordship', 22.

39. TNA, KB 9/166/1 mm. 90, 91; TNA, CP 40/487 m. 231; TNA, CP 40/490 m. 17.

40. Réville, *Soulèvement des Travailleurs*, p. 113; my translation.

41. Eiden, 'Joint Action against "Bad" Lordship', 22.

42. TNA, KB 9/166/1 mm. 60, 63; Barker, *England, Arise*, pp. 330, 344.

43. TNA, CP 40/485 m. 138;

44. TNA, KB 9/166/1 m. 54.

45. TNA, KB 9/166/1 m. 60.

46. TNA, KB 9/166/1 m. 58.

47. TNA, KB 9/166/1 m. 46.

48. TNA, CP 40/489 m. 395d.

49. Cohn and Aiton, *Popular Protest in English Towns*, pp. 325–7.

50. TNA, KB 9/166/1 m. 39.

51. Parfray is identified as vicar of All Saint's Sudbury in John Wraw's appeal and elsewhere: R. B. Dobson, *The Peasants' Revolt of 1381*, 2nd edn (London, 1983), p. 252.

52. TNA, KB 9/166/1 mm. 55, 93, 95.

53. Prescott, 'Great and Horrible Rumour', pp. 83–4, 87.

54. Dobson, *Peasants' Revolt*, p. 256.

55. A. W. Reid, 'The Rising of 1381 in South West and Central Norfolk', in Cornford (ed.), *Studies Towards a History of the Rising of 1381 in Norfolk*, pp. 11–33; B. Cornford and A. Reid, 'The Uprising of 1381', in P. Wade-Martins (ed.), *An Historical Atlas of Norfolk*, 2nd edn (Norwich, 1994), pp. 86–7; Eiden, 'Joint Action against "Bad" Lordship', 16–24; H. Eiden, 'The Social Ideology of the Rebels in Suffolk and Norfolk in 1381', in *Von Nowgorod bis London: Studien zu Handel, Wirtschaft und Gesellschaft im mittelalterlichen Europa; Festschrift für Stuart Jenks zum 60. Geburtstag* (Göttingen, 2008), pp. 425–40.

56. For convenient summaries of the development of the revolt in Norfolk, see Reid, 'The Rising of 1381 in South West and Central Norfolk', pp. 11–33, and Eiden, 'Joint Action against "Bad" Lordship', 16–24.

57. TNA, KB 9/166/1 m. 95.

58. Barker, *England, Arise*, p. 333.

59. Barker, *England, Arise*, pp. 334–6.

60. Dobson, *Peasants' Revolt*, pp. 258–9.

61. Eiden, 'Joint Action against "Bad" Lordship', 20.

62. TNA, KB 9/166/1 m. 76.

63. Eiden, 'Joint Action against "Bad" Lordship', 20; Ben McRee, 'Peacemaking and its Limits in Late Medieval Norwich', *English Historical Review*, 109 (1994), 836–7.

64. TNA, KB 9/166/1 m. 119.

65. L. S. Woodger, 'Fastolf, Hugh', in J. S. Roskell, L. Clark, C. Rawcliffe (eds), *The History of Parliament: the House of Commons 1386–1421*, *www.historyofparliamentonline.org/volume/1386-1421/member/fastolf-hugh-1392* (accessed 17 May 2017).

66. Eiden, 'Joint Action against "Bad" Lordship', 20; TNA, KB 9/166/1 mm. 83–6. The close similarity between these three indictments suggests some coordination in their preparation and that they emphasised aspects which affected the town's interests.

67. The records of the commission are TNA, KB 9/166/1. This file (and other commission records concerning the revolt) can now be consulted online via *The Anglo-American Legal Tradition* website: *http://aalt.law.uh.edu/* (accessed 1 September 2017).

68. TNA, KB 9/166/1 mm. 44–44d.

69. TNA, KB 9/166/1 m. 101.

70. TNA, KB 9/166/1 m. 44d.

71. TNA, KB 9/166/1 m. 97.

72. TNA, KB 9/166/1 m. 44d.

73. TNA, KB 9/166/1 m. 91.

74. Eiden, 'Joint Action against "Bad" Lordship', 22. I have been unable to locate the reference given by Eiden for the destruction of the records at Hautbois: no such case appears on TNA, CP 40/486 m. 426.

75. H. Eiden, *'In der Knechtschaft werdet ihr verharren …': Ursachen und Verlauf des englischen Bauernaufstands von 1381* (Trier, 1995), p. 346.

76. Andrew Prescott, 'The Judicial Records of the Rising of 1381' (unpublished PhD thesis, University of London, 1984), 253–91.

77. TNA, KB 27/497 m. 18d.

78. Andrew Prescott, 'The Hand of God: the Suppression of the Peasants' Revolt of 1381', in N. Morgan (ed.), *Prophecy, Apocalypse and the Day of Doom*, Harlaxton Medieval Studies, 12 (Stamford, 2004), p. 319.

79. TNA, KB 27/485 m. 45d.

80. Eiden, 'Joint Action against "Bad" Lordship', 23–4.

81. TNA, KB 27/488 m. 13.

82. TNA, KB 27/483 m. 27d.

83. Colin Richmond, *The Paston Family in the Fifteenth Century: The First Phase* (Cambridge, 1990), pp. 12–16.

84. Richmond, *Paston Family: The First Phase*, p. 13, n. 53.

85. Barker, *England, Arise*, pp. 343–9.

86. TNA, KB 9/166/1 m. 103.

87. Eiden, 'Joint Action against "Bad" Lordship', 22.

88. TNA, CP 40/487 m. 231.

89. TNA, KB 9/166/1 mm. 99, 101.

90. TNA, KB 9/166/1 m. 95.

91. TNA, KB 9/166/1 m. 97.

92. TNA, KB 9/166/1 m. 101.

93. TNA, KB 9/166/1 m. 119d.

94. TNA, KB 9/166/1 m. 88.

95. TNA, KB 9/166/1 m. 77.

96. Phillippa Maddern, 'Order and Disorder', in Carole Rawcliffe and Richard Wilson (eds), *Medieval Norwich* (London, 2004), p. 199.

97. McRee, 'Peacemaking', 840–5.

98. Christopher Baswell, 'Aeneas in 1381', in Rita Copeland, David Lawton and Wendy Scase (eds), *New Medieval Literatures*, 5 (2002), pp. 23–33.

99. TNA, KB 27/485 m. 54d; TNA, KB 27/486 m. 27; TNA, KB 27/487 m. 28; TNA, KB 27/488 m. 34; TNA, KB 27/489 mm. 43, 43d, 44, 44d, 47, 47d, 51, 51d, 52d; TNA, CP 40/483 m. 57d; TNA, CP 40/484 mm. 378d, 465.

100. Penelope Dunn, 'Trade', in Rawcliffe and Wilson (eds), *Medieval Norwich*, p. 214.

101. TNA, KB 27/489 m. 47.

102. L. S. Woodger, 'Limner (Lomynour), Henry', in J. S. Roskell, L. Clark and C. Rawcliffe (eds), *The History of Parliament: the House of Commons 1386–1421*, www.historyof parliamentonline.org/volume/1386-1421/member/limner-%28lomynour%29-henry-1409 (accessed 19 May 2017).

103. Cohn and Aiton, *Popular Protest in English Towns*, pp. 3–9.

104. B. Cornford, 'Events of 1381 in Flegg', in Cornford (ed.), *Studies Towards a History of the Rising of 1381 in Norfolk*, pp. 39–48.

105. H. Eiden, 'Norfolk, 1382: A Sequel to the Peasants' Revolt', *English Historical Review*, 114 (1999), 370–7.

106. Dobson, *Peasants' Revolt*, pp. 334–5.

107. TNA, CP 40/490 m. 17.

PART III

Women in the medieval monastic world

11

Looking for medieval female religious in Britain and Ireland: sources, methodologies and pitfalls

Kimm Curran

Medieval female religious and their communities in Britain and Ireland, for the most part, remain enigmatic. The reasons cited have been echoed throughout historical studies of monasticism: a lack of source material, poor economies and insignificant numbers of identifiable female religious throughout the entire medieval period. For many regions of England, the source material is vast and varied which has resulted in case studies for the dioceses of York, Norwich and London. For Ireland, Scotland and Wales, the source material about female religious presents more of a challenge. Whilst some communities may be lacking in surviving source material about them or by them, often pieces of information about the women who lived in cloistered religious communities can be found in the most unlikely and surprising places. This has resulted in researchers becoming more creative in approaching source material and applying new methods – such as prosopography – to the findings. Individual female religious have been identified as well as their interactions and networks with the secular world, and this has shattered preconceived stereotypes and assumptions of these women and their surrounding milieus.

Prosopography includes elements of family history, the study of names or naming patterns and demography in which the primary concern is the collection of data for several individuals in order to understand their connection to each other, their family or other groups and what their role was in society.[1] Applying prosopography as a method has enhanced our study of female religious communities and the individual identity of female religious, and contributed to discussions on women's agency, power and authority within religious communities and beyond; we have been able to identify and show the relationships between various female religious and their family, kin and locality within a specific historical or social context. This chapter looks at how prosopography has contributed to studies of individual female religious in Britain and Ireland who lived in female religious communities throughout the medieval period. Alongside this, a discussion is given of the challenges of using this methodology, especially in terms of source material and interpretation. It provides a sympathetic (and creative) approach in regards to source material, that can both hinder and enhance research approaches for the study of individual female religious. Lastly, it addresses some of the challenges we face working on female religious but also suggests the positive and exciting work that remains unfinished.

In 1987, Mary McLauglin noted that there was anticipation that the project, 'Women Religious Life and Communities, AD 500–1500', would 'contribute to the basic research needs in the two fields of growing interest to medievalists: monastic and religious history and the history of religious women'.[2] Its aims and scopes were to 'focus on the individual as well as the collective experiences of religious women ... with interests of prosopographers ... and foster their studies'.[3] This pioneering project became known as the Monastic Matrix. A large database was designed to be comprehensive, with biographical resources as well as the names of female religious and communities from the whole of Christendom. Today, it still addresses the needs of scholars and students and continues to provide updated material through the collaborative effort of an international group of scholars and volunteers.

The impact of the Matrix was felt with the proliferation of studies on medieval female religious in the late 1980s to 2000s.[4] One scholar who worked on the project in the early days was Marilyn Oliva and her work on female religious in the diocese of Norwich has made a large contribution to the study of individual female religious. With the use of a wide range of source material she was able to determine the social rank of female religious as well as show their interconnected networks to family and the world outside the cloister. Oliva also was able to prove that female heads of houses and the office-holding patterns of female religious within communities were not exclusive to the aristocracy but rather there were varied levels of social groupings within communities. Offices were given to those with experience or merit rather than based on social status; the percentage of office holders of higher rank in Norwich, for example, is very low.[5] Her research challenged preconceived ideas that all female religious were from the aristocracy or upper ranks, a stereotype that has continued in studies of female religious since the 1920s.[6]

The most prolific of medieval English monastic scholars, Janet Burton, has highlighted what kinds of material can be used to uncover recruitment patterns, links between founders and patrons and the environment of communities within the dioceses of York. For example, geographical patterns of recruitment emerge, as well as family and social origins, at Nun Appleton, Nun Monkton and Rosedale. Investigating these houses has shown that recruitment was spread across different houses, especially if houses were small or poor (or both).[7] Despite the negative press attributed to female religious from poor Yorkshire communities, the origins of female religious and their connections can be found when examining the material more closely and using a wide range of evidence. In Burton's study, she makes an important point: even though evidence is sporadic, there is sufficient reference to individual women to build up a 'group biography'.[8] What Burton has emphasised is that the clustering of members of the same family may be more common than was thought but that more research needs to be done to reveal these origins and connections.[9] Other case studies from Yorkshire of the communities at Appleton and Marrick in Yorkshire also indicate that female religious came from the locality and were related to local landowners where it is possible to ascertain their origins.[10] Other scholars such as Claire Cross and A. C. Macdonald have also contributed to this by identifying female religious, the consequences of the Dissolution of religious houses in the 1530s as well as the participation of female religious in activities such as pageant plays and confraternities in the diocese.[11]

Identifying female religious and their connections within the urban environment of London is the focus of Catherine Paxton's in-depth analysis of female religious communities in London. This provides a wide understanding of the myriad of intertwined and reciprocal relationships female religious maintained and fostered in surroundings and situations that were constantly changing.[12] Other case studies have been carried out on individual houses such as Paul Lee and the Dominican priory of Dartford where he identified the social origins of female religious and their role within the parish.[13] Similarly, Diane Coldicott's analysis of Hampshire female religious communities finds that female religious came from local prominent families and had parallel patterns of recruitment as in Yorkshire.[14]

For Ireland and Scotland, Dianne Hall and I used the established frameworks from other scholars to provide detailed studies of female religious. Ireland and Scotland's female religious are especially difficult to locate due to the lack of primary source material that has survived for the whole of the Middle Ages as compared to their neighbours. However, what has been discovered about these religious communities and individual female religious has provided us with evidence to suggest that despite geography, language and cultural difference, community recruitment patterns and the social backgrounds of female religious were similar to their counterparts in England during the same period. Dianne Hall points out that the backgrounds of female religious are sometimes hard to discover and their origins difficult to pinpoint. Female religious are rarely mentioned in family documents; nor are they related to patrons or donors. Establishing relationships is often speculative but the links are hard to discount.[15]

My own study relied on the multifaceted evidence from across the spectrum of sources and, most importantly, documents contained in family archives and collections. Individual female religious in Scotland were often related to prominent local families or families that had a direct relationship, contact or kin connection with the convent; strong kin groups and families were also present in the religious community itself. Both studies showed that despite poor source material, female religious were more present and visible than expected.

Marilyn Oliva remarked that there is fertile ground to pursue a prosopography of female religious by using a more wide-ranging collection of material.[16] Because of the variety this allows for widening the lens by which we can view communities, recruitment patterns and discover individual female religious. The task, however, is not easy. The approach to female religious communities still often begins with foundation and early histories, determining order, founders and patrons rather than individual women. The most common material used to start this search is charters to monastic communities. But, charters have limited use for identifying individual female religious as these women do not attest. Names of female religious in charters were more likely to be those whose entry into a community was accompanied by a grant of land or another gift. Even with this evidence comes a caution: grants to religious houses at the reception of a female religious may be concealed as dowry grants and were viewed as simony.[17]

Another widely used source is the collection of English episcopal registers as these provide information on communities, the movement of individual female religious to other houses, elections and entry into houses by women as well as their misdemeanours. But, visitations by bishops can also narrow the focus to only highlight offences by communities and individual female religious; these entries skew our understanding of the everyday experience of female religious in communities and of female religious more generally. The focus on wrongdoings, for example, also underestimates the authority and judgements made by female heads of houses on behalf of their communities.

But for Ireland, Scotland and Wales episcopal registers do not survive and reliance on other sources is essential. Burton reminds us that the thirteenth and fourteenth centuries are particularly difficult in regards to the survival of sources for female religious communities. Warfare, plague and economic hardship were endemic during this period and even more so for particular regions where continual conflicts between England and Scotland put smaller religious houses in harm's way: often communities could not recover.[18] Other material is more plentiful for the later medieval period such as: records of government, wills, consistory court, protocol books, land transfers or feu charters as well as records from burghs and towns. Female religious communities were often involved in litigation over the rights to land and their possessions in the later

Middle Ages with their heads of house appearing in legal records of court. For example, the community of Lismullin (Co. Meath) found itself in a protracted dispute with the priory of Little Malvern (Worchester) over dues on land given to the community at foundation and the records of the dispute are found in both Irish and English sources.[19] Yet, studies of later medieval female religious post-Black Death are relatively scarce.

Looking for female religious can be found in the most unlikely places and scholars searching for these allusive women often find them unexpectedly. For example, the name of an early thirteenth-century prioress was found on a folio of the Iona Psalter. Bethóc ingen Somairle (Bethoc Somerled) was the first prioress at the Augustinian community at Iona and it has been suggested that the Psalter was commissioned for Bethoc and the Iona community.[20] David Bell noted that finding books associated with female religious communities shows a level of benefaction. Books were valuable and expensive commodities; communities were not always able to purchase these items and were given the books by benefactors, patrons and family members.[21] Another fine example was found at Campsey Ash where the name of the sub-prioress, Catherine Babyngton, was inscribed in the *Life of St Catherine* (*c*.1446).[22]

For Wales, Jane Cartwright has also shown that finding individual female religious is not easy. There were only three established houses in Wales and the numbers of female religious were few; these women remain unknown. But evidence of poetry written to female religious or Bardic poetry about female religious has highlighted networks between individual women or abbesses and the outside world. The poem written on behalf of Annes, abbess of Llanllŷr in the mid-fifteenth century, for example, indicates possible connections to the royal court or family connection to Sir William Herbert, earl of Pembroke.[23] Whilst these occurrences are scarce, this points to opportunities for scholars to look at other poetic or Bardic traditions in Ireland and western Scotland, even if the results may turn out to be few.

Other places that have been overlooked when looking for medieval female religious are tomb effigies or grave slabs. It is rare to find surviving evidence for these pieces of material culture in general and even more so for those in religious communities.[24] Often men or women were buried in their communities but with no indication of who they were. Heads of religious houses may have been more likely to have attribution on markers, showing status and authority within the monastic community and beyond; but this was not always the norm. A rare surviving example of an Irish abbess indicates the status of the abbess, Elicia Butler of Kilculiheen. Although without direct attribution to her, the dating and location of the tomb at St Canice's Cathedral, Kilkenny makes a strong connection to the Butler family and Abbess Elicia.[25] Scotland has three examples of tomb effigies attributed to individual female religious as head of house, and two further examples linked to individual female religious: Anna Maclean was the prioress of Iona (1509–43); Blanche, prioress of Lincluden (*c*.1390); Elizabeth Lamb, prioress at Abbey St Bathans (1546–65); and Finnguala and Mariota MacInolly (sixteenth century) of Iona as female religious. Without these tomb effigies as evidence, we may not have known of these five individual female religious as they do not appear in documentary sources.[26]

There are other questions we have to ask of source material, most especially of survival. The nature of source material for medieval elites is more plentiful and groups of lesser ranks are often left out of sources and queries. For Marrick Priory, Tillotson argued that social origins are difficult to determine especially with such meagre surviving evidence: female religious may come from a variety of social backgrounds, making it difficult to find them especially as only exceptional cases leave a trace.[27] Because of the invisible nature of female religious in sources, assumptions are made about them; if they are not visible they must be from the lower social ranks of society. But, this comes with a word of warning: many female religious communities were relatively small with scanty resources suggesting that communities may have attracted women from middling or lower social rankings, not unlike their male counterparts.[28] The studies above indicate that sweeping generalisations about 'exceptional cases' need to be re-evaluated, especially as new source material is analysed and discovered.

The locations of many female religious communities were rural or marginal, making it difficult to recover details about women in these remote communities. Compiling a list of the most visible of female religious, for example, is problematic. Often the only members of the community that we find in the recorded material were the heads of house, but this was not always the case. Houses such as Iona (Western Isles), Abbey St Bathans (Scottish Borders) and Holystone (Northumbria) for example have either no complete record for their communities and, for some, no names of female religious have been found. For Ireland, many of the houses were rural and we have only a handful of women who can be attributed as heads of house for each community: seven women have been identified as prioresses at Graney Priory (Co. Kildare) between *c*.1200 and 1535, for example.[29] Female religious in Wales, in particular, are even scarcer to find.

Numbers of female religious and their ages at entry into the community or at death is also not easy to determine. The population of communities varied widely between different regions, orders and individual houses depending on locality, geography and economy. Burton notes that recruitment patterns are skewed due to resources available and calculating how many were in a community can be painstakingly difficult and prone to misinterpretation. The question we have to ask ourselves is how important are the numbers of female religious in any given community? Does the number of women prevent us from looking at the wider picture of community, settlement and kinship or family? Dismissing the myth of poverty and order, as well as a dearth of sources from the beginning of our investigations, focuses the investigation on looking for women rather than what is not left behind.

Those of us looking for enigmatic female religious spend the majority of our time debunking and refuting negative historiography and stereotypes that female religious were all from the upper ranks of society. Our focus can become distorted looking for reasons to disprove stereotypes rather than wider concerns of family and local community connections. Further difficulty lies in trying to gain an awareness of the experiences of female religious and connections to family and kin while at the same time keeping a tight rein on material sources – it can be difficult and time-consuming to manage them all. The other downside – and it is a big one – is that researchers may find nothing in archives and sources or may have to spend a lot of time looking for a local or family connection that may not exist. The frustration and barriers to discovering female religious feel all too tangible and we may rush to abandon the search.

Despite the difficulties, using varied sources and the 'needle in the haystack' approach when looking for female religious allows for prosopography to be applied more widely and group biographies to be discovered. Evidence of a name, for example, is sufficient to help us build a picture of recruitment in relation to geographic region.[30] Counting women allows us to project numbers in a particular region or community even when the total number of female religious found is relatively low. For example, the total number of female religious in Scotland is roughly 230. However, by using Oliva's methodology for calculating the numbers of female religious in Norwich during the same time period, estimation puts the total number of Scotland's female religious in the range of 1600 to 2000.[31] In identifying differences and similarities in communities, Oliva remarks that this facilitates a better understanding of the institution to which people belonged and exposes recruitment patterns.

But it can be a painstakingly slow process to go through the varied sources and train your eye for omissions, ellipses and small clues.[32] Perceptions can be skewed as often we have to apply a broad chronology to look for connections and traces of female religious and their families over time. Recognising female religious may be problematic, but prosopographical analysis allows for assumptions on family, kin and local connections to be more widely understood. We should not underestimate what we can learn from making these assumptions: women who have remained invisible for centuries become visible. Penelope Johnson remarked that even without firm family links 'those people whose sisters, aunts, cousins and mothers [who] had taken the veil were proud of their female kinfolk and did whatever they could to ensure the welfare of the [communities] hous- ing them'.[33] These relationships were reciprocal and, in many cases, inseparable. These linkages between the two were important to facilitate the channelling of information, affection and other resources; actions were interdependent.

Despite the work that has been done and the use of new methodologies, there is still much more that needs to be addressed. In England, for example, there are up to 100 communities that have not been investigated: roughly ninety-one have been completed or are near completion.[34] For the far north in areas of Northumbria and Cumbria, we know very little about these religious communities. Armathwaite, Seton (Lekeley), St Bartholomew (Newcastle) and Holystone, for example, are poorly documented and it is likely that records were destroyed during the continuous outbreak of border warfare from the late thirteenth century onwards. Devon and Cornwall have also been overlooked due to the lack of female religious communities founded in that region (much like Wales), yet there are documents we can consult to find individual names of female religious.[35] It is surprising that the diocese of Lincoln has not been attempted, especially as it has one of the richest collections of primary source material of a medieval diocese; whilst the number of communities may be few, the sources related to Fosse, Stixwould and Stainfield could provide us with an insight into the female religious of that diocese. If we look to other sources – family papers, borough registers as well as inventories, estate records or other deeds – we may find more than we realised, too. The English Monastic Archive database opens up the opportunity to search types and current locations of documents about individual houses contained in archives across England; some material has not been analysed in any great depth at all.[36]

Many names of female religious have been identified for a number of communities across Britain and Ireland but there has been no attempt to galvanise the field of monastic studies by constructing an interactive database to collate the wealth of material gathered by researchers and archivists. Many female religious remain hidden in articles, theses and books and small case studies. But, with the progress made in the digital humanities, a multifaceted online resource is possible to input the names of female religious that have already been identified.[37] Accomplishing this task takes time, collective energy, optimism and cooperation with a number of participants – which can prove to be a demanding task.

We have examples from scholars working on early modern female reli- gious that could prove useful. Looking at the project 'Who were the Nuns?' (WWtN) provides us with useful ways to organise material, documenting individual female religious, where possible, and making the resources available to the wider public.[38] Working collaboratively with projects like WWtN can give us new information hitherto unaddressed in Reformation or monastic studies. For example, the Dissolution of the monasteries by Henry VIII, carried out between 1535 and 1540, is rich in documentation identifying religious men and women receiving pensions and those alive or present at the time of the suppression of their communities. Very little work has been done on the consequences of the suppression on individual religious men and women and very little on where these men or women may have gone to live out the rest of their lives. There is evidence that some female religious stayed close to their community housed by relatives; some remained memorialised in legend like the prioress of Clonard (Co. Limerick), known as the Black Hag, who remained at the deserted convent living out her days gathering herbs.[39] There are some exceptions, however.

Paul Lee notes that post-Dissolution there were dynamic monastic communities which possessed a strong sense of identity and vocation. These communities were more likely to stay together and even seek re-enclosure elsewhere during the latter part of the sixteenth century. For example, the female religious of Dartford and Syon travelled to Flanders together in 1559 – in exile – and remained there; the Syon community later returned to England only to be forced to leave in 1594, settling in Portugal.[40] Looking at exiled female religious is outwith the scope of this chapter but, looking at the WWtN project can provide another way for medieval female religious to be identified, working backwards in time to uncover further local and family connections that may have been overlooked. Also, documents from exiled female religious in Europe occasionally make reference to the Dissolution and indicate a starting point for medievalists to start thinking about using early modern material more widely to study female religious. For some this may be challenging but, despite this, we could find useful insight into religious sentiments and continuity of religious life post 1560. For those working on medieval memory, for example, it is clear that the fracturing of religious life affected families, localities and individual female religious. The event may have still have been in the living memory of a generation: uncovering these snippets of medieval and post-Dissolution attitudes can provide us with much more than just a snapshot in time but also make female religious more visible and real.[41] Further to this, it could give a more detailed picture of the social make-up of some female religious communities, their family backgrounds and show the importance of kinship and extended networks both inside and outwith these communities.

By opening up discussions of post-Dissolution families and female religious, we allow opportunities to reflect back in time, using soft chronologies, which can free up limitations of periodisation revealing the more fluid aspects of relationships between communities, locality and family. Some families had long-standing relationships with female religious and monasteries. A good example of this was at Coldstream (Scottish Borders) where prioresses were from a particular local family, the Hoppringles, and this family held the office for over one hundred years.[42] The Hoppringles had strong ties to the locality and to the original founders and patrons of Coldsteam. Furthermore, some female religious inside the community were related to this family, too. Using a variety of sources from *c*.1150 to *c*.1582 a more complete picture of this religious community has been realised.

To conclude: we must take the hits and the misses, the pitfalls and the hidden gems when looking for female religious. The studies above show that by challenging the normal approaches and expanding the scope of the nature of source material, understanding and identifying female religious, their wider communities and connections to these communities are realised. Further developments in digital humanities and relational databases may assist in our pursuit of making known these connections as well as opening up new lines of enquiry in the study of everyday life, family and medieval memory. Burton reminds us that the history of female religious communities 'cannot be written in the same way for most of the monasteries' and we have to find new ways to uncover their past and their histories.[43]

Notes

1. *Oxford English Dictionary*, 2nd edn (1989), *s.v.* Prosopography.

2. M. M. McLaughlin, 'Looking for Medieval Women: an interim report on the project Women's Religious Life and Communities, A.D. 500–1500', *Medieval Prosopography*, 8 (1987), 61.

3. M. M. McLaughlin, 'Looking for Medieval Women', 61. The project has now expanded to AD 400 to 1600, see *https://monasticmatrix.osu.edu/*.

4. For a comprehensive list of the studies of female religious in Britain and Ireland, see the Medieval Bibliography of the History of Women Religious Britain and Ireland, *https://historyofwomenreligious.org/women-religious-bibliography/medieval/*.

5. Marilyn Oliva, 'Aristocracy or Meritocracy? Office-Holding Patterns in Late Medieval English Nunneries', in Derek Baker (ed.), *Women in the Church* (Oxford, 1990), p. 199.

6. Eileen Power, *Medieval English Nunneries c.1275–1535* (Cambridge, 1922).

7. Janet Burton, 'Documenting the Lives of Medieval Nuns', in J. Boffey and V. Davis (eds), *Recording Medieval Lives*, Proceedings of the 2005 Harlaxton Symposium (Donnington, 2009), p. 20. See also, Janet Burton, 'Yorkshire Nunneries in the Middle Ages: Recruitment and Resources', in J. Appleby and P. Dalton (eds), *Government, Religion and Society in Northern England, 1100–1700* (Stroud, 1997), pp. 104–17.

8. Burton, 'Documenting Lives', p. 21.

9. Burton, 'Documenting Lives', p. 24.

10. Marjorie Harrison, *The Nunnery of Nun Appleton* (York, 2001); John Tillotson, *Marrick Priory: A Nunnery in Late Medieval Yorkshire* (York, 1989).

11. Claire Cross and Noreen Vickers (eds), *Monks, Friars and Nuns in Sixteenth Century Yorkshire*, Yorkshire Archaeological Society, Record Series, 150 (1995); Noreen Vickers, 'The Social Class of Yorkshire Medieval Nuns', *Yorkshire Archaeological Journal*, 67 (1993), 127–32; A. C. Macdonald, 'Women and the Monastic Life in Late Medieval Yorkshire' (unpublished DPhil thesis, University of Oxford, 1997).

12. Catherine Paxton, 'The Nunneries of London and Its Environs in the Later Middle Ages' (unpublished DPhil thesis, University of Oxford, 1992).

13. Paul Lee, *Spirituality and Learning in Late Medieval English Society: The Dominican Priory of Dartford* (York, 2001).

14. Diane Coldicott, *Hampshire Nunneries* (Chichester, 1989).

15. Dianne Hall, 'Towards a prosopography of nuns in medieval Ireland', *Archivium Hibernicum*, 53 (1999), 3–15; Dianne Hall, 'The nuns of the medieval convent of Lismullin, County Meath, and their secular connections', *Rioct ne Midhe*, 10 (1999), 58–70.

16. Marilyn Oliva, 'All in the family? Monastic and Clerical Careers Among Family Members in the Late Middle Ages', *Medieval Prosopography*, 20 (1999), 161–80; Marilyn Oliva, 'Counting Nuns: A Prosopography of Late Medieval Nuns in the Diocese of Norwich', *Medieval Prosopography*, 16 (1995), 27–55.

17. Janet Burton, 'Looking for Medieval Nuns', in J. Burton and K. Stöber (eds), *Monasteries and Society in the British Isles in the Later Middle Ages*, Studies in the History of Medieval Religion, 35 (Woodbridge, 2008), pp. 114–16. See also Joseph Lynch, *Simonical Entry into Religious Life, 1000–1260: A Social, Economical and Legal Study* (Ohio, 1976).

18. Janet Burton, 'Cloistered Women and Male Authority: Power and Authority in Yorkshire Nunneries in the Later Middle Ages', in M. Prestwich, R. Britnell and R. Frame (eds), *Thirteenth Century England X: Proceedings of the Durham Conference 2003* (Woodbridge, 2005), p. 157; See also, K. Curran, 'Religious Women and their Communities in Late Medieval Scotland' (unpublished PhD thesis, University of Glasgow, 2005).

19. Hall, 'The nuns of the medieval convent of Lismullin', 63–4.

20. National Library of Scotland (NLS), Iona Psalter, MS 10000, fol. 9r.

21. David Bell, *What Nuns Read: Books and Libraries in Medieval English Nunneries*, Cistercian Studies Series, 158 (Kalamazoo, 1995), pp. 33–4.

22. BL, Arundel 396, fol. 130v.

23. Jane Cartwright, *Female Sanctity and Spirituality in Medieval Wales* (Cardiff, 2008), pp. 187–94.

24. Roberta Gilchrist indicates that there was a tomb effigy of the abbess of Romsey, but others are more difficult to trace: Roberta Gilchrist, *Gender and Material Culture: The Archaeology of Religious Women* (London, 1994), p. 20; see also the recent discovery of the

possible tomb slab of Abbot Hwyel (1295), abbot of Valle Crucis, 'Ornament' found to be 13th-century gravestone', *www.bbc.co.uk/news/uk-wales-north-east-wales-38228588* (accessed 6 December 2016).

25. Tracy Collins, 'An Archaeology of Female Monasticism in Medieval Ireland' (unpublished PhD thesis, National University of Ireland, Cork, 2015), vol. 1, 339–42.

26. Curran, 'Religious Women and their Communities', ch. 3 and appendix 2.

27. Tillotson, *Marrick*, p. 5.

28. Oliva, 'Aristocracy or Meritocracy?', p. 205.

29. Hall, 'Towards a prosopography', 4–14.

30. Burton, 'Looking for Medieval Nuns', p. 116.

31. Marilyn Oliva, *The Convent and the Community in Late Medieval England* (Woodbridge, 1998), pp. 220–9; Curran, 'Religious Women and Their Communities', appendix 2.

32. Dianne Hall, *Women and the Church in Medieval Ireland, c.1140–1540* (Dublin, 2003), p. 16.

33. Penelope Johnson, 'Mulier et Monialis: The Medieval Nun's Self Image', *Thought*, 64 (1989), 245.

34. Total taken from Power, *Medieval English Nunneries*, pp. 685–92; Ireland, Scotland and Wales as complete or at least majority completed with some updates and follow up needed.

35. See full listings here: The English Monastic Archive Project Database, *www.ucl.ac.uk/library/digital-collections/collections/monastic/* (accessed 15 August 2016), entry for Canonsleigh and Deed of Surrender, 1539.

36. The English Monastic Archive Project Database, *www.ucl.ac.uk/library/digital-collections/collections/monastic/* (accessed 15 August 2016).

37. For example the theses of A. C. Macdonald (York), Catherine Paxton (London) and Kimm Curran (Scotland).

38. See 'Who Were the Nuns? A Prosopographical study of the English Convents in exile 1600–1800', *https://wwtn.history.qmul.ac.uk/* (accessed 20 September 2016); see also 'Using Digital Resources for the Study of English Catholic Women', *Tulsa Studies in Women's Literature*, 31, 1/2 (2012), 229–36.

39. Gillian Kenny, *Anglo-Irish and Gaelic women in Ireland, c.1170–1540* (Dublin, 2007), p. 177.

40. Lee, *Spirituality and Learning*, pp. 125–33.

41. For a discussion on trauma and stress of the Dissolution see Peter Cunich, 'The Ex-Religious in Post-Dissolution Society: Symptoms of Post-Traumatic Stress Disorder?', in J. G. Clark, *The Religious Orders in Pre-Reformation England* (Woodbridge, 2002), pp. 227–38. For a wider consideration of the relationship between the impact of the Dissolution and its effect on collective memory, individual identity and place, see A. Walsham, *The Reformation of the Landscape: Religion, Identity and Memory in Early Modern Britain and Ireland* (Oxford, 2011).

42. Curran, 'Religious Women and their Communities', ch. 4 and appendix 2.

43. Janet Burton, *Yorkshire Nunneries in the Twelfth and Thirteenth Centuries*, Borthwick Papers, no. 56 (York, 1979), p. 36.

12

'As for a nun': corrodies, nunneries and the laity*

Brian Golding

Corrodies have had a poor press. Until comparatively recently they were seldom considered in discussions of monastic benefactions and donors, possibly because they were still subconsciously regarded as 'tainted' transactions. Certainly contemporaries had problems with them: they, more than other monastic negotiations, were dangerously close to, if not actually, simoniac (as Wycliffe certainly considered them).[1] Denounced in the sixteenth century by reformers, both within the Church and by more radical Protestants (perhaps most trenchantly, Latimer), later Protestant historians, most notoriously Coulton, regarded them as exemplifying the evils of the pre-Reformation church.[2] Conversely Catholic historians often ignored them, perhaps because they found them embarrassing and counter to monastic ideals: Knowles, for example, made no mention of them in either of his monumental volumes on monasticism before the Black Death. And most modern analysis of corrodies has taken place solely in the context of late medieval monasticism.[3] Yet corrodies had a longer, earlier, complex, but less examined history. This brief chapter explores these earlier developments particularly through the prism of corrodies provided for the laity within nunneries (as well as for women in male houses). It will argue that their functions were rather more nuanced than often assumed, that it is too simplistic to see corrodies as paradigmatic of a worldly monasticism, and that though open to abuse they continued to retain their eleemosynary role. Corrody, charity and community made up a major triad in the complex meshed relationship binding together cloistered and lay lives.

This is not to deny that corrodies were potentially transgressive and threatened good order. No other bond between benefactor and community so breached the barrier between the cloister and the world allowing the laity

---

* This chapter is offered to Janet with many thanks for over forty years of friendship, and for the generous provision of a corrody in Oxford of food and lodging, where it was surreptitiously completed!

to be permanently in, but not of, the convent, and problems were especially contingent on the presence of male corrodians (often with their servants) in nunneries, and, as seriously, female corrodians in male houses, which certainly posed a threat to monastic discipline.[4] Yet, a corrody was in origin no less an element of exchange than other commodities that made up the nexus of relationships between benefactors and religious, and frequently formed part of a wider assemblage of benefits: rather than being a trade in land this was one in goods and services. And for us to see (as diocesan bishops indeed tended to do) the corrodian merely as a paying guest, a hindrance to the community, a drain on resources and a worldly threat to the religious life is too reductive. Women (and men), for example, who were received might share to some measure in the cloister's spiritual world and liturgical round, attending or observing some services, while in their chambers they had the opportunity to follow their own devotions, structured or unstructured.

This chapter will suggest that there was a gradual transformation of the corrody's meaning and function. Originally an element of monastic almsgiving and often a component of a package of spiritual benefits, by the later Middle Ages it had become decoupled from confraternity, and was a free-standing, largely cash-based relationship benefitting the influential rather than the indigent.[5] At the same time there was a transition from 'outdoor' to 'indoor' relief.[6] So long as charity was dispensed at the abbey gate tensions inherent between the lay and spiritual realms could be resolved: these became much more complicated and intractable once played out within the precinct. This was particularly problematic in nunneries, which generally had fewer resources than their male counterparts, and were hence more subject to financial pressure and crisis, and where suspicion of sexual scandal was endemic.

But what was a corrody? Though Hamilton Thompson's definition that it was, or became, 'first and foremost a grant of money or victuals, or of other means of livelihood made by a monastery ... to dependents upon its bounty' cannot be bettered it is perhaps not sufficiently acknowledged that the term is a very fluid one.[7] Time-limited or in perpetuity (though very rarely heritable), they were extraordinarily varied in the benefits, spiritual and temporal, they offered, and many other provisions for lay benefactors were corrodies in all but name. Thus it is misleading to confine discussion solely to those settlements specifically styled *corredia*, and important to recognise that while the word *corredium*, meaning an allowance or annuity provided by a community to a non-religious, only became commonplace in the thirteenth century, there were certainly cognate arrangements in place well before then.[8] Though corrodians inhabited only a post-Conquest world, the pious women, widows, vowesses, occupying a liminal place between the religious and secular life in late Anglo-Saxon England with their highly individualised and flexible connections with religious houses of both men and women can plausibly be regarded as corrodians *avant la lettre*.[9] How, moreover, do we categorise the poor 'Maundy men' who received daily charity, ritualised but charity nevertheless, at many Old English Benedictine houses in return for their prayers?[10] Nor, of course, were corrodies solely an English phenomenon, and similar provisions are frequently found throughout western Europe.[11]

However, the earliest recognisable corrodies as later understood date from the first half of the twelfth century and were, perhaps significantly, for the benefit of women.[12] Though well known, they deserve further examination. Sometime between 1127 and 1134 the three women living an anchoretic life at Kilburn (which later became a nunnery) who were supervised by the monks of Westminster, were granted *beneficia*, the perpetual allowance previously given to Aimar, a hermit also once under Westminster's aegis, together with the daily portion of the monks of Westminster and Fécamp, living and dead. This quite lavish ration was supplemented a few years later by an additional grant of the commemorative *corredium* for Abbot Gilbert Crispin.[13] Three features need emphasis here. First, this was a grant in perpetuity. In other words it represented an endowment, a permanent element in the abbey's expenditure, still amounting to about £20 at the Dissolution.[14] This was the core of the women's income, lacking as they did landed property. Secondly, the grant of the customary monastic dishes was associative: by eating the same food, even if not in the refectory and outside the precinct, the women were incorporated into the Benedictine spiritual community, ties were consolidated and control more clearly demonstrated. Though the food (and wine) were doubtless welcome, the arrangement's essence was symbolic. Thirdly, they linked the living and the dead in collective memorialisation. They can be interpreted in the context of the monastic eleemosynary imperative, but as targeted almsgiving, rather than that indiscriminately dispensed at the abbey gate.[15] Charity was melded with commemoration. And, most significantly, the *beneficia* of the earlier charter have become *corredia* in the second. These temporal allowances were, and must be, seen as components in spiritual relationships. Nor was this settlement unique to Westminster. At the end of the century Abbot Warin of St Albans made very similar provision for the dependent nuns of St Mary de Pré and Norwich Cathedral Priory supplied the nuns of Thetford with their weekly bread and beer.[16]

From such agreements it was a short step to provide allowances due to nuns (or monks) to monastic servants. So, in the late twelfth century the abbess of Shaftesbury granted the hereditary office of nunnery cook to Durand Bardel, which his father had held before him. It was a handsome offer, and amongst the payments and perquisites included a nun's corrody.[17] Such was to become common practice in succeeding generations, and one prone to abuse as a means of rewarding favourites on their retirement: in the early fourteenth century the abbess of Malling was forbidden from giving a corrody to her maids, 'a bad old custom'.[18]

And if food allowances functioned to cement ties between the religious and their households there was no reason why they should not also reinforce lay patronal relationships. At Rochester the wife (widow?) of a Rochester cobbler gave a house to the cathedral priory in return for a food and clothing allowance, confraternity rights and the promise of prayers, as for a nun, on death. Shortly afterwards Robert Latimer's widow received a rather more lavish grant, appropriate to her higher status, of a food allowance due a monk, augmented with meat dishes, clothing in accord with her position and provision for two servants. Again this was associated with a detailed confraternity agreement, burial rights and the keeping of her anniversary, within the framework of a land settlement.[19] A very similar, and slightly later, example comes from the Augustinian priory of Christchurch. Here the canons granted Adeline, wife of Wyso Falconer, a life corrody, 'as for a canon', in settlement of a complicated land plea.[20] The frequent association of early corrodies with real or fictive litigation is unmistakeable: it was usually only later that such arrangements were adapted for purchasers or nominees. It is also clear that corrodies constructed for women were often connected with the buying-out of their interests or renunciation of any claim that they might have through dower or as unmarried heiress: it is notable, for instance, that about half of all corrodies granted by Westminster before 1300 were for women, sometimes single and/or widows, sometimes in conjunction with their husbands, mostly in association with quitclaims.[21]

The great majority of early corrodies provided by nunneries were for women (and it was probably only when a trade in corrodies divorced from any wider associative relationship with the community developed that men were generally admitted), perhaps being maintained there in their widowhood or old age by their family, as when Simon Luvel gave land in Eversden to Clerkenwell in return for a lifetime grant of food and clothing for his mother.[22] Such contracts were little different from those customarily made in manorial courts for the support of elderly or incapacitated labourers, except in one important respect, they normally also conveyed specific spiritual benefits, including, though this is rarely spelt out, burial.[23]

This provision of facilities *within* a religious house was, however, a slightly later development than those which offered sustenance outside the cloister. Indeed, early corrodians were sometimes allowed to remain in their own homes till death (comparable to today's equity release schemes), as when a citizen gave his house (which he then leased back) near London bridge to Clerkenwell nunnery in return for confraternity. On his death his wife would enjoy the same privileges, and have '*liberum bancum*', presumably in her house, for as long as she remained in 'honest widowhood'.[24] The first laypeople to be maintained within a community were generally those with which it had close ties. Thus Alice de Clare stayed over twenty years in St Osyth's Priory following the death of her husband in 1141: shortly after her own death her son, William de Vere (later bishop of Hereford) joined the priory as a canon.[25] At about the same time Ernald, *miles*, granted his land in Prestbury to Llanthony Secunda when he became a canon there. This created a problem both for the bishop of Hereford, whose tenant Ernald was, who stood to lose military service, and for Ernald's wife and children. In a series of agreements Ralph, Ernald's son, promised to provide for his mother and sisters, and to perform the service for his father's alienated land. In return for a further grant the obligation to look after Ernald's wife, who was received '*in sororem*' with a lifetime's provision of food and clothing was taken on by the priory.[26] That she was regarded as a sister of the community certainly suggests that she lived within its precincts. Even the Cistercians, who generally insisted that women be prohibited from their cloisters, were occasionally prepared to accept them as corrodians.[27] When the three daughters, and heiresses, of Nigel fitzGurwent collectively granted their land in Kirby Wiske to Fountains Abbey, the monks granted them food and clothing for life and gave 'counsel for their souls', spiritual guidance seemingly provided by one or more of the monks? When this grant was confirmed by a further quitclaim an alternative possibility, that the sisters be placed in religion, was added.[28] Their reception in a Yorkshire nunnery was perhaps deemed more appropriate than an ad hoc arrangement with an individual monk.

However, Cistercian corrodies were rare and subject to careful and nuanced negotiation. This is nowhere more clearly seen than at Waverley when in 1310 the diocesan bishop and abbey's chief patron, Henry Woodlock, wrote to the abbot of Cîteaux in support of his proctor, master Roger de Redenhale and his wife. Roger had done the bishop good service at the Canterbury court and his wife was of good reputation. They were now both elderly and had bought a corrody at Waverley and built a house *extra portam* at their own expense and situated next the chapel (perhaps emphasised to demonstrate their own piety) and wished with the abbot's consent to live out their days '*cum Deo*'. The bishop was writing to ask the abbot to write to the abbot of Waverley, if it could be done without offence, on the couple's behalf. Roger had given much to the order and abbey, and was minded to give much more.[29] There can be few clearer indications of the tensions between Cistercian ideals and economic advantage: in such circumstances the presence of an elderly woman might conveniently be permitted.

But when did commodification of corrodies occur?[30] It was undoubtedly a gradual process, and there had always been an element of calculated charity, gathering pace in the thirteenth century. The first recorded Gilbertine corrodies, for example, clearly signal that charity had to be paid for, by outright property grants or confirmations, by the sale of chattels. The spiritual associations explicit or implicit in earlier transactions have disappeared. Who profited more from these arrangements is difficult to say. William of Redbourn gained a substantial corrody of food, clothing and a house from the nuns of Alvingham, but the community obtained a large holding almost adjacent to the priory.[31]

Another factor in this trend was the growing practice of the Crown requiring corrodies to be provided for royal servants. This began during the reign of Henry III, but gathered pace during the reigns of his son and grandson, before tailing off in the reign of Edward III. A catalyst may have been the king's demands that Jewish *conversi* be housed in monasteries.[32] However, very few nunneries were so burdened, and the great majority of female converts, like the hapless Alice of Worcester discussed by Joan Greatrex, were consigned to male communities.[33] As the practice of royal requisition spread nominees were normally (though not exclusively) dispatched to the great long-established Benedictine nunneries, and even these were not as encumbered as their male counterparts. Though it was more usual for the king to send women, particularly widows, as corrodians to nunneries, it was far from unknown for male royal servants to be nominated, sometimes replacing a woman on the latter's death.[34] The women's lay status varied. In 1313 Edward II sent the niece of his old foster-mother to the Nunnaminster: others were relatives of loyal royal servants.[35] The widowed Agnes de Villers, for example, asked the newly crowned Edward III that he aid her and her children in regard for her husband's service to Edward I and II. Shortly afterwards she successfully requested a corrody at Barking.[36] Such plaintiffs were clearly in need, and though contemporary churchmen resented royal requisitions and were often genuinely placed in financial difficulties thereby, the corrody's original charitable function remained.

The economic temptations offered by corrody grants and sales were particularly alluring and dangerous to nunneries, the majority of which were comparatively poor and chronically indebted, and it is significant that the first synodal legislation to address (or even mention) the dangers of corrodies was directed at female houses, when these were forbidden by the 1222 council of

Oxford from selling or freely granting corrodies or stipends to clerics or the laity, 'in perpetuity or for a fixed term, unless forced by great necessity and with the diocesan's permission'.[37] This was the basis, and often the verbatim wording, of future episcopal injunctions. But who determined what defined necessity, and what influenced diocesan regulation? Moreover, this legislation is, of course, only a *terminus a quo* for a perceived problem, and the relative paucity of records from nunneries makes it difficult to establish a trajectory. It was only in 1268 that the London legatine council extended and strengthened the Oxford ruling to cover all religious communities, noting that the sale of *liberationes* meant that houses were so burdened by these demands that the sick and poor for whom benefactions had been specifically made were defrauded to the peril of the communities' souls and their great scandal. No such sales should be made in future and as earlier recipients surrendered their rights or died the corrodies should lapse, rather than being re-granted.[38] Thereafter, though the clergy complained at *royal* imposition of corrodians, there was no further reference to corrodies at the councils, and the problem was commonly addressed at an individual level via episcopal visitations, rather than more generally through diocesan or provincial synods.[39]

Though corrody sales could certainly offer short-term financial remedy their indiscriminate offer could seriously burden a nunnery. So it is no surprise to find the Gilbertine General Chapter of 1347 warning priors that they were not to encumber their houses with 'debts, corrodies, chantries or burdens of a similar kind'.[40] Typically the nuns of Cistercian Heynings complained in 1348 that they were impoverished by poor lands, too many guests and corrodians, and burdens laid on religious houses so that they had had to mortgage all their possessions.[41] Neither wealthy prestigious communities or poor insignificant nunneries were exempt from diocesan warnings and prohibitions. As early as 1252 we find Archbishop Gray forbidding any unauthorised sale of corrodies at Marrick.[42] At the same time as the bishops of Winchester were forbidding unlicensed corrodies at Romsey, at the other end of the country the archbishops of York were issuing identical prohibitions at the small nunneries of Moxby and Arden.[43] That in 1341 the king had complained that the abbess of Fontevraud was overburdening Amesbury with corrody requests may suggest that exploitative behaviour was not a royal monopoly, though (as Berenice Kerr points out) there were perhaps political motives behind the royal action.[44] And in 1364 even Nunnaminster, one of the wealthiest, and certainly one of the most prestigious, nunneries in the country was almost forced into liquidation partly as a result of the excessive charge of corrodies, and placed under special measures with a strict embargo on corrodians and the expulsion of all those whose stay was unnecessary.[45]

Corrodians were one in a constellation made up of various elements, surrounding, and to a greater or lesser extent, interacting with the cloistered nuns, who might themselves possess significant freedom of movement and independence if of high social status. As Berenice Kerr has observed, nuns of royal and high aristocratic family had their own private rooms, special allowances, wine (and cash) at Amesbury.[46] This is not, of course, to argue that real boundaries, conceptual and spatial, did not exist in the nunnery, but that frontiers between lay and religious could be fluid and negotiable, category distinctions could sometimes be unclear. Though known, almost subliminally, it is seldom explicitly recognised, or its implications followed through, that a medieval religious house generally contained considerably more lay than religious and was far more open to secular society than most contemplative counterparts today.[47] A guest (perhaps a local benefactor, or diocesan bishop on official visitation) might encounter cloistered nuns, novices, *ad succurrendum* entrants, teenage boarders sent for education and/or to wait till a suitable marriage was arranged, patrons with servants (and dogs and horses) on extended vacation, and women or men, who might, or might not, be elderly, perhaps married couples, or retired clergy, who might, or might not, be permanent residents or corrodians.[48] And an observer of Ilchester nunnery in the 1320s might query the exact status of Simonis wife of Gilbert Passeware who dwelt in a building she had had constructed at her own expense, as well as a living room, but who ate daily at the prioress' table, was attended by the community's servants and who wore the sisters' habit and veil: lay or religious?[49] In one sense, too, a corrody could be seen as a permanent extension of the lengthy hospitality often expected and enjoyed by patrons and which frequently stretched a nunnery's resources.

Sometimes a husband and wife might be received as corrodians together, living in their own house within the precincts.[50] Barbara Harvey has suggested convincingly that such corrodies were often taken by a husband to provide a secure jointure for his wife on widowhood, particularly if childless.[51] Corrodians clearly came and went at will, though how far the extraordinary case of a corrodian at St Mary's Clerkenwell is typical is impossible to determine. She was allowed to visit her husband should she marry, though he might not join her in the nunnery, and any children were to be born outside the house.[52] Staying at Clerkenwell, too, probably as a corrodian we find Nicholaa de Fulham making her will and bequeathing rents to her sister, Joanna, a nun who is likely to be identified as a later prioress of the community.[53] Nor was it unknown for whole families to be received, as happened at Bayham in 1290 when a couple were granted a corrody including lodging (and pasture for a cow) outside the precinct, alms at the abbey gate for their son who was intended as a priest, and who would serve the community if his health allowed, the employment of two younger sons within the precinct until they could support themselves, and monetary payments to the couple's daughters.[54]

It is clear, too, that corrodies were individually tailored for the needs and expectations of their recipients, calibrated both to their social status and the communities' calculated profit from the negotiation. Large estates or cash sums might change hands and risks were correspondingly high, though these risks could be mitigated if the corrodian also made an annual as well as a downpayment.[55] There was little scope for miscalculation when Margery, daughter of Bertram of Alderton, bought a lavish corrody (which included the provision of a chaplain to pray for her soul for one year, should she die within five years) from Winchcombe Abbey in 1317 for 140 marks.[56] Unsurprisingly these agreements were carefully drafted and their terms detailed, sometimes with sanctions on their non-performance.[57]

It is also important, though difficult, to distinguish between lay people nominated as novices to nunneries by the Crown, bishops or patrons, those sent as boarders (who might be long term, as was Alice of Ayote licensed to stay at Godstow nunnery in 1357 for two years at her own expense), and those as corrodians.[58] In some instances that distinction might be obscure to contemporaries, as it is to us. Who, for example, were the 'lay people of both sexes living in Markyate nunnery' accused in 1297 of incontinence without due evidence?[59] We do know that a few years later Markyate nuns made a violent protest against the imposition of *Periculoso*, and corrodies could be interpreted not only as simoniac, but flying in the face of demands for stricter claustration.[60] Just as benefactors might nominate a novice or a priest to serve in a monastic chantry chapel they might provide for a servant by a corrody. So, in settlement of a real or fictive land dispute in Chitterne between Ela, abbess of Lacock, and her attorney, Nicholas of Heddington, who was active in land transactions both on the abbey's and his own account, he was rented the land for a life term and on his death prayers were to be offered for him, 'and all his benefactors' (an interesting formulation) in the chapel of St Edmund Rich, and he might nominate one of his free servants in his will to receive 'all things necessary' during his lifetime.[61]

Before the closing days of monasticism it is extremely difficult to gauge how many corrodians were in a house at any one time, their gender, age or class.[62] Corrodies were individual, time-limited, rarely heritable: they are not always recorded in charters or cartularies unless exchanged for landed property, rather than a cash payment. That relatively few records survive for (or were perhaps produced by) for nunneries compared with male communities might indicate an even greater underestimate of the actual number of

corrodians in female houses. We do know that there were at least ten corrodians at Fontevraudine Amesbury in 1315–16, a significant proportion of this
high-status nunnery. These cost £8 4s. 8d over a six-month period. Two years
later at least three more were purchased for a total of nearly £70.[63] A very crude
calculation indicates that a corrodian would have to live for some twenty years
to 'show a profit': in other words at least at Amesbury the actuarial calculations
seem to the community's benefit. However these figures do not account for
accommodation or clothing (where provided) costs.[64]

Finally where were these early corrodians housed? Unfortunately little
is revealed in the archaeological and only infrequently in the documentary
record, though something can be inferred from late medieval practice. What
is certain is that there was no defined, regularised space for these long-term
lay residents in a sacred enclosure, nor could there be. It was common practice
for chambers to be provided for corrodians' long-term use. Thus, in 1399, two
men, at least one a former chaplain, were assigned a house within Lacock
Abbey formerly held by Christine Swayn.[65] As we have seen not all corrodians were permanently resident (or even maintained within the nunnery at all,
but were given houses outwith the precinct walls), sometimes they retained a
room for their use in the nunnery when needed.[66] The tensions inherent in the
physical juxtaposition of lay and religious were accentuated by the presence
of laymen in nunneries (or conversely of lay women in male communities)
and it made sense for corrodians' quarters to be close, if not integral, to guest
halls and ancillary buildings for visitors, well away from the central claustral
area. Alternatively, more prestigious (or generous) house guests might have
their own chamber, perhaps complete with private oratory, somewhere within
the precinct. The outer precinct, often extensive at nunneries, was particularly
suitable for male or married corrodians, where they might be neighbours of
lay or ecclesiastical tenants, or of the convent's senior lay officials, halfway
between the enclosed and secular world. Another option was the claustral
west range. At Lacock (and very probably elsewhere) it seems probable that
late medieval ground floor apartments on the west range of the cloister were
intended for corrodians, allowing easy access to a west gallery in the church.
This range was often the domain of lay brothers in sisters in both male and
female communities, and sometimes too of the abbess or abbot.[67] Gilchrist
has suggested that seculars used viewing galleries into the convent church.
Certainly there are indications of galleries in a number of nunneries but the
fact that some, at least, of these were accessed via the nuns' dormitory makes
it very unlikely that these were intended for lay use.[68] And whether they were
intended primarily for visiting patrons or long-stay residents (or both) cannot be determined.[69]

When observing corrodies from an early Tudor perspective and with a fiercely anti-monastic agenda Bishop Latimer launched his polemic arguing that rather than maintaining their own servants and relieving the poor themselves 'many people, especially widows, would give over housekeeping, and go to such houses' he was probably unaware, or ignored the fact, that they were not just a contemporary phenomenon, but that their contours were long-since drawn with roots reaching to late Anglo-Saxon times.[70] Both Latimer and the papal legate Ottobuono (whose canons became normative for the late medieval church) back in 1268 perceived that corrodies could distort and deflect the core charitable function of the monastery. Neither acknowledged that they also fulfilled a positive role in both literally and metaphorically providing a refuge for the laity within the religious community. By furnishing women and men with accommodation within the monastic enclosure the corrody had the potential to strengthen the association and bridge the divide between temporal and spiritual worlds.

Notes

1. John Wyclif, *On Simony*, trans. T. A. McVeigh (New York, 1992), pp. 132–4. As early as *c*.1200 corrodies were said to be *'non longe a simonya'*, see C. D. Ross and M. Devine (eds), *The Cartulary of Cirencester Abbey*, 3 vols (Oxford, 1964–77), I, no. 327/186 (p. 195); B. Harvey, *Living and Dying in England, 1100–1540: the Monastic Experience* (Oxford, 1993), p. 180.

2. G. G. Coulton, *Five Centuries of Religion*, 4 vols (Cambridge, 1923–50), 3, pp. 240–7.

3. There is now a very substantial literature. A. Hamilton Thompson, 'A corrody from Leicester Abbey, AD 1393–4, with some notes on corrodies', *Transactions of the Leicestershire Archaeological Society*, 19 (1925), 113–34, is the foundational study, but see, especially, Harvey, *Living and Dying*, pp. 179–209, 239–51. The fullest discussion of late medieval corrodies in nunneries remains E. Power, *Medieval English Nunneries c.1275–1535* (Cambridge, 1922), esp. pp. 194–200, 206–9. See also B. Golding, *Gilbert of Sempringham and the Gilbertine Order, c.1130–c.1300* (Oxford, 1995), pp. 154–8.

4. See, e.g. Archbishop Melton's prohibition on the servants of corrodian priests at Sinningthwaite who customarily carried their food and liveries straight through the cloister (W. Page (ed.), *VCH Yorkshire*, 3 (London, 1913), p. 177).

5. The distinction between 'corrody' and 'pension' is also a fluid one, and the terms were frequently interchangeable, though the latter tended to be cash-based and non-resident, necessary where an individual held allowances in several houses.

6. But these were not mutually exclusive. In 1313 the king stipulated that his nominee be given a nun's corrody by the Nunnaminster, Winchester, wherever she might be, with a suitable chamber whenever she chose to stay there (Power, *Medieval English Nunneries*, p. 196).

7. Thompson, 'A corrody from Leicester Abbey', 117.

8. See Burton, *Monastic Order*, p. 208; E. Amt (ed.), *The Latin Cartulary of Godstow Abbey* (Oxford, 2014), p. xxxvii.

9. S. Foot, *Veiled Women*, 2 vols (Aldershot, 2000), 1, esp. ch. 5, pp. 111–45.

10. T. Symons (ed.), *Regularis Concordia* (London, 1953), pp. xxxvii, 61–2; Harvey, *Living and Dying*, pp. 12–16; J. Kerr, *Monastic Hospitality: the Benedictines in England, c.1070–c.1250* (Woodbridge, 2007), pp. 29–32, 105.

11. G. Constable, *The Reformation of the Twelfth Century* (Cambridge, 1996), pp. 84–6, and see especially E. Lesne, 'Une source de la fortune monastique. Les donations à charge de pension alimentaire du VIIIᵉ au Xᵉ siècle', in *Mélanges de philosophie et d'histoire publiés à l'occasion du cinquentenaire de la faculté des lettres de l'Université catholique de Lille* (Lille, 1927), pp. 33–47. Particularly in this chapter's context see P. D. Johnson, *Equal in Monastic Profession: Religious Women in Medieval France* (Chicago, 1991), pp. 179–82 and L. V. Hicks, *Religious Life in Normandy, 1050–1300: Space, Gender and Social Pressure* (Woodbridge, 2007), esp. pp. 58–65, 135–44.

12. I am very grateful to Hirokazu Tsurushima and Katherine Blayney for discussing this material with me.

13. E. Mason (ed.), *Westminster Abbey Charters, 1066–c.1214*, London Record Society, 25 (1988), nos. 249, 264, pp. 117–19, 128; Harvey, *Living and Dying*, pp. 239–40; S. Thompson, *Women Religious: the Founding of English Nunneries after the Conquest* (Oxford, 1991), pp. 25–6, 63.

14. Harvey, *Living and Dying*, pp. 214, 240.

15. For which see Harvey, *Living and Dying*, pp. 7–33. See also M. Rubin, *Charity and Community in Medieval Cambridge* (Cambridge, 1987), esp. pp. 54–73. Cf. Giraldus Cambrensis's half-critical, half-admiring comments on Cistercian generosity, e.g. *Speculum Ecclesie* (*Giraldus Cambrensis Opera*, IV), p. 113 and *Itinerarium Kambriae* (*Giraldus Cambrensis Opera*, VI), pp. 43–6.

16. *Gesta abbatum monasterii sancti Albani*, ed. H. T. Riley, RS 28/4 (1867–9), I, pp. 202–3. See also Thompson, *Women Religious*, pp. 59, 63–4.

17. Did he have to cook his own corrody? N. E. Stacy (ed.), *Charters and Custumals of Shaftesbury Abbey 1089–1216* (Oxford, 2006), no. 16, pp. 50–1.

18. H. Wharton, *Anglia Sacra*, 2 vols (London, 1691), I, p. 364; Power, *English Nunneries*, p. 155.

19. Cf. J. Wardrop, *Fountains Abbey and its Benefactors 1132–1300* (Kalamazoo, 1987), pp. 255–7.

20. K. A. Hanna (ed.), *Christchurch Priory Cartulary*, Hampshire Record Society, 18 (2007), no. 248, p. 87. I am grateful to Katherine Blayney for bringing this case to my notice.

21. Harvey, *Living and Dying*, pp. 239–43. W. Urry, *Canterbury under the Angevin Kings* (London, 1967), p. 164 noted that all the twelfth-century corrodians at Christ Church were women, but thought that this 'had no particular significance'. All lived outside the monastic precincts, some were in settlement of claims, one was provided when her husband left her to become a monk.

22. W. O. Hassall (ed.), *Cartulary of St Mary Clerkenwell*, Camden Society, Third Series, 76 (1949), no. 138, pp. 88–9.

23. H. Tsurushima, 'The Fraternity of Rochester Cathedral Priory about 1100', *Anglo-Norman Studies*, 14 (Woodbridge, 1992), pp. 330–1; C. Dyer, *Standards of Living in the Later Middle Ages: Social Change in England, c.1200–1520* (Cambridge, 1989), pp. 151–6; E. Clark, 'The Quest for Security in Medieval England', in M. M. Sheehan (ed.), *Aging and the Aged in Medieval Europe* (Toronto, 1990), pp. 189–200; I. Metzler, *A Social History of Disability in the Middle Ages: Cultural Considerations of Physical Impairment* (London, 2013), pp. 123–6.

24. *Cartulary of Clerkenwell*, no. 200, p. 125.

25. L. Toulmin Smith (ed.), *Leland's Itineraries*, 5 vols (London, 1907–10), V, p. 171; J. Barrow (ed.), *English Episcopal Acta VII Hereford 1079–1234* (Oxford, 1993), p. xliv.

26. Barrow, *English Episcopal Acta VII*, nos. 43, 104, pp. 41–2, 71; A. Morey and C. N. L. Brooke (eds), *The Letters and Charters of Gilbert Foliot, Abbot of Gloucester (1139–48), Bishop of Hereford (1148–63), and London (1163–87)*, London (1967), no. 329 (p. 383).

27. By the later Middle Ages corrodians are recorded at e.g. Hampole, Heynings, Tarrant and Keldholme.

28. Wardrop, *Fountains Abbey*, pp. 255–6.

29. A. W. Goodman (ed.), *Registrum Henrici Woodlock Diocesis Wintoniensis*, 2 vols, Canterbury and York Society, 43, 44 (1940–1), I, p. 640.

30. By the early thirteenth century corrodies were being pledged to Jews, see G. H. Fowler (ed.), *A Digest of the Charters preserved in the Cartulary of the Priory of Dunstable*, Bedfordshire Historical Record Society, 10 (1926), no. 297, p. 103.

31. Golding, *Gilbert of Sempringham*, pp. 155–6.

32. J. Greatrex, 'Monastic Charity for Jewish Converts: the Requisition of Corrodies by Henry III', in D. Wood (ed.), *Christianity and Judaism*, Studies in Church History, 29 (1992), pp. 133–43.

33. Greatrex, 'Monastic Charity for Jewish Converts', pp. 141–2.

34. Power, *Medieval English Nunneries*, pp. 197–8; D. K. Coldicott, *Hampshire Nunneries* (Chichester, 1989), p. 124; V. G. Spear, *Leadership in Medieval English Nunneries*, Studies in the History of Medieval Religion, 24 (Woodbridge, 2005), pp. 74–8. On such royal corrodians, see especially H. Tillotson, 'Pensions, Corrodies and Religious Houses: an Aspect of the Relations of Crown and Church in Early Fourteenth Century England', *Journal of Religious History*, 8 (1974), 127–43.

35. Power, *Medieval English Nunneries*, p. 196; Spear, *Leadership*, p. 75.

36. TNA, SC 8/81/4013; 8/14/678.

37. Frederick M. Powicke and Christopher R. Cheney (eds), *Councils and Synods with Other Documents Relating to the English Church*, 2 vols (Oxford, 1964), II (i), p. 119. See also p. 152. Like any annuity the grants of a corrody was a calculated risk and it is (and was) usually difficult to determine whether the community or the recipient was the net gainer in such transactions. See the attempt at such a statistical calculation by A. Bell and

C. Sutcliffe 'Valuing Medieval Annuities: were Corrodies Underpriced?', *Explorations in Economic History*, 47 (2010), 142–57.

38. *Councils and Synods*, I, p. 788. See Harvey, *Living and Dying*, p. 180.

39. *Councils and Synods*, II (ii), pp. 1271–2. For a long, but incomplete, list of visitations of nunneries, see Power, *Medieval English Nunneries*, p. 226, n. 1. One of the earliest known visitations (of Cirencester, *c.*1200) condemned simony (see above, n. 1).

40. Bodl., MS Douce 136, fol. 96v.

41. W. Page (ed.), *VCH Lincolnshire*, 2 (London, 1906), p. 142.

42. Page (ed.), *VCH Yorkshire*, 3, p. 117.

43. Archbishop Greenfield seems to have been particularly concerned about the granting of corrodies to the Yorkshire nunneries without licence. See, e.g. W. Brown and A. H. Thompson (eds), *The Register of William Greenfield, Lord Archbishop of York, 1306–1315*, 5 vols, Surtees Society, 145, 149, 151–3 (1931–48), II, no. 962, pp. 124–5 (Hampole); III, no. 1210, p. 41 (Thicket) and no. 1379, p. 115 (Rosedale). He was only prepared to authorise a woman to be granted a corrody at Thicket in 1315 and to take a lay sister's habit provided it was the will of the community, that she was useful, and that it could be done without any detriment to the house (Brown and Thompson (eds), *The Register of William Greenfield*, III, no. 1275, p. 110).

44. B. M. Kerr, *Religious Life for Women, c.1100–c.1350: Fontevraud in England* (Oxford, 2000), p. 177.

45. Tillotson, 'Pensions, Corrodies and Religious Houses', 127–43; Spear, *Leadership*, pp. 68–9.

46. Kerr, *Religious Life*, pp. 110, 114–16, 166. Amesbury was, after all, the nunnery to which Malory has Guinevere retiring on Arthur's death.

47. But see, especially and for the later Middle Ages where evidence is greater, M. Oliva, *The Convent and the Community in Late Medieval England* (Woodbridge, 1998), pp. 125–38.

48. On canine disruption, see Golding, *Gilbert of Sempringham*, pp. 320–1. Horses could be as troublesome (and more expensive) than dogs. See, e.g. P. Greene, *Norton Priory: the Archaeology of a Medieval Religious House* (Cambridge, 1989), p. 15.

49. W. Page (ed.), *VCH Somerset*, 2 (London, 1911), p. 158.

50. See the case of the retired royal servant and his wife at Muchelney in the mid-thirteenth century (S. Wood, *English Monasteries and their Patrons in the Thirteenth Century* (Oxford, 1955), p. 108).

51. Harvey, *Living and Dying*, p. 208.

52. *Cartulary of Clerkenwell*, p. xv.

53. R. R. Sharpe (ed.), *Calendar of Wills Proved and Enrolled in the Court of Husting, London*, 2 vols (London,1889–90), I, p. 324; *Cartulary of Clerkenwell*, p. 282.

54. H. M. Colvin, *The White Canons in England* (Oxford, 1951), p. 313.

55. E.g. R. P. Bucknill, 'Wherwell Abbey and its Cartulary' (unpublished PhD thesis, London, 2003), 158.

56. D. Royce (ed.), *Landboc, sive registrum monasterii ... de Winchelcumbe*, 2 vols (Exeter, 1892–1903), I, p. 329.

57. See, e.g. two examples from Lacock, one dating from the late thirteenth century, the other from 1399, in K. H. Rogers (ed.), *Lacock Abbey Charters*, Wiltshire Record Society, 34 (1979), nos. 216, 399–400, pp. 57, 98.

58. W. Page (ed.), *VCH Oxfordshire*, 2 (London, 1907), p. 73. Perhaps the only difference between long-term boarders and corrodians was that the former paid regularly, the latter made a one-off payment. For the later Middle Ages, see Oliva, *Convent and the Community*, pp. 116–24.

59. R. M. T. Hill (ed.), *The Rolls and Register of Bishop Oliver Sutton, 1280–1299*, Lincoln Record Society, 64 (1969), p. 16.

60. Spear, *Leadership*, p. 53.

61. *Lacock Abbey Charters*, no. 302, p. 77.

62. J. Rosenthal, 'Retirement and the Life Cycle in 15th-century England', in Sheehan (ed.), *Aging and the Aged*, p. 175 suggests that 'we are prone to exaggerate their (i.e. corrodies') popularity'.

63. Kerr, *Religious Life*, pp. 144–6.

64. A lay brother received 8s. per annum for clothing (Kerr, *Religious Life*, p. 169).

65. *Lacock Abbey Charters*, no. 216, p. 57.

66. Bucknill, 'Wherwell Abbey', pp. 129–30.

67. J. Bond, 'English Medieval Nunneries: Buildings, Precincts and Estates', in D. Wood (ed.), *Women and Religion in Medieval England* (Oxford, 2003), pp. 67, 72; R. Gilchrist, *Gender and Material Culture: the Archaeology of Religious Women* (London, 1994), pp. 116–17.

68. Though lay servants frequently, and irregularly, slept in the dorter, and in 1440 one of them at Heynings was said to have purchased a corrody (Power, *Medieval English Nunneries*, p. 155).

69. Gilchrist, *Gender and Material Culture*, pp. 107–9. Of the examples cited the most likely possibilities are those at Lacock, Marrick and Aconbury, where the galleries were at the west end of the church.

70. Hugh Latimer, *Sermons and Remains*, 2 vols, ed. G. E. Corrie, Parker Society, 16, 20 (1844–5), I, p. 392.

13

Preaching to nuns in the Norwich diocese on the eve of the Reformation: the evidence from visitation records

Veronica O'Mara

It may be assumed that nuns in medieval England heard a sermon at their professions, on Sundays, on major holy days, during episcopal visitations and perhaps at other times, such as patronal feast days. Yet, unusually in a European context, there is very little surviving evidence for this.[1] There are only two Latin profession sermons from the fourteenth century; a Latin sermon for an undetermined occasion from the same century; a fifteenth-century English sermon for the feast of the Assumption; an English printed profession sermon from the late fifteenth century; and an English sermon written for a profession in the early sixteenth century.[2] In addition, there are merely about a dozen references to sermons or sermon collections associated with convent libraries in the post-Conquest period.[3] The absence of written evidence for preaching to English nuns is thus a major problem. It may be supposed that visitation sermons were written down in full or in part; whether this would have been in Latin or English we cannot say, though we may suspect it would have been Latin.[4] Such sermons are not extant in English and it can only be assumed (less certainly) that the Latin texts do not survive either. Nevertheless, we can piece some information together from visitations records, albeit that these should be treated with a degree of caution.[5]

This chapter will seek to unearth evidence for preaching to nuns from a systematic examination of visitation records from a particular part of the country, the diocese of Norwich. It builds on a previous study on the published Lincoln Visitation Records of William Alnwick.[6] In these visitations between 1437 and 1447 seventy-nine visits are described, almost all in great detail with the place of visitation, the order, the visitor and date provided. Fifty-seven were to male religious and twenty-two were to nuns. The preaching of a sermon is mentioned in forty-five of the visits to male religious and seventeen to female, which would mean a more or less equal treatment in preaching terms. In almost all cases the preacher's name, the theme of the sermon and the language (Latin or English) are specified. The sermons, whether to men or women, were almost consistently given by three of Alnwick's own staff, Thomas Duffeld (or Duffield), John Beverley and Thomas Twyer – all theologically trained university men. It depended upon who was 'on duty': on 3 July 1440 Thomas Duffeld preached to the nuns of Legbourne Priory and on 6 July 1440 to the monks of Humberstone Abbey; Duffeld preached to the brothers of Breedon Priory on 19 January 1441, Beverley to the nuns of Langley Priory on 20 January 1441, and Duffeld to the nuns of Gracedieu Priory on 21 January 1441. On various occasions the same preacher used the same theme in different locations: I Corinthians 14: 40 was chosen by Duffeld at Ulverscroft Priory on 29 July 1438 and at Markby Priory on 19 August of the same year, while Beverley was keen on Songs 3: 11 for female audiences as he used it for the nuns at Catesby Priory on 17 July 1442 and the nuns at Goring Priory on 21 May 1445. There was a slightly higher emphasis on themes from the New Testament than from the Old Testament in 'female' sermons. The themes chosen for sermons to nuns emphasised the more memorable biblical stories – Lot's wife as a pillar of salt (Genesis 19), the story of the fig tree (Luke 13) and so forth. In the texts selected there was a pronounced emphasis on virginal women, as well as a concentration on the physical and the corporeal. Most significantly, when specified, the language of the sermon was always English for the nuns and Latin for male religious with only two exceptions.[7]

There was a wealth of convents in the diocese of Lincoln, which stretched from south of York diocese to north of Salisbury diocese, and from the borders of Ely diocese in the east to the borders of Lichfield and Coventry diocese in the west. The diocese of Norwich, by contrast, merely comprised two counties (Norfolk and Suffolk), and had only eleven nunneries. In Norfolk there were the priories of Blackborough, Carrow, Crabhouse, Shouldham, Thetford and the abbey of Marham. In Suffolk there were the priories of Bungay, Campsey Ash, Flixton and Redlingfield, and the abbey of Bruisyard. With the exception of Bruisyard, which was founded in 1366, all the others were twelfth- or thirteenth-century foundations. At the time of their dissolution the *Valor Ecclesiasticus* valued the convents from £182 for Campsey Ash to £23 for Flixton.[8]

Most of the convents were Benedictine: Blackborough, Bungay, Carrow, Redlingfield and Thetford. Three were Augustinian: Campsey Ash, Crabhouse and Flixton, while Bruisyard was Franciscan/Poor Clares, Marham was Cistercian and Shouldham was Gilbertine. The order is significant because officially the local bishop only had jurisdiction over certain orders (male or female). Strictly speaking, episcopal visitation rights did not apply to the Cistercians as they came under the provenance of the General Chapter, although in practice a distinction was made in England between the fully incorporated houses of Marham in Norfolk and Tarrant Keynston in Dorset and the rest.[9] Therefore, in the comparisons below there is a difference between what was customary in the Norwich diocese where Marham was never visited, and in the Lincoln diocese where female Cistercian houses were routinely included in episcopal visitations. There was only ever a handful of Franciscan nunneries in the country (with only two others surviving at this time: Denney in Cambridgeshire and the Minories in London) and at this period fewer than a dozen houses of Gilbertine canons and nuns (mostly in Lincolnshire). Both orders came under the auspices of their General Chapters. It is therefore not surprising that neither Bruisyard nor Shouldham figure in the Norwich visitation lists.

This chapter will explore the later period of Norwich visitations by examining the published records of the bishops, James Goldwell (Oxford doctor of civil and canon law) between 1492 and 1494, and Richard Nykke (who studied at Oxford, Cambridge, Ferrara and Bologna where he was admitted as doctor of both civil and canon law) in 1514, 1520, 1526 and 1532.[10] Consideration will be given to the comparative aspects of preaching to men and women, that is: frequency, language, preacher and theme (see appendix 1). The aim of the chapter is to gain some idea – albeit from imperfect evidence – of the extent of monastic visitation preaching at the end of the fifteenth century and in the first decades of the sixteenth in a particular diocese so as to help cast some light on the issue of the 'decline' or otherwise of preaching in a monastic context on the eve of the Reformation.[11]

James Goldwell was bishop of Norwich from 1472 to 1499, but in the earlier part of his ministry he was engaged in the service of Henry VI and Edward IV, and it was not until after the accession of Henry VII that he withdrew from most public duties and concentrated on his diocese (with the help of his brother, Nicholas Goldwell, who represented him at many of the visitations). As may be seen from appendix 1, table 1, the total number of visits in James Goldwell's records for 1492 to 1494 was as follows. In 1492 there were sixteen visits from 5 October to 12 November: thirteen to men; two to women (Carrow and Thetford), plus Norman's Hospital, which consisted at this time of a master and sisters only. On seven of these visits sermons were preached. In this respect, with one exception, there is no difference between the male and female establishments in the manner in which the sermon is described. For those at the St Mary-in-the-Fields College (8 October), St Giles's Hospital (9 October), Norman's Hospital (9 October), Carrow (10 October), St Faith's Priory (11 October) and Wymondham Abbey (13 October) a variant of the same formulation is used: an unspecified preacher on an unspecified theme: '*Ubi verbo Dei proposito*'. At no point is the language of delivery stated, though from the explicit evidence of the Lincoln visitations above it must be assumed that the sermons to men were in Latin and that to the nuns at Carrow (and elsewhere) in the vernacular, although some qualification will be added below. Only the sermon at Norwich Priory, the first place to be visited (on 5 October), is delivered by a named preacher, Roger Framyngham (a Benedictine monk from the same house who was an Oxford scholar and, by 1499, a doctor of theology), though again without a specified theme.[12] In 1493 there were fourteen visits from 22 January to 27 September. Eleven were to male establishments and three to female (Campsey Ash on 24 January, Bungay on 31 January and Flixton on 20 June). On only one of these visits was a sermon preached: at Metyngham College on 18 June (with the usual formulation). Finally, in 1494 there were a mere six visits over a generous time frame (10 July to 15 September). All of these visits were to male religious and four sermons were preached: three by Henry Falke (a Cambridge doctor of canon law and the bishop's commissary): at Westacre Priory on 11 August, Walsingham Priory on 1 September and St Benet's at Hulme on 15 September, plus a sermon by an anonymous preacher at Butley Priory on 10 July.[13] Yet again nothing is known about themes or language of delivery.

After Goldwell's death on 15 February 1499, there was a vacancy during which time the Archbishop of Canterbury, John Morton, initiated a visitation of the Norwich diocese, but the evidence from this is insufficient for present research.[14] Richard Nykke took over in 1501. He straddled the medieval and renaissance periods as he was at the helm until 1535. In his records there are four rounds of visitations at six-yearly intervals in 1514, 1520, 1526 and 1532. Nykke was apparently a conscientious bishop, a scourge of Lollardy and Reformation tendencies, who was largely resident in his diocese. Given that his episcopacy started in 1501 and his first recorded visitation did not take place until 1514, it might be supposed that he likewise did a round six years earlier in 1508 and six years before that in 1502.

In 1514 (see appendix 1, table 2) there were thirty-six visits from 13 June to 30 August, with a standalone visit on 27 April. Twenty-nine were to male religious and eight to female (Thetford, Blackborough, Crabhouse, Campsey Ash, Redlingfield, Flixton, Bungay and Carrow) – all the convents subject to visitation. Fourteen sermons were preached of which only three were to women (Thetford, Campsey Ash and Carrow), which would indicate a slightly lower priority for preaching to nuns. The visitation to Norwich Priory on 27 April is noted as having not only a sermon, in Latin, but a theme (1 Corinthians 5: 7) and a named preacher, William Repps (natally named Rugg but also known by his locative name of Repps), who became Nykke's successor as bishop of Norwich (1536–50) after a short vacancy. Ten of the remaining sermons, including that at the convent in Thetford, were delivered by Henry Forth, formerly a fellow of Jesus College, Cambridge, who is described by Jessop as Nykke's chaplain.[15] This compares with the practice in the Lincoln visitations, in other words, the bishop's 'man', when on hand, delivered the sermon. It may therefore be presumed that Henry Forth was on duty between [16] June and 21 July; this would account for his addressing the nuns in Thetford on 22 June. In five cases the theme used by Henry Forth is given and in four other cases a blank was left for the theme, with the other one merely using the usual formulation. Various male religious had to focus respectively on Titus 2: 12; James I: 21; Ezechiel 18: 30 and Ecclesiasticus 43: 10, while the sisters at Thetford were focused on Luke 10: 42. Following 21 July, only the sermon at Butley on 30 July is delivered by a named preacher: the subprior of Westacre, on Acts 7: 3. In the remaining visits there are sermons only at Campsey Ash on 1 August and at Carrow on 25 August, though these are simply described in the usual formulaic way of 'proposito verbo Dei' and 'post verbum Dei propositum' respectively, with no mention of the preacher. It looks as if these convents are being discriminated against in some respect by not commanding the attention of someone of the calibre of Henry Forth – and this could be the case – it is equally likely that it was simply that Henry Forth was not then present in the bishop's entourage and that someone else (perhaps even the bishop himself) preached instead. Finally, at no point is the language of any of these sermons specified.

In 1520 (see appendix 1, table 3) there were thirty-six visits (plus a continuation of the visitation at Flixton), comprising one long stint from 14 June to 3 September; of these twenty-nine were to male religious and seven to female (Thetford, Crabhouse, Blackborough, Campsey Ash, Redlingfield, Flixton, Bungay, Flixton on 20 August, continued from 14 August). Twenty-one sermons were delivered of which nineteen were to men and two to women (Redlingfield and Flixton), once again a much lower proportion of sermons for women. Eleven of these sermons, including the two at the nunneries, were delivered by unspecified preachers in unknown languages with ten of them having the usual formulation of 'verbo Dei proposito' or a variant thereof. Most strikingly, the sermon on the unidentified theme of 'Vigilate' preached anonymously at St Olave's Priory on 24 July was actually preached in English, though there is no obvious explanation for this. Six of the remaining sermons were by John Roiston or more probably Royston (who has not been identified): Sudbury, on Titus 2: 12 (15 June); Stoke College, with the theme left blank (19 June), Walsingham on an unsourced theme preached in Latin (13/14 July); Ingham Priory again on Titus 2: 12 (18 July); Hickling Priory, with the theme left blank (18 July); and Butley, with no theme (30 July). Two others were by John Dry, an Oxford scholar and vicar of Wymondham: at Wymondham Abbey (29 June) on Luke 15: 6 and Pentney Priory (5 July) on an unsourced theme, while a 'Magister Brigat', whose identity is uncertain, preached at Westacre Priory on Songs 6: 10 (4 July) and the suffragan bishop, John of Chalcedon, at Coxford Priory on Ephesians 4: 3 at some point between 5 and 13/14 July.[16] Finally, in 1521 there was just one visitation on 9 April (to Stoke College) and no sermon.

In 1526 (see appendix 1, table 4) the number of visits stayed more or less the same but the number of sermons vastly declined. There were thirty-three visits (plus continuations at Stoke College and Sudbury College), comprising one long stint from 7 June to 25 August: twenty-seven were to male religious and six to female (Carrow, Campsey Ash, Redlingfield, Thetford, Bungay, Flixton). There were only four sermons preached, all to male establishments by named (but largely unidentified) preachers on mainly unspecified themes and in unspecified languages: Richard Bailwey preached at Ingham Priory on 18 June '*sub hoc themate*' (though it is then left blank); someone called 'Magister' Multon at Eye Priory on 5 July; John Clerk at Westacre Priory (to which he himself may have belonged) on 1 August; and Edmund Steward (a commissary of the bishop) at Metyngham College on 23 August.[17] No themes were specified, apart from that of John Clerk who preached on Hosea 11: 1 or Matthew 2: 15.

Finally, in 1532 (see appendix 1, table 5) there were thirty-five visits from 3 June to 22 August; of these twenty-seven were to male religious and seven to female convents (Carrow, Campsey Ash, Redlingfield, Thetford, Blackborough, Bungay and Flixton), in addition to Norman's Hospital. Once again the number of sermons was low, only five of them, though this time they include one to nuns. On 3 June 1532, at Norwich Priory, the monk Richard Norwich preached in Latin on Matthew 5: 48 while on 14 June 1532 in St Benet's at Hulme a sermon (with the theme left blank) was delivered by William Repps (whom we recall from his sermon at Norwich Priory on 27 April 1514 and who by this time was abbot of St Benet's). Repps's sermon was also in Latin. Then Giles Ferrers, the abbot of Wymondham (who was described by the monks of St Albans as 'a man of learning and virtue'), preached on 21 June 1532, at Butley Priory probably on Isaiah 52: 11 and on 25 June at Campsey Ash on Songs 3: 11, though without the language specified.[18] Finally, there was a sermon at Eye Priory on 2 July 1532 by an unspecified preacher on Romans 8: 18 but without mention of the language.

The level of detail in Alnwick's Lincoln records vastly exceeds that in the Norwich ones. In the latter there are only twenty examples where a biblical citation is given for the theme, five examples of the language cited and mention of fifteen named preachers. This means that we are not in a position to draw detailed conclusions about the sermons preached to nuns in Norfolk and Suffolk. Whether, like nuns in Lincoln diocese in the first half of the fifteenth century, they heard more about concrete narratives from the New Testament than male religious cannot be said, although the frequent use of the New Testament for men is in direct contrast to the earlier Lincoln visitations. For women we have only two examples of explicit themes: '*Maria optimam partem elegit*' (Luke 10: 42) and '*Egredimini filiae Sion*' (Songs 3: 11) so that on 22 June 1514 the nuns at Thetford would have been given the narrative of Martha and Mary from Luke 10 by Henry Forth (Goldwell's chaplain) and Giles Ferrers treated the nuns at Campsey Ash on 25 June 1532 to the erotic poetry of Songs. Otherwise whatever sermons they heard were by anonymous preachers, perhaps the bishop himself (if present), his suffragan or more likely someone from his household. (In the Lincoln visitations it was habitual for sermons to men and women to be delivered by one of Alnwick's staff.) Only on the two occasions above did the nuns have the same named preacher as their male equivalents. Of all the sermons mentioned, only three of them are in Latin, one by John Roiston at Walsingham Priory (13/14 July 1520), one by Richard Norwich at Norwich Priory (3 June 1532) and the third by William Repps in St Benet's at Hulme (14 June 1532). That there are only three gives pause for thought. Traditionally, as seen from the Lincoln visitations, preaching to women was in English and to men in Latin. Nevertheless, only three mentions of Latin *might* suggest that perhaps more preaching to men in English was carried out at this late stage than might have been the case hitherto. In England the emphasis is usually (and rightly) on the poor Latinity of nuns but this may also have applied to many male religious by the end of the medieval period. This might be supported by the one mention of English: on 24 July 1520, at St Olave's Priory, a male establishment.

If we attempt to compare the evidence from the Norwich diocese with the earlier results from Lincoln diocese, it is clear that William Alnwick in the latter diocese was far more rigorous about sermons than his Norwich equivalents, James Goldwell and Richard Nykke.[19] Yet to put this into another perspective, we might glance at Lincoln in the first decades of the sixteenth century. Substantial information survives from the visitation records of William Atwater (1514–21) and John Longland (1521–47) during the period from 1517 to 1531.[20] It is not possible to deal with these visitations in detail, but it may be noted that these bishops visited seventy-three houses with between one and three visits per house, a total of 122 visitations, of which thirty-nine were to the twenty-four female houses.[21]

Yet during this time in the Lincoln diocese there were only about eight sermons to female religious and about a dozen to men. The former sermons were given at Burnham (4 November 1521), Catesby (19 June 1520 and 10 September 1530), Greenfield (3 July 1525), Little Marlow (10 October 1530), Stixwould (15 May 1519) and Studley (26 April 1520), plus one that seems to have been intended for Godstow on 4 May 1520 but was apparently omitted because of time constraints. Only for four of these houses is the language specified: English is used for the sermons in Burnham (where the theme is left blank), Catesby (where the first theme is given as 2 Corinthians 4: 7) and Stixwould (without a theme), plus the one for Godstow on 4 May 1520 (also without a theme). This would strongly indicate that all preaching to nuns in the Lincoln diocese took place in English. Throughout all the sermons various preachers are mentioned, including the bishops themselves.

This later Lincoln sermon comparison puts Norwich diocese, with only eight convents, in a favourable light. Yet it is noticeable that in Norwich there is a severe fall-off in general sermon production as the period progresses: 1492–4 (twelve); 1514 (fourteen); 1520–1 (twenty-one); 1526 (four); and 1532 (five). With reference to nuns, there is a pronounced growth in visitations from the first of Goldwell's visitations in 1492, with two houses visited, and the first of Nykke's visitations in 1514 with all eight houses inspected (as may be seen from appendix 2, table 6). Apart from Blackborough and Crabhouse, all the other convents are visited between four and five times over the whole cycle. There is not, however, a corresponding growth in sermons: the figures for 1492 and 1532 are the same (one) and the only rise is around the period of 1514 and 1520 when there are two or three sermons in each round of visitations (while there were no sermons at convents in 1526).

Both Norwich and the later Lincoln figures compare very poorly with the earlier record from Lincoln as described in Alnwick's records, given that out of fifty-seven visits to men and twenty-two to women there were forty-five sermons to male religious and seventeen to nuns. If we can judge solely and roughly from the later Lincoln and the Norwich visitations, religious in the latter part of the fifteenth century and the first half of the sixteenth century were more likely to have had more visitations but correspondingly fewer sermons.[22] An obvious answer for this is the often cited excuse of the lamentable state of the monasteries in the run-up to the Reformation. Under this reasoning extra episcopal vigilance would have been necessary. And if the monasteries were in such a parlous state, then this might also imply an inadequacy on the part of the bishops when it came to sermon production. However, without entering into the tortuous debate about the state of the Church at this time, the evidence about these particular bishops or these nunneries only partially bears this out.[23] Neither is falling numbers the answer. While there was a decline during the plague years and variations over time in the numbers of nuns in each convent, by 1536 there was a total of 133 (named) nuns in the Norwich diocese, which indicated a slight rise over previous years.[24] There are also some personalised issues. For instance, by the time of his death in 1535 Richard Nykke was heading towards ninety and partially blind so he could hardly have been expected to preach himself (albeit that he could have got someone else to do so).

Moreover, in all the visits to convents in Norfolk and Suffolk between 1492 and 1532, there are very few that give obvious cause for concern. In most cases no need for reform was signalled, while in a few the visit would seem to have been done in a fairly cursory way: for example, in July 1520 all that is noted of Thetford is its poverty and for Crabhouse and Blackborough there is merely a line in each case: '*Omnia bene, juxta facultates*'.[25] In sum, injunctions are only provided after the following visitations: Campsey Ash on 1 August 1514, again on 27 June 1526, with *comperta* disclosed on 25 June 1532; Redlingfield on 7 August 1514; Flixton on 11 August 1514 and on 14/20 August 1520; and Carrow on 14 June 1526 and 10 June 1532.[26] In 1514 all was deemed well by the nuns at Campsey Ash; in his injunction the bishop merely asked that the prioress '*conficiat verum inventarium et exhibeat*'; the situation was the same in 1526 except that the precentrix, Margaret Harman, noted that the books for divine service needed repair to which the bishop acceded in his injunction. However, in 1532 there was a long litany of complaints on account of the strictness and parsimony of the prioress, Ela Buttery, who allowed very poor food to be served, including diseased animals, points that the bishop in his injunctions asked to be rectified. The nuns at Redlingfield complained about a host of troubles in 1514 ranging from the severity of the subprioress and the fact that the refectory was unused to the lack of curtains in the dormitories and the presence of children sleeping there – all of which were addressed in the injunctions. Likewise, the situation was not good at Flixton in 1514. The nuns had numerous complaints, among which were the non-observance of silence, the fact that John Wells was conversant with the prioress; that the nuns did not rise for divine office; and that discipline was not observed. In his injunctions the bishop saw to the removal of John Wells. By 1520 the complaints were fewer though the prioress, like her predecessors, did not render her accounts; and slept alone away from the dormitory. The bishop's representatives decreed that the number of dogs be reduced to one; that the prioress be accompanied by a sister chaplain when she slept outside the dormitory; that accounts be provided; and that Richard Carr be removed from her service within the month. There were some problems in Carrow in 1526 when there were complaints from the nuns about services being said and sung too quickly; the silence not being observed; the failure to observe certain feasts; the custom of a Christmas game where a junior nun assumed the role of the abbess (a variant of the Boy Bishop ceremony); and the liability of obedientaries for breakages – all of which were dealt with by the injunctions. However, by 1532 there would seem to have been more abuses at Carrow as the nuns reported, amongst other things, infringements of the habit, the behaviour of younger nuns, the lack of a screen between the nave and choir and of a lectern in the church, and the failure to observe certain feasts, some of which were addressed in the injunctions. With the exceptions of Flixton in 1514 and Carrow in 1526 and 1532, most of the faults were minor misdemeanours, and do not give much credence to any widespread spiritual inadequacy on the part of English convents, in the Norwich diocese at least, despite what we may have been led to believe from various lurid scandals about nuns in medieval England.[27] This contrasts very obviously with the more fundamental problems encountered in some of the male establishments, especially Norwich Priory and Walsingham Priory.[28]

That records do not inform us of everything we should like to know is one of the usual misfortunes of historical research. Overall, when compared with those of Lincoln (from the earlier period especially), the Norwich records do not enable us to amass detailed information about the precise sort or quality of sermons heard at visitations. Nevertheless, the records of James Goldwell and Richard Nykke are still a valuable resource when it comes to quantifying. Nuns in Norwich diocese on the eve of the Reformation were considerably less likely than their male equivalents to hear sermons at times of visitations. The reasons for this may have been partly due to a general reluctance on the part of the bishops to deal equally with male and female religious. In large measure it was also on account of the pronounced fall-off in visitation preaching at the time for reasons that may have had as much to do with the turbulence of the Reformation as anything else.[29] Yet another reason may be owing to the fact that, as far as these records demonstrate, the spiritual health of female religious in the Norwich diocese at this time was somewhat better than that of some of their male equivalents and so the need to preach them into increased godliness was perhaps not quite so pressing.[30]

Notes

1.   In mainland Europe an inordinate number of sermons addressed to and copied out by nuns survive in particular vernaculars, especially Dutch and German; for a comparative overview, see the introduction to Virginia Blanton, Veronica O'Mara and Patricia Stoop (eds), *Nuns' Literacies in Medieval Europe: The Antwerp Dialogue*, Medieval Women: Texts and Contexts, 28 (Turnhout, 2017), pp. xxi–lxvi.

2. For details, see V. M. O'Mara, 'Preaching to Nuns in Late Medieval England', in Carolyn Muessig (ed.), *Medieval Monastic Preaching*, Brill's Studies in Intellectual History, 90 (Leiden, Boston and Köln, 1998), pp. 93–119 (pp. 100–10).

3. See O'Mara, 'Preaching to Nuns in Late Medieval England', pp. 95–6, and David N. Bell, *What Nuns Read: Books and Libraries in Medieval English Nunneries*, Cistercian Studies Series, 158 (Kalamazoo, 1995), pp. 112–13, 118–19, 130, 134–5, 141, 158, 169–70, 185, 187–8, 203 and 216.

4. See the example of Alice Huntingfield's profession sermon in O'Mara, 'Preaching to Nuns in Late Medieval England', p. 101 and n. 26; this is preserved in Latin but internal evidence suggests English delivery.

5. See Valerie G. Spear, *Leadership in Medieval English Nunneries*, Studies in the History of Medieval Religion, 24 (Woodbridge, 2005), p. 116, who notes that such reports 'are not only tainted by the misogyny of the times, but hide the full circumstances of the visitation setting and environment'.

6. The reason for this choice was a pragmatic one; the Lincoln records, as with the Norwich ones below, have been fully edited. For the Lincoln visitations, see *Visitations of Religious Houses in the Diocese of Lincoln: Records of Visitations Held by William Alnwick*, ed. A. Hamilton Thompson, The Canterbury and York Society, 24 and 33, 2 vols (1919 and 1927), and for a breakdown of the detail below, see O'Mara, 'Preaching to Nuns in Late Medieval England', pp. 110–15 and the lists on pp. 117–19.

7. The two exceptions were the sermons on 7 July 1442 in St James's Abbey in Northampton and that in Bicester Priory on 28 May 1445; see Thompson (ed.), *Visitations of Religious Houses in the Diocese of Lincoln*, II, pp. 244–6 and I, pp. 34–6. The latter took place in the parish church and so the attendance of lay people would have been sufficient explanation for the vernacular; there is no obvious explanation for the first example.

8. Marilyn Oliva, *The Convent and the Community in Late Medieval England* (Woodbridge, 1998), table 1, p. 13.

9. The vexed position of the status of Cistercian nuns in England is carefully explained by Janet Burton; see her '*Moniales* and *Ordo Cisterciensis* in Medieval England and Wales', in Gert Melville and Anne Müller (eds), *Female vita religiosa between Late Antiquity and the High Middle Ages: Structures, Developments and Spatial Contexts*, Vita regularis: Ordnungen und Deutungen religiosen Lebens im Mittelalter, Abhandlungen, 47 (Zurich and Berlin, 2011), pp. 375–89, together with useful references therein.

10. See A. Jessopp (ed.), *Visitations of the Diocese of Norwich, A.D. 1492–1532*, Camden Society, New Series, 43 (1888). Nykke is also referred to as Nix by some modern commentators; see the entries by Rosemary C. E. Hayes and Norman P. Tanner for these bishops in the online *ODNB*.

11. A necessary caveat is that, when a sermon is not mentioned, this does not mean that it did not happen. Moreover, the visitations below were not always carried out

by the bishops themselves but sometimes by their suffragans and/or commissaries; when the identity of the preacher is not specified, it may be the bishop himself or his representative.

12. A. B. Emden, *A Biographical Register of the University of Oxford to A.D. 1500*, 3 vols (Oxford, 1957–9), II (1958), p. 721.

13. A. B. Emden, *A Biographical Register of the University of Cambridge to 1500* (Cambridge, 1963), p. 219.

14. For an overview of this visitation in 1499, see Christopher Harper-Bill, 'A Late Medieval Visitation – The Diocese of Norwich in 1499', *Proceedings of the Suffolk Institute of Archaeology and History*, 34 (1977–80), 35–47, who notes (37) that the *detecta* and *comperta* are omitted. The visitations conducted by the commissaries, Roger Church and John Vaughan, include Carrow, Bungay, Flixton, Campsey Ash and Redlingfield, but the accounts are skeletal and there is no mention of a sermon in any of the entries, male or female; see vol. 2, fols 79r–93r, of John Morton's register in London, Lambeth Palace Library. The material is calendared in Christopher Harper-Bill (ed.), *The Register of John Morton, Archbishop of Canterbury, 1486–1500*, III: *Norwich sede vacante, 1499*, The Canterbury and York Society, 89 (2000), pp. 160–8.

15. See Emden, *A Biographical Register of the University of Cambridge to 1500*, p. 238, and Jessopp (ed.), *Visitations of the Diocese of Norwich*, p. 325.

16. For Dry, see Emden, *A Biographical Register of the University of Oxford to A.D. 1500*, I (1957), p. 596. In Jessopp (ed.), *Visitations of the Diocese of Norwich*, p. 323, the unidentified Brigat is described as the bishop's chaplain.

17. Jessopp (ed.), *Visitations of the Diocese of Norwich*, p. 332.

18. A. B. Emden, *A Biographical Register of the University of Oxford A.D. 1501 to 1540* (Oxford, 1974), pp. 203–4 (p. 203).

19. At an early point in his career Alnwick was bishop of Norwich (1426–36), but all that remains in his register about visitations is an itinerary of houses (with the only convent included being Bungay on two occasions) to be visited during the ten years of his episcopate and a report of a visit to Redlingfield on 9 September 1427; see Thompson (ed.), *Visitations of Religious Houses in the Diocese of Lincoln*, II, pp. 409–13 for the list and pp. 413–17 for the visit.

20. A. Hamilton Thompson (ed.), *Visitations in the Diocese of Lincoln, 1517–1531*, The Lincoln Record Society, 33, 35 and 37, 3 vols (1940–7).

21. Atwater and Longland continued Alnwick's practice of visiting Cistercian houses, something that did not occur in the Norwich diocese (see above and n. 9 for references).

22. This is based on the overall figures rather than a statistical analysis of individual houses over time.

23. For an appraisal of the state of religious affairs in England, see G. W. Bernard, *The King's Reformation: Henry VIII and the Remaking of the English Church* (New Haven and

London, 2005) and references therein. See also Eamon Duffy, *The Stripping of the Altars: Traditional Religion in England c.1400–1580* (New Haven and London, 1992).

24. Oliva, *The Convent and the Community in Late Medieval England*, pp. 38–9 and table 6 (p. 39).

25. Jessopp (ed.), *Visitations of the Diocese of Norwich*, pp. 155 and 168.

26. For the respective visitations and injunctions, see Jessopp (ed.), *Visitations of the Diocese of Norwich, 1492–1532*, pp. 133–4, 219–20, 290–2, 138–40, 142–4, 190–1, 208–10 and 273–5.

27. See, for instance, the various stories in Eileen Power, *Medieval English Nunneries c.1275 to 1535*, Cambridge Studies in Medieval Life and Thought (Cambridge, 1922).

28. For a detailed discussion of the difficulties found in the male establishments, see the introduction to Jessopp (ed.), *Visitations of the Diocese of Norwich*.

29. It is questionable whether the fall-off was a sign of genuine decline or was itself caused in part by the uncertainty of the times; I am currently pursuing the issue of episcopal preaching in medieval England, particularly with regard to printed sermons, as well as preaching to nuns in general.

30. This chapter is based on a much revised and expanded version of a presentation entitled '"Lost Sermons": Visitation Preaching in Late Medieval England' that was delivered at a Journée d'étude internationale on 'Prédication et Société dans les Îles Britanniques aux XIVᵉ et XVᵉ siècles', at the Université de Poitiers in March 2014. It is dedicated now to Janet Burton as a very small token of appreciation to a tremendous scholar, a wonderful role model and a dear friend.

APPENDIX I

Key: M = male institution; F = female institution; U = unspecified

TABLE I: James Goldwell's visitations of 1492 to 1494

Date	Place	M/F	Preacher	Sermon/Theme	Language
5 Oct. 1492	Norwich Priory	M	Roger Framyngham	*'Ubi verbo Dei per ...'*	U
6 Oct. 1492	Carnary	M		No sermon mentioned	
8 Oct. 1492	St Mary-in-the-Fields College	M	U	*'Ubi verbo Dei proposito'*	U
9 Oct. 1492	St Giles's Hospital	M	U	*'Et verbo Dei ... proposito'*	U
9 Oct. 1492	Norman's Hospital	F	U	*'Et verbo Dei proposito'*	U
10 Oct. 1492	Carrow Nunnery	F	U	*'Ubi verbo Dei ... proposito'*	U
11 Oct. 1492	St Faith's Priory	M	U	*'Et verbo Dei ... proposito'*	U
13 Oct. 1492	Wymondham Abbey	M	U	*'Et verbo Dei ... proposito'*	U
16 Oct. 1492	Bokenham Priory	M		No sermon mentioned	
23 Oct. 1492	Hickling Priory	M		No sermon mentioned	
23 Oct. 1492	Ingham Priory	M		No sermon mentioned	
2 Nov. 1492	Coxford Priory	M		No sermon mentioned	
7 Nov. 1492	Pentney Priory	M		No sermon mentioned	
10 Nov. 1492	Thompson College	M		No sermon mentioned	
12 Nov. 1492	Thetford Priory	M		No sermon mentioned	
12 Nov. 1492	Thetford Nunnery	F		No sermon mentioned	
22 Jan. 1493	Trinity Priory, Ipswich	M		No sermon mentioned	

Date	Place	M/F	Preacher	Sermon/Theme	Language
23 Jan. 1493	St Peter's Priory, Ipswich	M		No sermon mentioned	
24 Jan. 1493	Campsey Ash Nunnery	F		No sermon mentioned	
25 Jan. 1493	Snape Priory	M		No sermon mentioned	
28 Jan. 1493	Attleborough Priory	M		No sermon mentioned	
30 Jan. 1493	St Olave's Priory	M		No sermon mentioned	
31 Jan. 1493	Bungay Nunnery	F		No sermon mentioned	
5 Feb. 1493	Eye Priory	M		No sermon mentioned	
8 Feb. 1493	Sudbury College	M		No sermon mentioned	
9 Feb. 1493	Stoke College	M		No sermon mentioned	
13 Feb. 1493	Ixworth Priory	M		No sermon mentioned	
18 Jun. 1493	Metyngham College	M	U	'Et verbo Dei ... proposito'	U
20 Jun. 1493	Flixton Nunnery	F		No sermon mentioned	
27 Sept. 1493	Wingfield College	M		No sermon mentioned	
10 Jul. 1494	Butley Priory	M	U	'Et verbo Dei ... proposito'	U
11 Aug. 1494	Westacre Priory	M	Henry Falke	'Et verbo Dei per ...'	U
25 Aug. 1494	Beeston Priory	M		No sermon mentioned	
25 Aug. 1494	Weyburne Priory	M		No sermon mentioned	
1 Sept. 1494	Walsingham Priory	M	Henry Falke	'Ubi verbo Dei per...'	U
15 Sept. 1494	St Benet's, Hulme	M	Henry Falke	'Ubi verbo Dei per ... proposito'	U

TABLE 2: Richard Nykke's visitations of 1514

Date	Place	M/F	Preacher	Sermon/Theme	Language
27 Apr. 1514	Norwich Priory	M	William Repps	1 Corinthians 5: 7	L
13 Jun. 1514	Sudbury College	M		No sermon mentioned	
[16] Jun. 1514	Stoke College	M	Henry Forth	Titus 2: 12	U
20 Jun. 1514	Ixworth Priory	M	Henry Forth	James 1: 21	U
20 Jun. 1514	Bromehill Priory	M		No sermon mentioned	
21 Jun. 1514	Thetford Priory	M		No sermon mentioned	
22 Jun. 1514	Thetford Nunnery	F	Henry Forth	Luke 10: 42	U
23 Jun. 1514	Rushworth College	M	Henry Forth	Ezechiel 18: 30	U
24 Jun. 1514	Thompson College	M		No sermon mentioned	
? Jun. 1514	Attleborough College	M		No sermon mentioned	
26 Jun. 1514	Bokenham Priory	M	Henry Forth	'proposito . . . sub hoc themate [. . .]'	U
28 Jun. 1514	Wymondham Abbey	M	Henry Forth	Ecclesiasticus 43:10	U
5 Jul. 1514	Westacre Priory	M	Henry Forth	'proposito . . . sub hoc themate [. . .]'	U
6 Jul. 1514	Pentney Priory	M	Henry Forth	'proposito . . . sub hoc themate videlicet [. . .]'	U
7 Jul. 1514	Blackborough Nunnery	F		No sermon mentioned	
10 Jul. 1514	Crabhouse Nunnery	F		No sermon mentioned	
12 Jul. 1514	Flitcham Priory	M		No sermon mentioned	
12 Jul. 1514	Coxford Priory	M		No sermon mentioned	
13 Jul. 1514	Hempton Priory	M		No sermon mentioned	

Date	Place	M/F	Preacher	Sermon/Theme	Language
14 Jul. 1514	Walsingham Priory	M	Henry Forth	'*Et proposito verbo Dei …*'	U
18 Jul. 1514	Weyburne Priory	M		No sermon mentioned	
18 Jul. 1514	Beeston Priory	M		No sermon mentioned	
21 Jul. 1514	Hickling Priory	M	Henry Forth	'*exposito verbo Dei … sub hoc themate* […]'	U
23 Jul. 1514	Weybridge Priory	M		No sermon mentioned	
24 Jul. 1514	St Benet's, Hulme	M		No sermon mentioned	
27 Jul. 1514	St Olave's Priory	M		No sermon mentioned	
30 Jul. 1514	Butley Priory	M	Subprior of Westacre	Acts 7: 3	U
1 Aug. 1514	Campsey Ash Nunnery	F	U	'*proposito verbo Dei*'	U
2 Aug. 1514	Woodbridge Priory	M		No sermon mentioned	
3 Aug. 1514	Trinity Priory, Ipswich	M		No sermon mentioned	
4 Aug. 1514	St Peter's Priory, Ipswich	M		No sermon mentioned	
7 Aug. 1514	Redlingfield Nunnery	F		No sermon mentioned	
8 Aug. 1514	Eye Priory	M		No sermon mentioned	
11 Aug. 1514	Flixton Nunnery	F		No sermon mentioned	
12 Aug. 1514	Bungay Nunnery	F		No sermon mentioned	
25 Aug. 1514	Carrow Nunnery	F	U	'*post verbum Dei propositum*'	U
30 Aug. 1514	Walsingham Priory	M		No sermon mentioned	

TABLE 3: Richard Nykke's visitations of 1520/1

Date	Place	M/F	Preacher	Sermon/Theme	Language
14 Jun. 1520	Ixworth Priory	M		No sermon mentioned	
15 Jun. 1520	Sudbury College	M	John Roiston	Titus 2: 12	U
19 Jun. 1520	Stoke College	M	John Roiston	'*proposuit verbum Dei sub hoc themate*'	U
21 Jun. 1520	Bromehill Priory	M	U	'*proposito verbo Dei*'	U
22 Jun. 1520	Thetford Priory	M	U	'*verbo Dei tunc proposito*'	U
22 Jun. 1520	Thetford Nunnery	F		No sermon mentioned	
23 Jun. 1520	Rushworth College	M		No sermon mentioned	
26 Jun. 1520	Attleborough College	M		No sermon mentioned	
27 Jun. 1520	Bokenham Priory	M	U	'*proposito verbo Dei*'	U
29 Jun. 1520	Wymondham Abbey	M	John Dry	Luke 15: 6	U
4 Jul. 1520	Westacre Priory	M	? Brigat	Songs 6. 10	U
5 Jul. 1520	Pentney Priory	M	John Dry	'*Fraternitatem diligite*'; unsourced	U
U	Crabhouse Nunnery	F		No sermon mentioned	
U	Blackborough Nunnery	F		No sermon mentioned	
U	Flitcham Priory	M		No sermon mentioned	
U	Coxford Priory	M	Suffragan	Ephesians 4: 3	U
13/14 Jul. 1520	Walsingham Priory	M	John Roiston	'*Nolite conformari huic seculo*'; unsourced	L
U	Weyburnee Priory	M		No sermon mentioned	
18 Jul. 1520	Ingham Priory	M	John Roiston	Titus 2: 12	U

Date	Place	M/F	Preacher	Sermon/Theme	Language
18 Jul. 1520	Hickling Priory	M	John Roiston	'*Proposito verbo … sub hoc themate*'	U
20 Jul. 1520	St Benet's Abbey, Hulme	M	U	'*verbo Dei proposito*'	U
24 Jul. 1520	St Olave's Priory	M	U	'*Vigilate*'; unsourced	E
U	Blythburgh Priory	M		No sermon mentioned	
U	Snape Priory	M		No sermon mentioned	
30 Jul. 1520	Butley Priory	M	John Roiston	'*post verbum Dei propositum per …*'	U
U	Campsey Ash Nunnery	F		No sermon mentioned	
31 Jul. 1520	Woodbridge Priory	M	U	'*verbo Dei proposito*'	U
2 Aug. 1520	St Peter's Priory, Ipswich	M	U	'*verbo Dei propositoque*'	U
6 Aug. 1520	Wingfield College	M		No sermon mentioned	
7 Aug. 1520	Redlingfield Nunnery	F	U	'*verbo Dei proposito*'	U
8 Aug. 1520	Eye Priory	M		No sermon mentioned	
14 Aug. 1520	Flixton Nunnery	F	U	'*verbo Dei proposito*'	U
16 Aug. 1520	Metyngham College	M	U	'*exposito verbo Dei*'	U
17 Aug. 1520	Bungay Nunnery	F		No sermon mentioned	
20 Aug. 1520	Flixton Nunnery	F		[continuation]	
22 Aug. 1520	St Faith's Priory	M	U	'*verbo Dei proposito*'	U
3 Sep. 1520	Norwich Priory	M		No sermon mentioned	
9 Apr. 1521	Stoke College	M		No sermon mentioned	

TABLE 4: Richard Nykke's visitations in 1526

Date	Place	M/F	Preacher	Sermon/Theme	Language
7 Jun. 1526	Norwich Priory	M		No sermon mentioned	
11 Jun. 1526	St Giles's Hospital	M		No sermon mentioned	
12 Jun. 1526	St Mary-in-the-Fields College	M		No sermon mentioned	
14 Jun. 1526	Carrow Nunnery	F		No sermon mentioned	
18 Jun. 1526	Ingham Priory	M	Richard Bailwey	'*exposito verbo Dei per ... sub hoc themate* [...]'	U
19 Jun. 1526	Hickling Priory	M		No sermon mentioned	
U	St Benet's Abbey, Hulme	M		No sermon mentioned	
22 Jun. 1526	St Olave's Priory	M		No sermon mentioned	
23 Jun. 1526	Blythburgh Priory	M		No sermon mentioned	
26 Jun. 1526	Butley Priory	M		No sermon mentioned	
27 Jun. 1526	Campsey Ash Nunnery	F		No sermon mentioned	
29 Jun. 1526	Trinity Priory, Ipswich	M		No sermon mentioned	
2 Jul. 1526	St Peter's Priory, Ipswich	M		No sermon mentioned	
5 Jul. 1526	Eye Priory	M	[?] Multon	'*proposito verbo Dei per ...*'	U
6 Jul. 1526	Wingfield College	M		No sermon mentioned	
7 Jul. 1526	Redlingfield Nunnery	F		No sermon mentioned	
10 Jul. 1526 [cont. later]	Sudbury College	M		No sermon mentioned	

Date	Place	M/F	Preacher	Sermon/Theme	Language
12 Jul. 1526 [cont. later]	Stoke College	M		No sermon mentioned	
16 Jul. 1526	Ixworth Priory	M		No sermon mentioned	
U	Bromehill Priory	M		No sermon mentioned	
18 Jul. 1526	Thetford Priory	M		No sermon mentioned	
18 Jul. 1526	Thetford Nunnery	F		No sermon mentioned	
20 Jul. 1526	Rushworth College	M		No sermon mentioned	
21 Jul. 1526	Thompson College	M		No sermon mentioned	
24 Jul. 1526	Bokenham Priory	M		No sermon mentioned	
26 Jul. 1526	Wymondham Abbey	M		No sermon mentioned	
1 Aug. 1526	Westacre Priory	M	John Clerk	Hosea 11: 1 or Matthew 2: 15	U
2 Aug. 1526	Pentney Priory	M		No sermon mentioned	
8 Aug. 1526	Coxford Priory	M		No sermon mentioned	
11 Aug. 1526	Walsingham Priory	M		No sermon mentioned	
23 Aug. 1526	Metyngham College	M	Edmund Steward	'propositoque verbo Dei … per'	U
23 Aug. 1526	Bungay Nunnery	F		No sermon mentioned	
25 Aug. 1526	Flixton Nunnery	F		No sermon mentioned	

TABLE 5: Richard Nykke's visitations in 1532

Date	Place	M/F	Preacher	Theme	Language
3 Jun. 1532	Norwich Priory	M	Richard Norwich	Matthew 5: 48	L
7 Jun. 1532	St Mary-in-the-Fields College	M		No sermon mentioned	
8 Jun. 1532	St Giles's Hospital	M		No sermon mentioned	
8 Jun. 1532	Norman's Hospital	F		No sermon mentioned	
10 Jun. 1532	Carrow Nunnery	F		No sermon mentioned	
12 Jun. 1532	Ingham Priory	M		No sermon mentioned	
13 Jun. 1532	Hickling Priory	M		No sermon mentioned	
14 Jun. 1532	St Benet's, Hulme	M	William Repps	'... *sub hoc themate* [...]'	L
18 Jun. 1532	St Olave's Priory	M		No sermon mentioned	
19 Jun. 1532	Blythborough Priory	M		No sermon mentioned	
21 Jun. 1532	Butley Priory	M	Giles Ferrers	cf. Isaiah 52: 11	U
25 Jun. 1532	Campsey Ash Nunnery	F	Giles Ferrers	Songs 3: 11	U
26 Jun. 1532	Woodbridge Priory	M		No sermon mentioned	
27 Jun. 1532	Trinity Priory, Ipswich	M		No sermon mentioned	
2 Jul. 1532	Eye Priory	M	U	Romans 8: 18	U
4 Jul. 1532	Wingfield College	M		No sermon mentioned	
5 Jul. 1532	Redlingfield Nunnery	F		No sermon mentioned	
7 Jul. 1532	Sudbury College	M		No sermon mentioned	

Date	Place	M/F	Preacher	Theme	Language
10 Jul. 1532	Stoke College	M		No sermon mentioned	
15 Jul. 1532	Ixworth Priory	M		No sermon mentioned	
16 Jul. 1532	Thetford Priory	M		No sermon mentioned	
18 Jul. 1532	Rushworth College	M		No sermon mentioned	
21 Jul. 1532	Thetford Nunnery	F		No sermon mentioned	
23 Jul. 1532	Bokenham Priory	M		No sermon mentioned	
23 Jul. 1532	Wymondham Abbey	M		No sermon mentioned	
31 Jul. 1532	Westacre Priory	M		No sermon mentioned	
1 Aug. 1532	Blackborough Nunnery	F		No sermon mentioned	
1 Aug. 1532	Pentney Priory	M		No sermon mentioned	
U	Coxford Priory	M		No sermon mentioned	
9 Aug. 1532	Walsingham Priory	M		No sermon mentioned	
? [Aug. 1532]	Beeston Priory	M		No sermon mentioned	
17 Aug. 1532	St Faith's Priory	M		No sermon mentioned	
21 Aug. 1532	Metyngham College	M		No sermon mentioned	
21 Aug. 1532	Bungay Nunnery	F		No sermon mentioned	
22 Aug. 1532	Flixton Nunnery	F		No sermon mentioned	

APPENDIX 2

TABLE 6: Visitations and sermons* preached to nuns in Norwich diocese

	1492	1493	1514	1520	1526	1532
Blackborough			7 Jul.	? Jul.		1 Aug.
Bungay		31 Jan.	12 Aug.	17 Aug.	23 Aug.	21 Aug.
Campsey Ash		24 Jan.	1 Aug.*	? Jul.	27 Jun.	25 Jun.*
Carrow	10 Oct.*		25 Aug.*		14 Jun.	10 Jun.
Crabhouse			10 Jul.	? Jul.		
Flixton		20 Jun.	11 Aug.	14* & 20 Aug.	25 Aug.	22 Aug.
Redlingfield			7 Aug.	7 Aug.*	7 Jul.	5 Jul.
Thetford	12 Nov.		22 Jun.*	22 Jun.	18 Jul.	21 Jul.

SELECT BIBLIOGRAPHY

Primary sources

Aelred of Rievaulx, *Mirror of Charity*, trans. Elizabeth Connor (Kalamazoo, 1990)

Chartularies of St Mary's Abbey, Dublin, ed. J. T. Gilbert, 2 vols, RS (London, 1884)

Chronica Monasterii de Melsa a fundatione usque ad annum 1396, auctore Thoma de Burton, Abbate, ed. E. Bond, RS, 43, 3 vols (1866–8)

The Chronicle of St Mary's Abbey, York, ed. H. Craster and M. Thornton, Surtees Society, 148 (1934)

Daniel of Beccles, *Urbanus Magnus Danielis Becclesiensis*, ed. J. Gilbart Smyly (Dublin, 1939)

Dugdale, W., *Monasticon Anglicanum*, ed. J. Caley, H. Ellis and B. Bandinel, 6 vols in 8 (London, 1817–30)

Eadmer, *The Life of St Anselm Archbishop of Canterbury by Eadmer*, ed. R. W. Southern (Oxford, 1962; repr. 1972)

—— *Eadmeri Historia Novorum in Anglia*, ed. Martin Rule, RS, 81 (London, 1884)

Foundation History of the Abbeys of Byland and Jervaulx, ed. J. Burton, Borthwick Texts and Studies, 35 (York, 2006)

Gerald of Wales, *Giraldi Cambrensis Opera*, ed. J. S. Brewer. J. F. Dimock and G. F. Warner, 8 vols, RS (London, 1861–91)

Gesta abbatum monasterii sancti Albani, ed. H. T. Riley, RS, 28, 4 (1867–9)

Lanfranc, *The Monastic Constitutions of Lanfranc*, ed. D. Knowles (London, 1951)

Letters and Papers of the Reign of Henry VIII, ed. J. S. Brewer, J. Gairdner and R. H. Brodie 23 vols in 38 (London, 1862–1932)

Liber Ordinis Sancti Victoris Parisiensis, ed. Lucas Jocqué and Ludovicus Milis (Turnhout, 1984)

Matthew Paris, *Matthaei Parisiensis monachi Sancti Albani Chronica Majora*, ed. H. R. Luard, RS, 7 vols (London, 1872–83)

The Observances in Use at the Augustinian Priory of S. Giles and S. Andrew at Barnwell, Cambridgeshire, ed. J. Clark (Cambridge, 1897)

Register of the Abbey of St Thomas, Dublin, ed. J. T. Gilbert (London, 1889)

Robert Grosseteste, *Letters of Robert Grosseteste bishop of Lincoln*, ed. F. A. C. Mantello and J. Goering (Toronto, 2010)

The Rule of St Benedict in Latin and English, ed. J. McCann (London, 1952)

Statuta Capitulorum Generalium Ordinis Cisterciensis ad anno 1116–1786, ed. Joseph
    Marie Canivez, 8 vols (Louvain, 1933–41)
Visitations of the Diocese of Norwich A.D. 1492–1532, ed. A. Jessopp, Camden
    Society, New Series, 43 (1888)
*Visitations of Religious Houses in the Diocese of Lincoln: Records of Visitations Held by
    William Alnwick*, ed. A. Hamilton Thompson, The Canterbury and York
    Society, 24 and 33, 2 vols (1919 and 1927)
Walter Daniel, *The Life of Aelred of Rievaulx*, ed. and trans. Maurice Powicke,
    Cistercian Fathers Series, 57 (Kalamazoo, 1994)

Secondary sources
Andrews, Frances, *The Other Friars: Carmelite, Augustinian, Sack and Pied Friars in
    the Middle Ages* (Woodbridge, 2006)
Austin, David, 'The Archaeology of Monasteries in Wales and the Strata
    Florida Project', in Janet Burton and Karen Stöber (eds), *Monastic Wales,
    New Approaches* (Cardiff, 2013), pp. 3–20
——, 'Strata Florida and its Landscape', *Archaeologia Cambrensis*, 153 (2004),
    192–201
Bell, David, *What Nuns Read: Books and Libraries in Medieval English Nunneries*,
    Cistercian Studies Series, 158 (Kalamazoo, 1995)
Bhreathnach, Edel, 'Benedictine Influence in Ireland in the Late Eleventh
    and Early Twelfth Centuries: A Reflection', *Journal of Medieval Monastic
    Studies*, 1 (2012), 63–91
—— and Małgorzata Krasnodębska-D'Aughton and Keith Smith (eds),
    Monastic Europe: Landscape and Settlement (Turnhout, forthcoming)
Browne, Martin and Colmán Ó Clabaigh (eds), *The Irish Benedictines: A History*
    (Dublin, 2005)
Burton, Janet, *The Monastic Order in Yorkshire, 1069–1215* (Cambridge, 1999)
—— and Emilia Jamroziak (eds), *Religious and Laity in Western Europe, 1000–1400*
    (Turnhout, 2006)
—— and Julie Kerr, *The Cistercians in the Middle Ages* (Woodbridge, 2011)
—— and Karen Stöber, *Abbeys and Priories of Medieval Wales* (Cardiff, 2015)
—— and Karen Stöber (eds), *Monastic Wales: New Approaches* (Cardiff, 2013)
—— and Karen Stöber, *The Regular Canons in the Medieval British Isles* (Turnhout,
    2011)
—— and Karen Stöber, *Monasteries and Society in the British Isles* (Woodbridge,
    2008)
Cariboni, Guido, 'Hospitality in a Cistercian Context: Evidence for
    Customary Attitudes and Identity in Legislation', *Bulletin for International
    Medieval Research*, 19 (2013), 58–82

Carter, Michael, '"*So it was abowte iiiic yeres agoo*". Retrospection in the Art and Architecture of the Cistercian in Northern England in the Late Middle Ages', *Journal of Medieval Monastic Studies*, 4 (2015), 107–32

Cartwright, Jane, *Female Sanctity and Spirituality in Medieval Wales* (Cardiff, 2008)

Cassidy-Welch, Megan, *Monastic Spaces and their Meanings: Thirteenth-Century English Cistercian Monasteries* (Turnhout, 2001)

Clark, J. G., *A Monastic Renaissance at St Albans. Thomas Walsingham and his Circle, c.1350–c.1440* (Oxford, 2004)

— (ed.), *The Religious Orders in Pre-Reformation England* (Woodbridge, 2002)

Constable, Giles, *The Reformation of the Twelfth Century* (Cambridge, 1996)

Coppack, Glyn, *The Cistercians in Britain 1128–1540* (Stroud, 1998)

Cross, Claire and N. Vickers (eds), *Monks, Friars and Nuns in Sixteenth Century Yorkshire*, Yorkshire Archaeological Society, Record Series, 150 (1995)

Dunn, Marilyn, *The emergence of monasticism: from the Desert Fathers to the early Middle Ages* (Oxford, 2003)

Dutton, Marsha (ed.), *Aelred of Rievaulx: A Companion (1110–1167)*, Brill's Companions to the Christian Tradition, 76 (Leiden and Boston, 2017)

Fergusson, Peter, *The Architecture of Solitude: Cistercian Abbeys in Twelfth-Century England* (Princeton, 1984)

— and Stuart Harrison, *Rievaulx Abbey: Community, Architecture and Memory* (New Haven and London, 1999)

Flanagan, Marie Therese, *The Transformation of the Irish Church in the Twelfth Century* (Woodbridge, 2010)

—, 'Hiberno-papal relations in the late twelfth century', *Archivium Hibernicum*, 34 (1977), 55–70

France, James, *Separate but Equal: Cistercian Lay Brothers, 1120–1350* (Kalamazoo, 2012)

Freeman, E., *Narratives of a New Order: Cistercian Historical Writing in England, 1150–1220*, Medieval Church Studies, 2 (Turnhout, 2002)

Gilchrist, Roberta, *Gender and Material Culture: The Archaeology of Religious Women* (London, 1994)

Golding, Brian, *Gilbert of Sempringham and the Gilbertine Order, c.1130–c.1300* (Oxford, 1995)

Grant, Lindy, 'The architecture of the early Savignacs and Cistercians in Normandy', *Anglo-Norman Studies*, 10 (1987), 111–43

Greatrex, Joan, *The English Benedictine Cathedral Priories: Rule and Practice, c.1270–c.1420* (Oxford, 2011)

Gwynn, Aubrey and R. Neville Hadcock, *Medieval Religious Houses: Ireland* (London, 1970)

Hall, Dianne, *Women and the Church in Medieval Ireland, c.1140–1540* (Dublin, 2003)

Harvey, Barbara, *Living and Dying in England, 1100–1540: the Monastic Experience* (Oxford, 1993)

Heale, Martin, *The Abbots and Priors of Late Medieval and Reformation England* (Oxford, 2016)

— (ed.), *Monasticism in Late Medieval England, c.1300–1535* (Manchester, 2009)

Hoskin, Philippa, *Robert Grosseteste as Bishop of Lincoln: the episcopal rolls 1235–1253*, Kathleen Major Series of Medieval Records, 1 (Woodbridge, 2015)

Jamroziak, Emilia, *The Cistercian Order in Medieval Europe, 1090–1500* (London, 2013)

—, *Rievaulx Abbey and its Social Context, 1132–1300: Memory, Locality, and Networks* (Turnhout, 2005)

Jurkowski, Maureen and Nigel Ramsay (eds), *English Monastic Estates, 1066–1540: a List of Manors, Churches and Chapels*, List & Index Society, Special Series 42 (2007)

Kehnel, Annette and Sabine von Heusinger (eds), *Generations in the Cloister: Youth and Age in Medieval Religious Life* (Wien, 2007)

Kerr, Julie, *Monastic Hospitality: the Benedictines in England, c.1070–c.1250* (Woodbridge, 2007)

Kinder, Terryl (ed.), *Perspectives for an Architecture of Solitude: Essays on Cistercians, Art and Architecture in Honour of Peter Fergusson* (Turnhout, 2004)

Knowles, David, *The Monastic Order in England. A History of its Development from the Times of St Dunstan to the Fourth Lateran Council, 940–1216*, 2nd edn (Cambridge, 1966)

— and R. Neville Hadcock, *Medieval Religious Houses. England and Wales*, 2nd edn (Harlow, 1971)

Lafaye, Annejulie, 'The Dominicans in Ireland: A Comparative Study of the East Munster and Leinster Settlements', *Journal of Medieval Monastic Studies*, 4 (2015), 77–106

Luxford, Julian, *The Art and Architecture of English Benedictine Monasteries, 1300–1540: a Patronage History* (Woodbridge, 2005)

Müller, Anne, *Bettelmönche in islamischer Fremde: institutionelle Rahmenbedingungen franziskanischer und dominikanischer Mission in muslimischen Räumen des 13. Jahrhunderts* (Münster, 2002)

Norton, Christopher and David Park (eds), *Cistercian Art and Architecture in the British Isles* (Cambridge 1986)

Ó Clabaigh, Colmán, *The Friars in Ireland, 1224–1540* (Dublin, 2012)

—, 'The Benedictines in Medieval and Early Modern Ireland', in Browne and Ó Clabaigh (eds), *The Irish Benedictines: A History*, pp. 79–121

Oliva, M., *The Convent and the Community in Late Medieval England* (Woodbridge, 1998)

O'Mara, V. M., 'Preaching to Nuns in Late Medieval England', in Carolyn Muessig (ed.), *Medieval Monastic Preaching*, Brill's Studies in Intellectual History, 90 (Leiden, Boston and Köln, 1998)

Power, Eileen, *Medieval English Nunneries c.1275 to 1535* (Cambridge, 1922)

Prescott, Andrew, '"Great and Horrible Rumour": Shaping the English Revolt of 1381', in Justine Firnhaber-Baker with Dirk Schoenaers (eds), *The Routledge History Handbook of Medieval Revolt* (London, 2017), pp. 76–103

Robson, Michael, *The Franciscans in the Middle Ages* (Woodbridge, 2006)

Röhrkasten, Jens, *The Mendicant Houses of Medieval London, 1221–1539* (Münster, 2004)

Signori, Gabriela, 'Cell or Dormitory? Monastic Visions of Space amidst the Conflict of Ideals', *Journal of Medieval Monastic Studies*, 3 (2014), 21–49

Sommer, Petr, P. Vlček and D. Foltýn, *Encyklopedie českých klášterů* (Praha, 1997)

Spear, Valerie G., *Leadership in Medieval English Nunneries*, Studies in the History of Medieval Religion, 24 (Woodbridge, 2005)

Stöber, Karen, *Late Medieval Monasteries and their Patrons: England and Wales, c.1300–1540*, Studies in the History of Medieval Religion, 29 (Woodbridge, 2007)

Thomason, Richard, 'Hospitality in a Cistercian Context: Evidence for Customary Attitudes and Identity in Legislation', *Bulletin for International Medieval Research*, 19 (2013), 58–82

Thompson, S., *Women Religious: the Founding of English Nunneries after the Conquest* (Oxford, 1991)

Wardrop, Joan, *Fountains Abbey and its Benefactors 1132–1300* (Kalamazoo, 1987)

BIBLIOGRAPHY OF
JANET BURTON'S PUBLICATIONS

BOOKS AND EDITIONS

1978 (ed.), *The Cartulary of the Treasurer of York Minster and related documents*, Borthwick Texts and Calendars (York)

1988 (ed.), *English Episcopal Acta V, York 1070–1154* (Oxford)

1994 *Monastic and Religious Orders in Britain, 1000–1300*, Cambridge Medieval Textbooks (Cambridge; repr. 1995, 1997, 2000)

1996 *Medieval Monasticism from its Origins to the Coming of the Friars*, Headstart History Papers (Bangor)

1999 *The Monastic Order in Yorkshire 1069–1215*, Cambridge Studies in Medieval Life and Thought, 40 (Cambridge)

2004 (ed.), *The Cartulary of Byland Abbey*, Boydell Press for the Surtees Society, vol. 208 (Woodbridge)

2006 (ed. and trans.), *The Foundation History of the Abbeys of Byland and Jervaulx*, Borthwick Texts and Studies, 35 (York)

2011 with Julie Kerr, *The Cistercians in the Middle Ages* (Woodbridge)

2013 *Historia Selebiensis Monasterii, The History of the Monastery of Selby*, Oxford Medieval Texts (Oxford)

2015 with Karen Stöber, *Abbeys and Priories of Medieval Wales* (Cardiff)

EDITED COLLECTIONS

2004 with William Marx (eds), *Readers, Printers, Churchmen and Travellers: essays in honour of David Selwyn* (Lampeter)

2005 with Björn Weiler, Phillipp Schofield and Karen Stöber (eds), *Thirteenth Century England XI* (Woodbridge)

2006 with Emilia Jamroziak (eds), *Religious and Laity in Western Europe 1000–1300: interaction, negotiation and power*, Europa Sacra, 2 (Turnhout)

2008 with Karen Stöber (eds), *Monasteries and Society in the British Isles in the Later Middle Ages*, Studies in the History of Medieval Religion, 35 (Woodbridge)

2009 with Phillipp Schofield and Björn Weiler (eds), *Thirteenth Century England XII* (Woodbridge)
2010 with William Marx and Veronica O'Mara (eds), *Essays in Honour of Oliver Pickering, Leeds Studies in English*, 41 (Leeds)
2011 with Frédérique Lachaud, Phillipp Schofield, Karen Stöber and Björn Weiler (eds), *Thirteenth Century England XIII* (Woodbridge)
2011 with Karen Stöber (eds), *The Regular Canons in the Medieval British Isles* (Turnhout)
2013 with Karen Stöber (eds), *Monastic Wales: New Approaches* (Cardiff)
2013 with Phillipp Schofield and Björn Weiler (eds), *Thirteenth Century England XIV* (Woodbridge)
2015 with Phillipp Schofield and Björn Weiler (eds), *Thirteenth Century England XV* (Woodbridge)
2015 with Karen Stöber (eds), *Women in the Medieval Monastic World* (Turnhout)

ARTICLES AND PAPERS

1978 'The election of Joan Fletcher as prioress of Basedale, 1524', *Borthwick Institute Bulletin*, 1, 4, 145–53
1979 *The Yorkshire Nunneries in the Twelfth and Thirteenth Centuries*, Borthwick Papers, no. 56
1979 'A confraternity list from St Mary's Abbey, York', *Revue Bénédictine*, 89, 325–33
1979 'A roll of charters for Lenton Priory', *Borthwick Institute Bulletin*, 2, 1, 13–26
1979 'Charters of Byland Abbey relating to the grange of Bleatarn, Westmorland. Two Twelfth-Century Agreements made between Newburgh Priory and Byland Abbey', *Transactions of the Cumberland and Westmorland Antiquarian and Archaeological Society*, 79, 29–50
1982 'Monastic Building in twelfth-century Yorkshire: some documentary evidence', *Trivium*, 17, 67–86
1983 'The settlement of disputes between Byland Abbey and Newburgh Priory', *Yorkshire Archaeological Journal*, 55, 67–72
1985 'Inventories of the property of the treasurer of York, 1297–8', *Borthwick Institute Bulletin*, 3, 3, 141–56
1986 'The foundation of the British Cistercian houses', in Christopher Norton and David Park (eds), *Cistercian Art and Architecture in the British Isles* (Cambridge), pp. 24–39; and with Roger Stalley, 'Tables of Cistercian affiliations', Norton and Park (eds), *Cistercian Art and*

Architecture in the British Isles, pp. 394–401; repr. 1988, and in paperback, 2012

1987 'Monasteries and parish churches in eleventh- and twelfth-century Yorkshire', *Northern History*, 23, 39–50

1988 with Christopher Wilson, *St Mary's Abbey, York* (York)

1988 'St Mary's Abbey and the City of York', *Yorkshire Philosophical Society Annual Report for 1988*, pp. 62–72

1988 'Hatfield Peverel, prieuré bénédictine dans le comté d'Essex', in R. Aubert (ed.), *Dictionnaire d'Histoire et de Géographie Ecclesiastiques* (Paris), fasc. 133–4, 571–8

1988 'Hatfield Regis ou Hatfield Broadoak, prieuré bénédictine dans le comté d'Essex', in Aubert (ed.), *Dictionnaire d'Histoire et de Géographie Ecclesiastiques*, fasc. 133–4, 518–19

1988 'Haverfordwest, prieuré de chanoines reguliers dans le comté de Pembroke', in Aubert (ed.), *Dictionnaire d'Histoire et de Géographie Ecclesiastiques*, fasc. 133–4, 615

1988 'Healaugh Park, prieuré de chanoines de S Augustin dans le comté et le diocèse d'York', in Aubert (ed.), *Dictionnaire d'Histoire et de Géographie Ecclesiastiques*, fasc. 133–4, 682–3

1989 *The Religious Orders in East Yorkshire in the Twelfth Century*, East Yorkshire Local History Series, 42 (Beverley)

1990 'Henry Murdac, archevêque d'York', in Aubert (ed.), *Dictionnaire d'Histoire et de Géographie Ecclesiastiques*, fasc. 136, 1188–9

1991 'Byland, Jervaulx, and the problems of the English Savigniacs *c*.1134–*c*.1155', *Monastic Studies*, II, 119–31

1991 'The eremitical tradition and the development of post-Conquest religious life in northern England', in N. Crossley-Holland (ed.), *Eternal Values in Medieval Life*, *Trivium*, 26, 18–39

1991 'Reform or Revolution? Monastic movements of the eleventh and twelfth centuries', *Medieval History*, 1, 2, 23–36

1991 'The Knights Templar in Yorkshire in the twelfth century: a reassessment', *Northern History*, 27, 26–40

1994 'The monastic revival in Yorkshire: Whitby and St Mary's York', in David Rollason, Margaret Harvey and Michael Prestwich (eds), *Anglo-Norman Durham 1093–1193* (Woodbridge), pp. 41–51

1995 *Kirkham Priory from Foundation to Dissolution*, Borthwick Paper, 86 (York)

1995 'New Light on the Summergame', *Notes & Queries*, 240, 428–9

1996 'St Andrew, Fishergate, York: historical report', in R. Kemp with C. Pamela Graves (eds), *The Church and Gilbertine Priory of St Andrew, Fishergate*, The Archaeology of York, vol. 11, fasc. 2, *The Medieval*

Defences and Suburbs (Council for British Archaeology for the York Archaeological Trust), pp. 49–67

1997 'Yorkshire Nunneries in the Later Middle Ages: Recruitment and Resources', in J. Appleby and P. Dalton (eds), *Government, Religion and Society in Northern England, 1000–1700* (Stroud), pp. 104–16

1998 'The Cistercian Adventure', in D. Robinson (ed.), *The Cistercian Abbeys of Britain: Far from the Concourse of Men* (London), pp. 7–33

1998 'The estates and economy of Rievaulx Abbey in Yorkshire', *Cîteaux: Commentarii Cistercienses*, 49, 29–94

1999 'Archbishop William Melton's Visitations of St Mary's Abbey and St Clement's Priory, York, 1317–1324', in D. M. Smith (ed.), *The Church in Medieval York: records edited in honour of Professor Barrie Dobson*, Borthwick Texts and Calendars, 24 (York), pp. 29–49

1999 'Priory and Parish: Kirkham and its parishioners, 1496–7', in Benjamin Thompson (ed.), *Monasteries and Society in Medieval Britain*, Harlaxton Medieval Studies, VI (Stamford), pp. 329–47

2000 'Rapport sur L'Espace Anglais', in *Unanimité et Diversité Cisterciennes: filiations, réseaux, relectures du IIᵉ au XVIIᵉ siècle. Actes du quatrième colloque international du CERCOR, 1998*, C.E.R.C.O.R., Travaux et Recherches, Publications de l'Université de Saint-Etienne, pp. 301–19

2001 'The Chariot of Aminadab and the Yorkshire nunnery of Swine', in R. Horrox and S. Rees Jones (eds), *Pragmatic Utopias: Ideals and Communities 1200–1630* (Cambridge), pp. 26–42

2002 'The monastic world', in B. Weiler and I. W. Rowlands (eds), *England and Europe in the Reign of Henry III* (Aldershot), pp. 121–36

2003 'Selby Abbey and its twelfth-century historian', *Learning and Literacy in England and Abroad*, Utrecht Studies in Medieval Literacy, 3 (Turnout), pp. 49–68

2004 'Commemoration and memorialization in a Yorkshire context', in D. Rollason, A. J. Piper, Margaret Harvey and Lynda Rollason (eds), *The Durham Liber Vitae and its Context*, Regions and Regionalism in History, 1 (Woodbridge), pp. 221–31

2004 'Rievaulx Abbey: the Early Years', in Terryl N. Kinder (ed.), *Perspectives for an Architecture of Solitude: Essays on Cistercians, Art and Architecture in Honour of Peter Fergusson* (Turnhout), pp. 47–53

2004 *New DNB* articles on: Archbishops Gerard, Thomas II, Thurstan, Henry Murdac and William Fitzherbert of York; Hugh the Chanter; Hugh of Kirkstall; Osbert of Bayeux

2005 'Cloistered Women and Male Authority: power and authority in Yorkshire nunneries in the later Middle Ages', in Michael Prestwich,

Richard Britnell and Robin Frame (eds), *Thirteenth Century England X: Proceedings of the Durham Conference 2003* (Woodbridge), pp. 155–65

2005 'Convent and community: cause papers as a source for monastic history', in Philippa Hoskin, Christopher Brooke and Barrie Dobson (eds), *A Contribution to the Foundations of Historical Research* (Woodbridge), pp. 63–76

2005 'Renunciation', in Rosemary Horrox and Mark Ormrod (eds), *A Social History of England, 1200–1500* (Cambridge), pp. 356–68

2006 'Roger de Mowbray as a founder and patron of monasteries', in Emilia Jamroziak and Janet Burton (eds), *Religious and Laity in Western Europe 1000–1300: interaction, negotiation and power*, Europa Sacra 2 (Turnhout), pp. 23–39

2007 '*Homines sanctitatis eximiae, religionis consummatae*: The Cistercians in England and Wales', *Archaeologia Cambrensis*, 154 (for 2005), *Cistercians in Wales and the West*, 27–49

2008 'Confraternities in the Durham *Liber Vitae*', and 'Charters in the Durham *Liber Vitae*', in David and Lynda Rollason (eds), *The Durham Liber Vitae: London, British Library, MS Cotton Domitian A.VII*, vol. I (London), pp. 73–7

2008 'English monasteries and the continent in the reign of King Stephen', in Paul Dalton and Graeme White (eds), *King Stephen's Reign, 1135–1154* (Woodbridge), pp. 98–114

2008 'Looking for Medieval Nuns', in Burton and Stöber (eds), *Monasteries and Society in Britain and Ireland in the Later Middle Ages*, pp. 113–23

2008 'Past models and current concerns: the origins and growth of the Cistercian Order', in Kate Cooper and Jeremy Gregory (eds), *Revival and Resurgence in Christian History, Studies in Church History*, 44 (Woodbridge), pp. 27–45

2009 'Les Chanoines reguliers en Grande-Bretagne', in M. Parisse (ed.), *Les Chanoines reguliers: émergence et expansion (xie–xiiie siècles)* (St Etienne), pp. 477–98

2009 'Citadels of God: monasteries, violence, and the struggle for power in Northern England, 1135–1154', in Chris Lewis (ed.), *Anglo-Norman Studies XXXI: Proceedings of the Battle Conference 2008* (Woodbridge), pp. 17–30

2009 'Constructing a corporate identity: the *Historia Fundationis* of the Cistercian abbeys of Byland and Jervaulx', in Anne Müller and Karen Stöber (eds), *Self-Representation of Medieval Religious Communities: the British Isles in Context, Vita Regularis: Ordnungen und Deutungen religiosen Lebens in Mittelalter, Abhandlungen*, 40 (Berlin), pp. 327–40

2009 'Documenting the Lives of Medieval Nuns', in J. Boffey and V. Davies (eds), *Recording Medieval Lives*, Proceedings of the 2005 Harlaxton Symposium (Donnington), pp. 14–24

2009 'Material Support: religious orders', in Miri Rubin and Walter Simons (eds), *The Cambridge History of Christianity: Christianity in Western Europe c.1100–1500* (Cambridge), pp. 107–13

2010 'The Cistercians in England', in Franz J. Felten and Werner Rösener (eds), *Norm und Realität: Kontinuität und Wandel der Zisterziener in Mittelalter* (Mainz), pp. 379–409

2011 '*Moniales* and *Ordo Cisterciensis* in Medieval England and Wales', in Gert Melville and Anne Müller (eds), *Female vita religiosa between Late Antiquity and the High Middle Ages: Structures, Developments and Spatial Contexts*, Vita regularis: Ordnungen und Deutungen religiosen Lebens im Mittelalter, Abhandlungen, 47 (Zurich and Berlin), pp. 375–89

2011 with Karen Stöber, 'What lay behind those monastery walls?', in H. V. Bowen (ed.), *A New History of Wales* (Llandysul), pp. 42–8

2011 'The Regular Canons and Diocesan Reform', in Burton and Stöber (eds), *The Regular Canons in the Medieval British Isles* (Turnhout), pp. 41–57

2013 'Furness, Savigny and the Cistercian world', in Clare Downham (ed.), *Jocelin of Furness: Essays from the 2011 Conference* (Stamford), pp. 7–16

2013 'Transition and Transformation: the Benedictine Houses', in Burton and Stöber (eds), *Monastic Wales: New Approaches*, pp. 21–37

2014 'After Knowles: new directions in monastic studies in England and Wales', in Dominic Aidan Bellenger and Simon Johnson (eds), *Keeping the Rule: David Knowles and the Writing of History* (Stratton-on-the-Fosse), pp. 117–38

2015 'Medieval nunneries and male authority; female monasteries in England and Wales', in Burton and Stöber (eds), *Women in the Medieval Monastic World*, pp. 123–43

2016 with Karen Stöber, 'The Monastic Wales Project', *Imago Temporis, Medium Aevum* 10, 339–55

GENERAL EDITORSHIPS

Boydell and Brewer, Monastic Orders Series

The Journal of Medieval Monastic Studies (Turnhout: Brepols), with associated book series, Medieval Monastic Studies

INDEX

D

Q

R

S

TABULA GRATULATORIA

The following have kindly associated themselves with the publication of this book through subscription.

Frances Andrews, Fife
Ian Bass, Hereford
Peter Borsay, Aberystwyth
Guido Cariboni, Milan
Jane Cartwright, Lampeter
Emma Cavell, Swansea
Miriam Clyne, Galway
Giles Constable, Princeton
Glyn Coppack, Barrow Upon
  Humber
Martin Crampin, Aberystwyth
Colin Eldridge, Lampeter
Claude and Paul Evans, Toronto
Lindy Grant, Reading
Isobel Harvey and Oliver Padel,
  Liskeard
Michael Hicks, Winchester
Kurt Villads Jensen, Stockholm
Maureen Jurkowski, London

Annette Kehnel, Mannheim
Anne-Julie Lafaye, Dublin
William Marx, Lampeter
Anne Müller, Eichstätt
Helen J. Nicholson, Cardiff
Helen Palmer and Richard W.
  Ireland, Aberystwyth
Ben Pink, Oswestry
Daniel Power, Swansea
Huw Pryce and Nancy Edwards,
  Bangor
Hedwig Röckelein, Göttingen
Araceli Rosillo-Luque, Barcelona
Phillipp Schofield, Aberystwyth
Petr Sommer, Prague
Martial Staub, Sheffield
Richard J. A. Thomason, Canterbury
Paul and Claire Watkins,
  Carmarthen